AF632886

NEPAL : A BIBLIOGRAPHY

NEPAL
A bibliography

COMPILED BY
DINA NATH WADHWA

EDITED BY
SATKARI MUKHOPADHYAYA

SHARADA

Sharada Publishing House
DELHI - 110052

Wadhwa, Dina Nath, 1943-

Nepal : a bibliography/compiled by Dina Nath Wadhwa ; edited by Satkari Mukhopadhyaya. — Delhi : Sharada Publishing House, 1991.

xii, 344 p. ; 23 cm.

Includes Index

ISBN: 81-85616-00-0

LCCN: 91-905035

SHARADA ₹ 950/-

1. Bibliography. 2. Nepal—Bibliography.

I. Mukhopadhyaya, Satkari.

First Published 1991

© DINA NATH WADHWA, 1943—

Published by

SHARADA PUBLISHING HOUSE
E-239, Shastri Nagar,
DELHI - 110052 Phone : 516539

Printed by

Amar Printers at FTAD Printing Press, Delhi-110052

CONTENTS

INTRODUCTION

Nepal is one of the world's most isolated countries, ocated in the Himalayas. It is bordered by two of Asia's giants—China and India. Partly on account of its location and partly on account of the policy of discouraging foreign contacts pursued by its government until recently, Nepal has not had many visitors from abroad.

It is one of the most beautiful countries in the world with breath-takingly high mountains (Mount Everest is located here), scenic valleys, and picturesque temples. It is the meeting place of two of Asia's great art traditions—Indian and Chinese.

The people reflect the mixing of the Mongol and Indo-Aryan races and the presence of many tribes, each with its quaint customs provides opportunities for the anthropologist to polish his science.

The population is predominantly Hindu including a sizeable Buddhist population with smaller numbers of Muslims and animists. The government was monarchical but now democratic norms have been introduced and Nepal is in fact the world's only Hindu kingdom.

Nepal has within its boundaries the birth-place of Gautama, the Buddha, the founder of one of the world's great religions. On another plane, the Gurkha warriors have fought with distinction in many of Britain's wars. The Sherpas who specialize in helping mountain climbers are noted for their skill and daring.

A small and isolated country as Nepal is, it has drawn no less attention of the world. Its history, culture, art, architecture, literature, ethnic variety, and economy have created keen interest among scholars. As a result a vast literature in English and some other European languages has grown. The bulk of writings in Nepali and Newari is also considerable. It is therefore in the fitness of things that a bibliography of works on Nepal be compiled to facilitate Nepal studies in India and abroad. The following pages contain the results of a modest but sincere effort in that direction.

The major sources for the material in this Bibliography are: (1) Publications acquired by the U.S. Library of Congress Office, New Delhi for American universities; (2) the personal collections of Mr. E. Gene Smith, presently Field Director of the U.S. Library of Congress Office, Jakarta; (3) Reference collections of the U.S. Library of Congress Office, New Delhi. Apart from these a number of reference sources have been consulted. These include (1) Works on Nepal in the National Library : an annotated bibliography (Kirtipur); (2) Annotated bibliography on women in Nepal (Kathmandu); (3) Contributions to Nepalese studies (Kirtipur); (4) Kailash : a journal of Himalayan studies (Kathmandu); (5) Journal of the Nepal Research Centre (Wiesbaden/BRD); (6) Praśāsana; the Nepalese journal of public administration (Lalitpur); (7) Journal of Tribhuvan University (Kirtipur).

This Bibliography aims at an audience ranging from the informed general reader to the scholar who wishes to obtain information regarding Nepal. Most of the publications included in this Bibliography are available in the university libraries of the English speaking world.

The compiler is aware of several omissions; he, nevertheless, hopes that this volume will prove useful to the audience. This Bibliography covers the period from 1951 to 1981 and efforts are being made to update this by another volume next year.

Seope

This Bibliography includes books, periodicals, and articles on Nepal published in Nepal and other countries. The entries are related to all aspects of Nepal, e.g., agriculture, art, history, literature, etc. It was, however, not possible to cover titles of creative literature in the native languages of Nepal in the Bibliography.

In general the Bibliography covers the period 1951 to 1981 but it includes some monographs of the earlier period also. There are 1180 entries in this Bibliography consisting of 906 monographs, 52 periodicals, and 222 articles published in periodicals. Among the monographs, 209 are published outside Nepal. There are 132 monographs in vernaculars and 14 in European languages other than English. The Bibliography also includes 182 government publications.

Articles are included as a means of giving the varied potential readership more than one option; a reader may not have the time or interest to read a 250 page book on a topic, whereas a 20 page article will answer his needs. Several titles listed in the Bibliography are bi or multilingual and cover multiple subjects.

In Nepal the book production is limited and limited number of copies of publications are produced. An attempt was made to see an actual copy of every title listed in this Bibliography but in some cases this proved impossible. Those entries were given with such information as was available from secondary sources.

Annotations

Annotations are provided to most of the entries, with a view to drawing the readers' attention to its importance, so that their interest is aroused. Annotations are of varied length and in some cases they are a purely objective summary of contents. An attempt is made to explain in the annotation certain terms relating to objects, persons, organizations, places, or events with local or vernacular names, whose accurate meaning is not generally known to the persons residing outside Nepal. So maximum and current information s given in abridged form. That is why, in several cases, the annotations are lengthy. In a few cases where the title is self-explanatory or the publication could not be located, an annotation has not been attempted.

Section references

There are certain publications which cover more than one subject. In those cases, the entry is listed under the main subject and references are included under other subject(s) which are covered by the publication.

Arrangement

The entries in this Bibliography are organized under the subjects. Some subjects are further sub-divided to make the material easily accessible. Under each subject, the entries are arranged in one alphabetical sequence.

Index

The index includes all the possible access points: authors, joint authors, editors, compilers, titles, parallel titles, alternate titles, etc. The index is arranged in one alphabetical sequence and all the index entries are referred to the entry numbers in the text of the Bibliography. Initial articles are ignored in filing.

ACKNOWLEDGEMENTS

I am thankful to Mr. Jerry R. James, who was Field Director of the U.S. Library of Congress Office, New Delhi upto August 1980 for granting me permission to work on Nepal bibliography. I am grateful to Mr. Jerry R. James and Mr. E. Gene Smith, Field Director, U.S. Library of Congress Office, New Delhi (September 1980-September 1985) for allowing me to use the material acquired from Nepal by the Office for American universities. It is a pleasure for me to put on record my deep sense of gratitude to Mr. E. Gene Smith for allowing me to use his valuable personal collection of monographs and periodicals pertaining to Nepal as well as for his valuable guidance. I will fail in my duty if I do not thankfully mention the encouragement I received from Mrs. Lygia M. Ballantyne, Field Director and Miss Alice L. Kniskern, Deputy Field Director of the U.S. Library of Congress Office, New Delhi at the final stage of my work.

I am grateful to Dr. Satkari Mukhopadhyaya, Deputy Secretary, Sahitya Akademi, New Delhi, for his unfailing guidance, support and encouragement. It is because of his efforts, this Bibliography is now available in book form.

I am also thankful to Shri Achal Rangaswami for editorial advice; Shri K. Subramaniyan for guiding me on several occasions; Shri Ram Saran Wadhwa for helping me in arranging and checking the entries; Shri Manga Ram Kashyap for his ungrudging assistance in locating books; and to my brother, Shri Nand Kishore Wadhwa, who is no more, for helping me in a number of ways.

My special appreciation is for Shri B.L. Bansal of Sharada Publishing House for his enthusiasm to publish this Bibliography.

August 15, 1991 DINA NATH WADHWA

1

ADMINISTRATION AND LOCAL GOVERNMENT

1. **Abullaish**. An evaluation of administrative decentralization in Nepal. Kathmandu : Centre for Economic Development and Administration, Tribhuvan University, 1980. 81 p. bibliog.

   Administrative decentralization has been a major concern in Nepal since the overthrow of oligarchic Rana rule in 1951. Public participation in the development process is not possible unless there is proper decentralization of administrative decision-making and so over the last three decades a number of commissions, expert groups, and committees have prescribed various policies for decentralization. This research report evaluates the impact of the process of decentralization.

2. **Agrawal, Govind Ram**. Personnel management—a system approach. *Praśāsana : The Nepalese Journal of Public Administration*, vol. 6 (1975), pp. 5-11. illus.

   The author argues that personnel management must shed is myopic attitudes and become systems-oriented. He supports his study with illustrations and charts.

3. **Bhatta, Bhim Dev**. Administrative problems of project implementation in Nepal, with assistance from Babu Ram Shrestha; Bijaya Kumar. Kathmandu : Centre for Economic Development and Administration, Tribhuvan University, 1980. 79 p. bibliog.

Lack of effective implementation is one of the most critical constraints in the development process in Nepal, and the prime reason for this seems to be poor administrative capability. This study was undertaken to identify the operational problems of project management and to suggest solutions. The research team paid a number of visits to various project sites in order to gain deeper insight into the problems. This study will be useful to those concerned with project formulation as well as with implementation.

4. **Bhatta, Bhim Dev.** Development administration in Nepal. Kathmandu : Indira Bhatta, 1979. 177 p. bibliog.

The study of development administration has become a vital concern in Nepal as in all the underdeveloped and developing nations. This book is an attempt to remedy the dearth of reading material in this field. It contains : Concept of development; Development administration in Nepal : an institutional approach; Organization; Personnel administration; Financial administration; Leadership; Communication; Motivation : conceptual frame work and its role in Nepalese bureaucracy; and Problems of Nepalese administration.

5. **Bhatta, Bhim Dev.** Development administration in Nepal : an appraisal. *Prāśasana : the Nepalese Journal of Public Administration*, vol. 6 (1975), pp. 42-57.

An analysis of the growth of development administration in Nepal.

6. **Edwards, Daniel W.** The daudaha (inspection tour) system under the Ranas. *Contributions to Nepalese Studies*, vol. 3, no. 2 (Sept. 1976), pp. 7-34. illus.

In the past, there were no good means of transportation and communication and rulers found it difficult to maintain control over the different parts of their realms and to prevent the fragmentation of their authority. The *daudaha* (inspection tour) therefore evolved as a means of checking all aspects of government and investigating specific conditions in the districts. The chiefs of the *daudahas* were selected by the prime minister and given charters defining the nature of their work and authority. They were to submit their reports upon return to Kathmandu. In this paper, the author discusses the different types of *daudahas* and the tasks they were to perform; what the inspection teams were able to accomplish and the problems they encountered in the field; the effectiveness of *daudaha* system in the context of central-district relations; and some general characteristics of administration during those times in view of the centre's reliance upon *daudaha*.

7. **Gongol, Sushila Devi.** Foreign experts in the administration of Nepal : a survey on their reports. Kathmandu : Centre for Economic Development and Administration, 1973. 168 p. bibliog.

   Describes the problems and prospects of administrative reform in Nepal through the advice of foreign experts who have submitted reports on the various administrative problems and on how to improve them. It is a comprehensive survey and includes a full bibliography on the subject.

8. **His Majesty's Government of Nepal** : Organization charts of the executive, the judiciary, and other official bodies and list of zonal and district personnel and other information. Kathmandu : American Embassy, 1966. 54 leaves.

   This mimeographed publication is based on the *Nepal Gazette, The Gorkhapatra,* and other official sources and newspaper reports.

9. **Joshi, Krishna.** Sārvajanika praśāsana, ādhunika adhyayana : Nepālako vyāvahārika adhyayanasahita. Kathmandu : Ratna Pustak Bhandar, 1979. 373 p. bibliog.

   Public administration of any state is the outcome of continuous development, experiment, and reform. This work is a historical study of the various principles underlying such development and the problems which can arise from such experiments. Though the study generalized, it has particular application to Nepal, where various experiments in the form of government and public administration are going on. The author offers some suggestions to administrators, particularly about the co-ordination of administrative departments. In Nepali.

10. **Joshi, Nanda Lal.** Evolution of public administration in Nepal, experience and lessons. Kirtipur, Nepal : Centre for Economic Development and Administration, 1973. 122 p. bibliog.

    Includes chapters on Administration before 1951; Major development since 1951; Organisation, planning, and general administrative reforms; Training; Civil service system; and Challenges for the 1970's.

11. **The Journal of Development and Administrative Studies.** Kirtipur, Nepal : Centre for Economic Development

and Administration, Tribhuvan University, 1978- semiannual.

Centre for Economic Development and Administration is a part of Tribhuvan University but it works independently. The Centre does number of surveys, studies, and undertakes research project. The Centre has produced the largest numbers of books on economy of Nepal. This journal contains scholarly articles on development and administrative studies of Nepal, based on the surveys, studies, and research undertaken by the Centre.

12. **Malhotra, Ram C.** Decentralization of public administration in Nepal. Kathmandu : Ministry of Information and Broadcasting, Department of Information, 1966. 15 p. (Nepal today series, no. 3).

This leaflet is based on a talk delivered on 20 April 1966 and was first published in the daily paper *Rising Nepal.*

13. **Pradhan, Paras Mani.** Sarakārī kāmakāja garne vidhi. Handbook of official correspondence, drafting, noting, etc. Kalimpong, India : Bhagya Lakshmi Prakashan, 1973. 160 p. bibliog.

A useful handbook which includes an English-Nepali glossary of administrative terms.

14. **Pradhan, Prachand.** Ecology of development administration. *Praśāsana : the Nepalese Journal of Public Administration,* vol. 6 (1975), pp. 22-24.

A discussion of public administration in Nepal using an ecological model as a basis.

15. **Pradhan, Prachand.** Problems of decentralization of power in Nepal. *Nepalese Perspective,* vol. 9, no. 6 (Dec. 1973), pp. 49-54.

The article is in two parts : 'Needs of decentralization' and 'Decentralization of power : a case study of Pokhara'.

16. **Pradhan, Prachand.** Public administration in Nepal. Kathmandu : Curriculum Development Centre, Tribhuvan University, 1976. 192 p.

A collection of articles, previously published in various periodicals by the author, an expert in public administration.

17. **Praśāsana** : *the Nepalese Journal of Public Administration.*

    For full entry refer to Professional periodicals section.

18. **Rajbhandari, Bharat Lall.** Partners for progress in Nepal : a study on the task of personnel management for socio-economic progress with special reference to conditions in Nepal. Lalitpur, Nepal : Savitri Devi, 1971. 298 p.

    A collection of articles previously published in various periodicals.

19. **Regarding Nepal Public Service Commission.** Kathmandu: Nepal Public Service Commission, 1963. 35 p.

    An account of the history and activities of the Nepal Public Service Commission. Includes legislation.

20. **Regmi, Mahesh C.** Preliminary notes on the nature of Rana law and government. *Contributions to Nepalese Studies*, vol. 2, no. 2 (June 1975), pp. 103-115.

    On 15 September 1846, Jung Bahadur was appointed Prime Minister of Nepal, a position he held for thirty-one years. During this period he laid the foundation of a political system which, notwithstanding occasional inter-family conflicts and political conspiracies, survived until 1951. This period is called the Rana period. This article describes the conditions leading to Rana rule, the status of the Rana family and the growth of the civil administration under Rana rule. It also discusses the merits and faults of the 1854 legal code.

21. **Seminar-cum-Workshop on Development Administration,** *November 17, 1971-December 17, 1971.* Kathmandu : Centre for Economic Development and Administration, [1971?]. 232 p.

    A collection of papers on the administrative system of Nepal, presented at a seminar organized by the Centre for Economic Development and Administration.

22. **Seminar-cum-Workshop on Project Analysis & Management** : *selected papers.* Kirtipur, Nepal : Centre for Economic Development & Administration, 1971. 340 p.

    The papers include some Nepalese case studies.

23. **Shrestha, C.B.** The system of central places in the Arniko Rajmarga area of Nepal. *Himalayan Review*, vol. 6 (1973-74), pp. 19-39.

An investigation into how the pattern of central places can be studied in Nepal. The data and information were collected in connection with the feasibility study sponsored by the National Planning Commission.

24. **Shrestha, Nutan R.** Need for position classification in HMG, civil service. *Praśāsana, the Nepalese Journal of Public Administration*, vol. 3, no. 2 (Oct. 1972), pp. 67-78.

An analysis of the Nepalese civil service and some suggestions for improvement.

25. **Shrestha, Tulsi Narayan.** Nepalese administration : an image. Kathmandu : Sajha Prakashan, 1981. 455 p. map. bibliog.

The contents are : The backdrop; Law and other administration; Development administration; Area administration; Decentralization programme : an experiment; Personnel administration; Financial administration; The disease of corruption; and An image. Includes appendixes.

26. **Shrestha, Tulsi Narayan.** A study of panchayat training in Nepal. Lalitpur, Nepal : Central Panchayat Training Institute, 1980. 164 p.

The emergence of the panchayat system in 1960 led to the development of panchayat training in Nepal. Under this programme, several thousand people, both officials and non-officials, have been trained in order to ensure that man-power is available to strengthen political as well as rural development. But how far such training has proved to be effective is still a moot question. This mimeographed study is one of the few evaluations of the programme. Includes appendix.

27. **Wildes, M.E., ed.** Top Management Seminar, June 20, 1972-June 24, 1972. Kathmandu : Centre for Economic Development and Administration [1972?]. 105 p.

Papers and discussions on the role of senior management in economic development. Both theoretical considerations and practical applications are considered. The seminar was organized by the Centre for Economic Development and Administration.

2

AGRICULTURE

28. **Agriculture census reports,** 1971/72, Bagamati Zone, districts, Sindhu Palchok, Rasuwa, Nuwakot, Dhading, Kavre Palanchok, Bhaktapur, Kathmandu, Lalitpur. Central Bureau of Statistics, Nepal. Kathmandu : His Majesty's Government of Nepal, National Planning Commission Secretariat, Central Bureau of Statistics, 1976. approx. 400 p.

    The economy of Nepal is predominantly agrarian. Agricultural sector contributes to more than two thirds of the Gross National Product. Central Bureau of Statistics, Nepal decided for Agricultural census reports, one for each zone of Nepal in order to have comprehensive and reliable statistics covering its various components for each zone. These reports consist of statistical tables only. The census reports are second of its kind to be conducted in Nepal. These census reports aimed at the collection of quantitative data on areas under different crops by size of holding, tenure, mode of operation, and land utilization and productivity. The sampling plan adopted for these census reports was a stratified random sampling. The coverage of the country was achieved by taking a fifteen percent sample of Wards. Agricultural households living in ihe selected Ward served as reporting units using a holding as an enumeration unit. These census reports will serve the basic requirements for planning, formulation of agricultural policy, and appraising agricultural development projects in the country. Has cover title : National sample census of agriculture, 1971/72, Nepal, Bagamati Zone.

29. **Agriculture census reports,** 1971/72, Bheri Zone, districts, Jajarkot, Dailekh, Surkhet, Banke, Bardia. Central

Bureau of Statistics, Nepal. Kathmandu : His Majesty's Government of Nepal, National Planning Commission Secretariat, Central Bureau of Statistics, 1976. approx. 135 p.

Same as for Agriculture census reports, 1971/72, Bagamati Zone. Has cover title : National sample census of agriculture, 1971/72, Nepal, Bheri Zone.

30. **Agriculture census reports**, 1971/72, Dhaulagiri Zone, districts, Mustang, Dolpa, Myagdi, Banglung. Central Bureau of Statistics, Nepal. Kathmandu : His Majesty's Government of Nepal, National Planning Commission Secretariat, Central Bureau of Statistics, 1976. approx. 200 p.

Same as for Agriculture census reports 1971/72, Bagamati Zone. Has cover title : National sample census of agriculture, 1971/72, Nepal, Dhaulagiri zone.

31. **Agriculture census reports**, 1971/72, Gandaki Zone, districts, Gorkha, Manang, Lamjung, Kaski, Parbat, Tanahun, Syangja. Central Bureau of Statistics, Nepal. Kathmandu : His Majesty's Government of Nepal, National Planning Commission Secretariat, Central Bureau of Statistics, 1976. approx. 330 p.

Same as for Agriculture census reports, 1971/72, Bagamati Zone. Has cover title : National sample census of agriculture, 1971/72, Nepal, Gandaki Zone.

32. **Agriculture census reports**, 1971/72, Janakpur Zone, districts, Dolakha, Ramechhap, Sindhuli, Dhanusha, Mahotari, Sarlahi. Central Bureau of Statistics, Nepal. Kathmandu : His Majesty's Government of Nepal, National Planning Commission Secretariat, Central Bureau of Statistics, 1976. approx. 280 p.

Same as for Agriculture census reports, 1971/72, Bagamati Zone. Has cover title : National sample census of agriculture, 1971/72, Nepal, Janakpur Zone.

33. **Agriculture census reports**, 1971/72, Karnali Zone, districts, Humla, Mugu, Tibrikot, Jumla. Central Bureau of Statistics, Nepal, Kathmandu : His Majesty's Government of Nepal, National Planning Commission Secretariat, Central Bureau of Statistics, 1976. approx. 200 p.

Same as for Agriculture census reports, 1971/72, Bagamati Zone. Has cover title : National sample census of agriculture, 1971/72, Nepal, Karnali Zone.

34. **Agriculture census reports**, 1971/72, Koshi Zone, districts Sankhuwa Sabha, Terhathum, Dhankuta, Morang, Sunsari. Central Bureau of Statistics, Nepal. Kathmandu : His Majesty's Government of Nepal, National Planning Commission Secretariat, Central Bureau of Statistics, 1976. approx. 230 p.

Same as for Agriculture census reports, 1971/72, Bagamati Zone. Has cover title : National sample census of agriculture, 1971/72, Nepal, Koshi Zone.

35. **Agriculture census reports**, 1971/72, Lumbini Zone, districts, Nawalparasi, Palpa, Gulmi, Arghakhanchi, Rupendehi, Kapilbastu. Central Bureau of Statistics, Nepal. Kathmandu : His Majesty's Government of Nepal, National Planning Commission Secretariat, Central Bureau of Statistics, 1976. approx. 280 p.

Same as for Agriculture census reports, 1971/72, Bagamati Zone. Has cover title : National sample census of agriculture, 1971/72, Nepal, Lumbini Zone.

36. **Agriculture census reports**, 1971/72, Mahakali Zone, districts, Dharchula, Baitadi, Dandel Dhura, Kanchanpur. Central Bureau of Statistics, Nepal. Kathmandu : His Majesty's Government of Nepal, National Planning Commission Secretariat, Central Bureau of Statistics, 1976. approx. 200 p.

Same as for Agriculture census reports, 1971/72, Bagamati Zone. Has cover title : National sample census of agriculture, 1971/72, Nepal, Mahakali Zone.

37. **Agriculture census reports**, 1971/72, Mechi Zone, districts, Taplejung, Panchther, Illam, Jhapa. Central Bureau of Statistics, Nepal. Kathmandu : His Majesty's Government of Nepal, National Planning Commission Secretariat, Central Bureau of Statistics, 1976. approx. 200 p.

Same as for Agriculture census reports, 1971/72, Bagamati Zone. Has cover title : National sample census of agriculture, 1971/72, Nepal, Mechi Zone.

38. **Agriculture census reports**, 1971/72, Narayani Zone, districts, Makwanpur, Chittwan, Rautahat, Bara, Parsa. Central Bureau of Statistics, Nepal. Kathmandu : His Majesty's Government of Nepal, National Planning Commission Secretariat, Central Bureau of Statistics, 1976. approx. 230 p.

    Same as for Agriculture census reports, 1971/72, Bagamati Zone. Has cover title : National sample census of agriculture : 1971/72, Nepal, Narayani Zone.

39. **Agriculture census reports**, 1971/72, Rapti Zone, districts, Rukum, Ropla, Salyan, Pyuthan, Dang Deukhuri. Central Bureau of Statistics, Nepal. Kathmandu : His Majesty's Government of Nepal, National Planning Commission Secretariat, Central Bureau of Statistics, 1976. approx. 235 p.

    Same as for Agriculture census reports, 1971/72, Bagamati Zone. Has cover title : National samrle census of agriculture, 1971/72, Nepal, Rapti Zone.

40. **Agriculture census reports**, 1971/72, Sagarmatha Zone, districts, Solukhumbu, Bhojpur, Khotang, Okhaldhunga, Udaypur, Saptari, Siraha. Central Bureau of Statistics, Nepal. Kathmandu : His Majesty's Government of Nepal, National Planning Commission Secretariat, Central Bureau of Statistics, 1976. approx. 320 p.

    Same as for Agriculture census reports, 1971/72, Bagamati Zone. Has cover title : National sample census of agriculture, 1971/72, Nepal, Sagarmatha Zone.

41. **Agriculture census reports**, 1971/72, Seti Zone, districts, Bajura, Bajhang, Achham, Doti, Kailali. Central Bureau of Statistics, Nepal. Kathmandu : His Majesty's Government of Nepal, National Planning Commission Secretariat, Central Bureau of Statistics, 1976. approx. 230 p.

    Same as for Agriculture census reports, 1971/72, Bagamati Zone. Has cover title : National sample census of agriculture, 1971/72, Nepal, Seti Zone.

42. **Agriculture credit and banking** : papers and proceedings of the National Seminar held at National Vocational Training Centre, Sanothimi, Kathmandu, December 17-31, 1970. Kathmandu : Agricultural Development Bank, Nepal, 1972. 254 p.

The seminar was organized under the auspices of Agricultural Development Bank, in collaboration with FAO/UNDP. Has cover title : Papers and proceedings of the National Seminar on Agricultural Credit and Banking, Kathmandu, December 17-31, 1970. Includes illustrations.

43. **Agricultural credit survey, Nepal.** Research Department, Nepal Rastra Bank. Kathmandu : Research Department, Nepal Rastra Bank, 1972. 4 vols.

Vols. 1-2 deal with the survey report, vol. 3 deals with the technical report, and vol. 4 deals with summary and recommendations.

44. **Alirol, Philippe**. Animal husbandry in the Ganesh Himal region : an essay in ecological synthesis. *Contributions to Nepalese Studies*, vol. 3, no. 1 (January 1976), pp. 47-61.

Ganesh Himal is a range of mountains to the northwest of Kathmandu, reaching an altitude of 7,402 m. The massif is bounded in the east by the Trisuli river and by the Buri Gandaki in the west. It is the source of the entire river basin which feeds the Ankhu Khola. Animal husbandry in the Ganesh Himal Range is not very different than that practised in other ranges of Nepal. The principal interest in doing this study was to produce a model of the ecological milieu (the ecosystem). This essay was translated from the original French by Andrew Manzardo. Includes maps and illustrations.

45. **Banskota, Mahesh.** The Nepalese hill agro-ecosystem. Place and publishers not given, 1979. 168 leaves. maps. bibliog.

A simulation analysis of alternate policies for food production and environmental change. Ph.D. Dissertation presented to Cornell University.

46. **Clark, G.C.** et al. First annual progress report on Nepal's small farmers' project. *Contributions to Nepalese Studies*, vol. 5, no. 2 (June 1978), pp. 69-86.

Workshops on Development Support for Small Farmers in cooperations with FAO/UNDP were held in several countries. Regional Follow-up Seminar held in Bangkok in August 1974. The seminar formulated a broad strategy based on a number of activities considered essential for programmes for small farmer development. At the same time, the delegates from Nepal together with FAO/ASARRD members and observers from international organizations prepared an indicative outline for follow-up Field Action Projects in the (1) Dhanusha and (2) Nuwakot Districts. Based on this plus subsequent discussions with officials of the Agriculture Ministry and the Agricultural Development Bank of Nepal, the present Field Action Project (FAP) was developed and initiated from November 1975. This is the first progress report of this project.

47. **Credit**. Agricultural Documentation Centre.

For full entry refer to Bibliographies section.

48. **Dedgaun Tar Irrigation Project** : irrigation impact evaluation study. Agricultural Project Services Centre. Kathmandu : Agricultural Projects Services Centre, 1978. 39 leaves.

Dedgaun Tar Irrigation Project is a project in Nawalparasi District of Lumbini Zone. The main objects of this study was : (i) to evaluate the contribution of irrigation project in agricultural development; (ii) to study the impact of project on various categories of farmers; (iii) to offer suggestions regarding the development of irrigation. The scope of the study was limited to socio-economic and engineering aspect of the project only. Mimeographed.

49. **FAO, Nepal.** Agricultural Documentation Centre.

For full entry refer to Bibliographies section.

50. **Feasibility study of Livestock Development Project, Lamjung and Tanahu.** Agricultural Projects Services Centre. Kathmandu : Agricultural Projects Services Centre, 1980. 44, 119 leaves. 2 maps.

The Livestock Development Project is especially designed to increase the meat production in Lamjung and Tanahu to meet the increasing demand for meat in Kathmandu and Pokhara markets. The project mainly focusses on introducing improved breed, upgrading of economically low productive animals, and the development of necessary marketing infrastructure. This project is largely concerned with meat animals such as goat, sheep, buffaloes, and swine. The study was sponsored by Nepal Rastra Bank. Mimeographed.

51. **Gokarna Irrigation Project** : irrigation impact study. Agricultural Projects Services Centre. Kathmandu : Agricultural Projects Services Centre, 1979. 46 leaves.

The Gokarna Irrigation Project constructed in the fiscal year 1951/52, is in Kathmandu District of Bagmati Zone. The project aimed at irrigating 90 hectares of land covering a few wards of Gokarna, Atrakhel, Jorpati, and Baudha villages. The objectives of this study was (1) to evaluate the contribution of irrigation project in agricultural development; (2) to study the impact of irrigation project on various categories of farmers; (3) to study the problem associated with fuller utilization of irrigation potential, and (4) to offer suggestion regarding development of irrigation. The scope of this study was limited to socio-economic and engineering aspect of the project. This mimeographed publication has cover title : Irrigation impact evaluation study, Gokarna Irrigation Project. Includes illustrations.

52. **Hand book of agricultural statistics of Nepal.** Compiled by: Agricultural Statistics Division. Kathmandu : His Majesty's Government, Department of Food and Agricultural Marketing Services, Agricultural Statistics Division, 1979. 45 p.

Gives statistical information on land use, population, gross domestic product, cultivated physical area and cropping intensity, agriculture, irrigation, agricultural inputs, Agricultural Development Bank, Fifth Plan, and miscellaneous.

53. **Impat, P.** Phewa watershed : soil survey interpretation and land capability. Kathmandu : Department of Soil Conservation and Watershed Management, Integrated Watershed Management, Torrent Control, and Land Use Development Project, 1980. 87 leaves. 3 maps. bibliog. (Phewa Tal technical report ; no. 14).

This survey was conducted with the following objectives : to describe and map the soil resource to interpret the various soils with respect to their suitability for various land uses within their capabilities; to provide basic data for making decisions of land use development of the area. Mimeographed.

54. **Integrated rural development.** Agricultural Documentation Centre.

For full entry refer to Bibliographies section.

55. **Irrigation.** Agricultural Documentation Centre.

For full entry refer to Bibliographies section.

56. **Joshi, Chandni**. Profile of women in agriculture and rural development in Nepal, 1980, for FAO's Study-cum-Planning Group Country Workshop. Lalitpur, Nepal : His Majesty's Government, Home Panchayat Ministry, Training Material Production Centre, 1980? 78 p.

Rural women in Nepal have been handicapped socially and not been able to fully contribute towards rural development. In order to utilize the human resources of the women properly, social status have to be improved. This profile recommends several programmes for this purpose. This will fulfill the objectives set by FAO. This profile has cover title: Country review and analysis on the role and participation of women in agriculture & rural development, Nepal, 1980.

57. **Joshi, Durga Datt**, Compiler and editor. Livestock trade statistics of Nepal, 1956/57 to 1974/75. Kathmandu : Kaushalya Devi Joshi, 1979. 159 p.

In Nepal, planning is being done in all fields. It was difficult for livestock planners to make their plans on account of lack of livestock statistics. This book claims to be the first book on the subject. Statistical tables provide information on various aspects of import and export statistics of livestock and livestock products between Nepal-Tibet, Nepal-India, and Nepal-Overseas countries. Particular attention is paid to leather and wool export.

58. **Khageri Irrigation Project** : irrigation impact evaluation study. Agricultural Projects Services Centre. Kathmandu : The Centre, 1978. 60 leaves.

The Khageri Irrigation Project is a project in Chitwan District of Narayani Zone. The objectives of this study was (1) to evaluate the contribution of irrigation project in agricultural development; (2) to study the impact of project on various categories of farmers; (3) to study the problems associated with fuller utilization of irrigation potential; and (4) to offer suggestions regarding development of irrigation. The scope of this study is limited to socio-economic and engineering aspect of the project. Mimeographed.

59. **Levenson, Burt**. Fuelwood utilization : a study of the demand and available fuelwood resources at six selected villages. Kathmandu : Ministry of Forest, Department of Soil and Water Conservation, Integrated Watershed

Management, Torrent Control, and Land Use Development Project, 1979. 65 leaves. 1 map. bibliog. (Phewa Tal technical report ; no. 9)

Bhadaure panchayat, in the Phewa Tal Catchment area, was chosen as the study area. Specifically, six villages were selected as representative of the total population that uses the forests in Bhadaure panchayat. It was intended to present data which would further help to construct and narrow the parameters of a model for fuelwood consumption. By having information available from which to create such a model, sound management decisions can be derived concerning the extraction and use of the forest resources in the Hill region of Nepal. The author also lived in the panchayat for a period of two years and was able to affirm many of the conclusions reached by the study through observations over this period of time.

60. **Mahakali Irrigation Project** : irrigation impact evaluation study. Agricultural Projects Services Centre. Kathmandu : The Centre, 1979. 53 leaves.

The Mahakali Irrigation Project is a project in Kanchanpur District of Mahakali Zone. The objectives of this study was (1) to evaluate the contribution of irrigation project in agricultural development; (2) to study the impact of irrigation project on various categories of farmers; (3) to study the problem associated with fuller utilization of irrigation potential; and (4) to offer suggestions regarding development of irrigation. The scope of this study was limited to socio-economic and engineering aspect of the project. This mimeographed publication has cover title : Irrigation impact evaluation study, Mahakali Irrigation Project. Includes illustrations.

61. **Manushmara Irrigation Project** : irrigation impact evaluation study. Agricultural Projects Services Centre. Kathmandu : The Centre, 1978. 60 leaves.

The Manushmara Irrigation Project is a project in Sarlahi District of Janakpur Zone. The barrage was constructed in the year 1966/67. The canal system from barrage of Manushmara river was expected to irrigate 2,000 ha. of land. The main object of this study was : (1) to evaluate the contribution of irrigation project in agricultural development; (2) to study the impact of irrigation project on various categories of farmers; (3) to study the problem associated with fuller utilization of irrigation potential; and (4) to offer suggestions regarding development of irrigation. The scope of this study was limited to socio-economic and engineering aspect of the project. Mimeographed.

62. **March, Kathryn S.** Of people and naks : the management and meaning of high altitude herding among contemporary Solu Sherpas. *Contributions to Nepalese Studies*, vol. 4, no. 2, (June 1977), pp. 83-97.

High altitude herding remains an integral part of contemporary Solu Sherpa life. In this article, the author has examined the econmic and management aspects of high altitude herding in Solu. In particular, the daily labour and personnel requirements and the diversity, value and distribution, as well as seasonal variations and movements, are discussed with reference to the types of pastoralism currently widely practised. But herding is more than purely economic activity to Sherpas. It is tied throughout to the life of the village and its inhabitants, not only through the sale of its products but also by important ritual activities. The article also presents several examples of the ritual and symbolic value of the herds.

63. **Marketing.** Agricultural Documentation Centre.

For full entry refer to Bibliographies section.

64. **Mathema, Pushpa Ram Bhakta.** Agricultural development in Nepal. Kathmandu : Jaya Shree Mathema, 1966. 84 p.

The people of Nepal are basically dependent on agriculture. Eighty-five percent of the manpower is employed in agriculture. The author has traced the agricultural development in Nepal to date in this publication.

65. **Mathema, Pushpa Ram Bhakta.** Ratna Feed Industries, its role in promoting poultry farming in the Kathmandu Valley, Nepal. Kathmandu : Department of Food and Agricultural Marketing Services, 1976. 30 p. bibliog.

This case study was prepared to present in the "F.A.O./RED Small Farmers Marketing Seminar" to be held in Bangkok in May 1976. This study highlights the role of the use of agricultural business in promoting and sustaining the poultry business. In addition, better understanding and cooperation between public and private sectors have contributed significantly to the effort to develop organized poultry farming business in the Valley.

66. **National sample census of agriculture, A.D. 1962.** Agriculture Division, Central Bureau of Statistics, Nepal. Kathmandu : His Majesty's Government, National Planning Commission Secretariat, Central Bureau of Statistics, 1963? 26, 12 leaves.

Report on the census of agriculture, 1962 have been published already. This report is a supplement to 1962 report and is in English and Nepali. This is for the whole country and is the sum total of district estimates, based on the data collected by the method of sampling. Northern parts of Himalayan and trans-Himalayan regions and the entire Jumla District which were considered unimportant from the agricultural point of view were excluded. This census was conducted according to the guidelines issued by Food and Agriculture Organization of the United Nations for modern statistical sampling.

67. **National sample census of agriculture**, B.S. 2018, 1962 A.D. : yield data for principal crops. Agricultural Section, Central Bureau of Statistics, Nepal. Kathmandu : Central Bureau of Statistics, 1965. 15 p.

This census is the first of its kind and contains tables. This is based on the data collected by sampling. Northern parts of Himalayan and trans-Himalayan regions and the entire Jumla District which were considered unimportant from agricultural point of view were excluded. This census is conducted according to the guidelines issued by Food and Agriculture Organisation of the United Nations for modern statistical sampling. Includes appendices. The supplement to this report is published in 1963? In English and Nepali.

68. **Nepal Agricultural Extension Project, Phase II.** Agricultural Projects Services Centre. Kathmandu : The Centre, 1978. 4 vols. 2 maps.

This is the Phase II report of the Nepal Agricultural Extension Project. The Phase I report has already been appraised by the World Bank. This report is an investment proposal for the extension activities in the remaining fourteen Tarai districts. This proposal is similar to that in the Phase I report. The study also incorporates recommendations for consolidating the supporting institutional services relating to agricultural research, credit, and inputs. For a proper understanding of the backdrop against which the proposed extension network is to operate, the current agricultural situation has also been reviewed as an integral component of the report. Mimeographed.

69. **Nepal, Grain Storage Project :** preparation report. Agricultural Projects Services Centre. Kathmandu : The Centre, 1979. 3 vols. 1 map.

The foodgrain sector plays a dominant role in the Nepalese economy and is of fundamental importance in the context of long term national interests. The public sector agencies responsible for administering the government's foodgrain policies are characterised by insufficient and poor quality infrastructure. The project proposes an investment programme for improving the infrastructure of these agencies. It is hoped that the report will provide an adequate base for an investment appraisal, that it will subsequently make a contribution towards establishing the required infrastructure and that the supporting data presented will prove a useful source of information for planners, policy makers, and those implementing plans and policies. Mimeographed.

70. **Nepal, Small Farmers Development Programme,** Field Action Project : evaluation study, Dhanusha and Nuwakot districts. Agricultural Projects Services Centre. Kathmandu : The Centre, 1980. 53, 99 leaves. 1 map.

This study was conducted at the request of U.N. Economic and Social Commission for Asia and the Pacific. This programme is making a unique contribution towards solving probably the major problem Nepal is facing today, that of raising income levels, standards of living, and self-reliance among the rural poor, by involving them in the development process. This study provides an important insight into the successes and problems of the programme. Mimeographed.

71. **Nepal, Small Farmer Development Project :** preparation report. Agricultural Projects Services Centre (Nepal), Kathmandu : The Centre, 1980. 4 vols.

The programme has demonstrated that it is possible to involve people with a traditional outlook in the development process. The proposed expansion programme represents a substantial step in increasing the level of infrastructure needed to reach the rural poor and would enable a considerable number of rural poor to benefit from the programme. This report will provide an adequate base for an investment appraisal and will ultimately made a contribution towards establishing the required infrastructure. Mimeographed.

72. **Nepalese Journal of Agriculture.**

For full entry refer to Professional periodicals section.

73. **Pant, Y.P.** and **Jain, S.C.** Agricultural development in Nepal; a search for new strategy. Bombay : Vora & Co., 1979. 2nd rev. & enl. ed. 162 p. bibliog.

The geographical setting of Nepal into the Tarai Plain Hills and High Mountains from south to north provides an excellent opportunity for crops, livestock, and horticulture development in an integrated manner. This work is conceived with the major problems of agricultural development in a wider context of economic planning in Nepal. Underlying the work as a whole is an emphasis on a balanced and integrated approach to the problems of agricultural development in the country. The study is supported by statistics.

74. **Proceedings of Workshop on 'Development Support for Small Farmers', Nepal, January 4-14, 1974**. Kathmandu : Agricultural Development Bank, 1974. 183 p. maps.

The Workshop was held at Janakpur and Kathmandu under the joint auspices of Ministry of Food, Agriculture, and Irrigation, Ministry of Land Reform, and Agricultural Development Bank of Nepal.

75. **Report on evaluation of the fisheries development program** : conducted jointly by National Planning Commission Secretariat, His Majesty's Government of Nepal, American Peace Corps in Nepal, Fisheries Section, Department of Agriculture, His Majesty's Government of Nepal. Kathmandu : National Planning Commission Secretariat, 1975. 201 p. bibliog.

This study has evaluated the problems of the fishery development due to the ignorance of farmers, paucity of literature in scientific farming, and poor communication. It has also enlightened the problems of marketing and co-ordination, etc. The report has suggested some broad measures for improvement. Mimeographed. Incldes illustrations.

76. **Resource use and productivity in the Narayani Irrigation Development Project area**. Agricultural Projects Services Centre (Nepal). Kathmandu : The Centre, 77 leaves.

Narayani Irrigation Development Project covers Bara and Parsa districts. But it was found that eastern canal which was started in 1967/68 under Indo-Gandak project and was completed in 1976 by His Majesty's Government needed major improvement. To carry out these activities the project was again started under the name of Narayani Irrigation Development Project. This report states that the first phase of this project is completed in 1978/79. This phase will provide irrigation to about 18,710 hectares, construct tubewells and canals, and improve the old system in 1 to 6 Blocks. The second phase upon completion will provide irrigation to additional 12,730 hectares. An intensive agricultural system will also be introduced in Bara and Rautahat districts. Mimeographed.

77. **Scientific results of the Japanese Expedition to Nepal Himalaya, 1952-53.**

For full entry refer to Flora & Fauna section.

78. **Small farmer development.** Agricultural Development Centre.

For full entry refer to Bibliographies section.

79. **Soil, Nepal.** Agricultural Documentation Centre.

For full entry refer to Bibliographies section.

80. **Suwal, Rajendra.** Small farmer's development programme: a case study. Kathmandu : Centre for Economic Development and Administration, 1980. 26, 12 leaves. bibliog.

Nepal is basically country of small farmers. The "Small Farmer's Developmenl Programme" has appeared as an interesting model for effecting improvements in the quality of life of small farmers. However, this programme so far has remained confined to projects of experimental nature. Preparations are underway to launch this programme on massive scale in various parts of the country in near future. This case study about small farmers development programme is an attempt to objectively assess the pros and cons of the programme. It was sponsored by the UN Asian and Pacific Development Administration Centre (ADPAC) of Malaysia. Mimeographed.

81. **Tika Bhairab Irrigation Project** : irrigation impact evaluation study. Agricultural Projects Services Centre. Kathmandu : The Centre, 1978. 60 leaves.

The Tika Bhairab (TB) Irrigation Project is a project in Lalitpur District of Bagmati Zone and it consists of two projects namely TB 1 and TB 2. TB 1 was started in 1954 and was completed in 1960. This project was expected to irrigate 500 ha. of land.

TB 2 was started in 1973 and completed in 1976. This project was expected to irrigate 300 ha. of additional land. The objectives of this study was (1) to evaluate the contribution of irrigation project in agricultural development; (2) to study the impact of irrigation project on various categories of farmers (small, medium, and large); (3) to study the problem associated with fuller utilization of irrigation potential, and (4) to offer suggestions regarding development of irrigation. The study is limited to socio-economic and engineering aspect of the project. Mimeographed.

82. **Yadav, Ram Prakash**. Case study of small farmers in Naktajhijh Dhanukha, Nepal. *Contributions to Nepalese Studies*, vol. 5, no. 1 (Dec. 1977), pp. 15-39.

Naktajhijh Panchayat is located along the Janakpur-Mahendranagar Road which meets the East-West Highway at Dhalkebar. Naktajhijh is about 19 kilometers north of Janakpurdham, the headquarters of Janakpur Zone and only 5 kilometers off the East-West Highway. This panchayat is idealy situated with respect to transport networks. It is only 4 kilometers away from the Sakhuwa Village, the FAO Field Action Project Area. This case study is of small farmers in Naktajhijh Village Panchayat and is to determine the attitude and reactions of small owner operators share croppers and landless agricultural labourers towards the rural institutions. It deals mainly with six institutions and their organizational set-up, their mode of operations and interaction with the farmers at the village level. These institutions are : agricultural extension, credit, cooperative, land reform, marketing, and village government. This study also provides the basis for a meaningful comparison between areas with and without the FAO Field Action Project. Includes three appendices.

83. **Yadav, Ram Prakash**. A glance at the present agricultural research, education, and extension in Nepal. Kathmandu : Agricultural Projects Services Centre, 1976. 14 p. (APROSC staff paper ; no. 1)

Discusses the priorities, progress, and revisal of objectives and strategies. The author concludes that the agricultural research, education, and extension being corner stones of agricultural development, a compatable nexus among them is highly essential. The focus of these components should be to uplift the rural population who are largely small holders and tenants, rather than to meet or achieve the physical targets of agricultural input and output ignoring the equity aspect completely.

84. **Zollinger, F.** Analysis of river problems and strategy for flood control in the Nepalese Terai. Kathmandu : Ministry of Forest, Department of Soil and Water Conservation, Integrated Watershed Management, Torrent Control, and Land Use Development Project, 1979. 130 p. 2 maps.

In Nepal, Terai area presents a dramatic picture of the destructive nature of rivers. The Terai is exposed to serious floods with the onset of every monsoon. This, together with the great amount of sediment which is deposited daily, the continuous erosion of river banks, and the periodic change in the course of many rivers has brought about a situation which demands serious attention. This report deals in detail with the problems mentioned above. The report tries to define that why these problems exist and what might be done to alleviate some of them. This report also examined the activities already being undertaken by various ministries and foreign agencies to avoid this situation. Some recommendations are also suggested in this report.

3

ARCHAEOLOGY

85. **Amatya, Saphalya.** Nepālamā purātattva. Kathmandu : Sajha Prakashan, 1979. 258 p.

    This publication is in Nepali and deals with the art, architecture, and archaeological remains of Nepal, with special reference to temple art, iconographs, etc.

86. **Ballinger, Thomas O.** Simraongarh revisited : a report on some observations made at the ruins of the former capital of Mithila in the Terai of Nepal. *Kailash : a Journal of Himalayan Studies*, vol. 1, no. 3 (Sept. 1973), pp. 180-184. illus.

    A revised version of a paper presented on 23 May 1970 at the Pacific North West Art History Association Conference, University of California at Davis. The article describes the condition of this ancient site as it stands today and gives several examples of sculpture and carving at Simraongarh.

87. **Burghart, Richard.** The disappearance and reappearance of Janakpur. *Kailash : a Journal of Himalayan Studies*, vol. 6, no. 4 (1978), pp. 257-284. bibliog.

    Janakpur was thecapital of Mithila. Ancient Mithila was ruled by the Vaidehi dynasty but during a war Janakpur was destroyed, and the dynasty became extinct. What the opposing armies did not destroy, the jungle covered over, and Janakpur disappeared without a trace. Until the end of the 17th century, for the Vaisnavites, Janakpur existed as an object of devotion and meditation but site remained unknown. In this essay, the author reconstructs the reappearance of Janakpur and the events which led to the founding of the modern town of Janakpurdham in the early 18th century, He considers three aspects : the oral testimony of the ascetics; Archaeological and documentary evidence; and analysis of the oral testimony.

88. **Deo, Shantaram Bhalchandra**. Archaeological excavations in Kathmandu, 1965. Kathmandu : Department of Archaeology, His Majesty's Government of Nepal 1968. 46 p. illus.

This report deals with the excavations at Lazimpet and Hadigaon, and includes information on the ancient history of Nepal. The project was jointly undertaken by the Department of Archaeology and the Indian Cooperation Mission, Nepal.

89. **Deo, Shantaram Bhalchandra**. Archaeological investigations in the Nepal Tarai, 1964. Kathmandu : Department of Archaeology, Government of Nepal, 1968. 32+27 p. map. illus.

A report of the work undertaken jointly by the Department of Archaeology and the Indian Cooperation Mission, Nepal. Includes 27 pages of illustrations, some folded.

90. **Lumbini, Kapilavastu.** Kathmandu: His Majesty's Government, Lumbini Development Committee, Publicity Sub-Committee, 1979. 28 p. 2 maps. illus. (Lumbini year: 1979).

A collection of articles on two ancient sites associated with early Buddhism. The articles are : 'Buddhism in Nepal' by Dr. Billi Raman Regmi (extracted from *Everest Weekly*, vol. 9, no. 27, 1 Oct. 1978); 'Sakyamuni's birth-place' by Dr B.C. Law (from *The Maha Bodhi* : *Journal of the Mahabodhi Society*, vol. 55, no. 5-6, May-June 1947); 'Kapilavastu conundrum' by A.D.T.E. Perera. Includes five plates.

91. **Lumbini, Kapilavastu, Ramagrama**. Kathmandu : His Majesty's Government, Lumbini Development Committee, Publicity Sub-Committee, 1979. 16 p. map. bibliog. illus. (Lumbini year : 1979).

A collection of four articles on three ancient sites associated with early Buddhism. The articles are : 'The discovery of Lumbini' by Rishikesh Shaha (from *Lumbini*, vol. 1, no. 2, 17 May 1973); 'Lest we forget; Lumbini and its message to the modern world' by Rt. Hon. Prof. Rama Prasad Manandhar (from *Lumbini*, vol. 1, no. 2, 17 May 1973); 'Identification of Ramagrama' by Dr. Tulsi Ram Vaidya; 'Sakya token of Kapilavastu' by Babu Krishna Rijal. Includes four plates.

92. **Rajvanshi, Shankarman,** ed. Purātattva-patrasaṅgraha. Kathmandu : His Majesty's Government, Archaeology and Cultural Department, 1961-63. vols. 2-3. (Purātattvaprakāśanamālā, 7, 19).

The publication contains not only letters, but also stone and copper inscriptions. This meterial is quite useful for research on the socio-economic conditions and government of mediaeval Nepal during the Malla and Shaha periods. The stone and copper inscriptions (generally found in temples) and the letters are arranged chronologically in one sequence. Many of the copper inscriptions are royal charters : documents of land grants to temples or religious orders or exemptions from taxes granted to such bodies. There are 183 letters and inscriptions, in Newari or Devanagari scripts, and in Sanskrit, Newari, Nepali, Hindi, or Maithili languages. Includes a brief introduction of the archaeological places in Nepal.

93. **Rau, Heimo.** The Pūjārī Maṭha of the Dattātreya Temple, Bhaktapur, and its restoration : a preliminary report. *Journal of the Nepal Research Centre*, vol. 1 (Humanities) (1977), pp. 117-129.

The Dattātreya Temple in Bhaktapur is situated in the centre of the area of artisans and traders in the city. On the south side of the temple is the *Pūjārī Maṭha*; a monastery which is the most outstanding *maṭha* in the area in terms of size and facilities. The *maṭha* was founded by Gosvami Gurubaksha Giri, a saint from Mahuragarh, India who returned through Nepal, laden with treasure from his pilgrimage to Tibet. This article describes the *maṭha* and its manifold functions, and also examines the restoration work, undertaken between September 1971 and May 1972 with the advice of the German government.

94. **Rijal, Babu Krishna.** Archaeological activities in Lumbini, 1976-78. Kathmandu : His Majesty's Government of Nepal, Lumbini Development Committee [1979 ?]. 19 p. map. bibliog. illus.

Lumbini, which is situated in the western Terai of Nepal, was a pleasure-garden for the people of Kapilavastu and Devadaha, even before it gained importance as the birthplace of Lord Buddha. This publication is a brief study of the archaeological activities in Lumbini during 1976-78. There are 12 plates.

95. **Rijal, Babu Krishna.** Archaeological remains of Kapilavastu, Lumbini, and Devadaha. Kathmandu : Educational Enterprises, 1979. 88 p. 5 maps. bibliog.

These three places are important historical Sites because of Gautama Buddha. The identification of Kapilavastu, based on ample archaeological evidence and historical record, has been accepted, although of late certain archaeologists have challenged the findings. In the early 1960s, the Nepalese Government's Department of Archaeology started excavation work in Kapilavastu (now known as Tilaurakot), Paisa, Banjarahi, and Lumbini, collaborating at first with the Archaeological Survey of India and later with the Rissho University of Japan. From the beginning, the author, a research officer of the Department of Archaeology, Nepal worked at these sites. In this book, the author examines these ancient sites, particularly Kapilavastu and Lumbini, and uses recent archaeological evidence to present his conclusions in a most convincing way.

96. **Rijal, Babu Krishna.** Introduction to Tilaurakot as Kapilavastu. *Nepalese Culture*, vol. 1 (1979), pp. 21-28.

Kapilavastu, the capital town of Lumbini where Gautama Buddha was born, is considered by Buddhists to be the first of the four great holy places of pilgrimage. According to legend, Kapilavastu was also the dwelling-place of the saint Kapilmuni. This article discusses the origin of Kapilavastu and its history and culture. Archaeological excavations have been undertaken for the last 125 years to find out the exact location of Kapilavastu, and the author has carried out his own surveys since 1972. In this article the author shows that most studies confirm Tilaurakot's claim to be the exact site of ancient Kapilavastu.

97. **Slusser, Mary Shepherd.** The Saugal-ṭol Temple of Patan. *Contributions to Nepalese Studies*, vol. 2, no. 1 (Feb. 1975), pp. 39-46. illus.

This small temple at Saugal-ṭol is a typical Nepalese, or Newar, construction of brick and wood; it is built to a square plan, with two roofs. It is difficult to date the shrine, but it probably belongs to 16th or 17th century. In this article, the author comments on the temple and the images in it from the archaeological point of view. Includes three illustrations of Sankara Narayana.

98. **Vaidya, T.R.** Identification of Ramagrama. *Nepalese Culture*, vol. 1 (1979), pp. 9-13.

Attempts to identify the date of the Ramagrama and the stupa constructed by the Koliyas in Nepal. The stupa of Ramagrama is one of the holy places visited by all eminent Buddhist pilgrims.

4

ARTS

99. **Alsop, Ian** and **Charlton, Jill.** Image casting in Oku Bahal. *Contributions to Nepalese Studies,* vol. 1, no. 1 (Dec. 1973), pp. 22-49. bibliog.

The two centres of image casting in Patan, the city of fine arts, are two Newari Buddhist communities of the Bare or Vanras caste at Oku Bahal and Nag Bahal. Oku Bahal is the more productive of the two in terms of the fine quality pieces. The whole process of image casting in Nepal as witnessed by the authors in Oku Bahal in Patan is described with photo plates. This article also describes a brief history of image casting in Nepal, India, and Tibet and the survival of casting in Nepal and the decline of surrounding traditions.

100. **Bajracharya, Harsha Purna** and **Shrestha, K. M.** Nepal : history, arts, crafts, and temples. Kathmandu : Nepal National Commission for UNESCO, 1974. 37 p. (Different aspects of Nepalese way of life ; 2).

This publication includes two essays: 'Arts, crafts, sculpture, and temples in Nepal', by P.H, Bajracharya and 'An outline history of Nepal', by K. M. Shrestha.

101. **Banerjee, Nil Ratan.** Nepalese architecture. Delhi : Agam Kala Prakashan, 1980. 272 p. bibliog.

While serving Archaeological Survey of India, the author was on deputation to His Majesty's Government of Nepal as an advisor in Archaeological Studies from 1966 to 1972. He utilized this opportunity to study Nepal's great artistic heritage. In this publication, the author has discussed systematically the cultural background, the unique features of temple architecture in Nepal, and an account of its general architectural norms. The study draws heavily the inscriptional evidence. Ample documentation of the construction, repairs, and restoration of structures of several kinds are provided. The author has also drawn a close parallel between the architecture of India and Nepal. Includes 35 leaves of plates.

102. **Bernier, Ronald M.** A bibliography of Nepalese art.

For full entry refer to Bibliographies section.

103. **Bernier, Ronald M.** Metaphorical canons and the early development of the Buddha image. *The Nepalese Perspective*, vol. 9, no. 3 (Sept. 1973), pp. 13-34.

This article describes that the body of Buddha in early Indian art is provided as background to the Nepalese style in sculpture.

104. **Bernier, Ronald M.** The Nepalese pagoda : origins and style. New Delhi : S. Chand, 1979. 219 p. bibliog

Several studies are undertaken on architecture of Nepal and the Himalaya, but the origin of pagoda temple is not made clear so far. This study attempts to deal with this question and links widely separated visual traditions as parts of an artistic tradition that is unique to the Himalaya. The study searches for the essence as well as the image of sacred architecture in the mountain region. Author has also discussed pagodas relationship to domestic buildings while defining their significance within the context of geography, society, and art.

105. **Bernier, Ronald M.** Notes on Chusya-Bahāl in Kathmandu. *Kailash : a Journal of Himalayan Studies*, vol. 6, no. 4 (1978), pp. 233-236.

Like pagoda temples of Nepal, the *bahāl* or *vihāra* monastery are also important. The vihāra of Chausya-Bahal is located a short walk from King's Way and behind the National Theatre. This bahāl is amongst the oldest and best preserved Buddhist monastery buildings in Nepal, dated by inscriptions to 1662 A.D. and the regin of Pratapa Malla. In this study, the author has discussed Chausya-Bahāl from architectural point of view. The study is supported by four pages of illustrations.

106. **Bernier, Ronald M.** The temples of Nepal : an introductory survey. New Delhi : S. Chand, 1978. 2nd rev. ed. 171 p. bibliog.

This publication which is an introductory survey describes Historical sketch; Notes on religious background; Elements of Nepalese temples architecture; The monuments of Patan; The monuments of Bhaktapur; The monuments of Kathmandu; and Other monuments. There are 10 leaves of illustrations of major monuments discussed in the book. Includes index of temples.

107. **Chandra, Jagdish.** Bibliography of Nepalese art.

For full entry refer to Bibliographies section.

108. **Chittadhar, Tuladhar.** Chitta Dhar 'Hridaya's Nepalese music=Nepāla saṅgīta. Translated by : Thakurlal Manandhar. Kathmandu : Nepal Bhasha Parishad, 1957, 18 p. (Nepal-bhasha series ; no. 20)

Address delivered at the prize-giving ceremony inside the Hanuman Dhoka (Layekuli) under the auspices of the Santi-Raksha-Swayam Sevaka-Sangh. The address was delivered in Newari and now translated into English.

109. **Connally, Ernest A.** An art that conciliates gods and men. *UNESCO Courier*, vol. 27 (Dec. 1974), pp. 16-18.

A general description of Nepalese art and architecture.

110. **Deo, Shantaram Bhalchandra.** Glimpses of Nepal wood-work. *The Journal of the Indian Society of Oriental Art*, new series, vol. 3 (1968/69). 48 p. of text with 38 p. of illustrations and a map.

This essay describes the structural and ornamental woodworking tradition of the Newar craftsmen of Nepal. The author has presented a general account of the distinctive ornamental features of traditional architecture found in the several centres of the Kathmandu Valley. Some of these structure belong to 14th and 15th centuries. The author has also described the artisans, their tools, apparatus, and techniques.

111. **A glimpse of the Nepalese numismatography**. Compiled by National Museum of Nepal. Kathmandu : The Museum, 1975. 19 p.

Describes about the collection of numismatics in the Museum. Includes illustrations.

112. **Gut, Paul.** Architecture in the national parks of Nepal : documentation. Kathmandu : National Parks and Wildlife Conservation Office, His Majesty's Government, Nepal, 1980. 75 p. 1 map. fully illustrated.

The National parks of Nepal are situated in various parts of the country which differ highly in geography and climate. The National Parks & Wild Life Conservation Office in Nepal was founded in 1972 and is supported by FAO. In 1974 the Project received support from Swiss Association for Technical Assistance which provided architects and engineers and the work was started by Jean Wuethrich and was succeeded by the author in 1976. Another person, Willi Bielser worked with the project from 1975 till beginning of 1979. The buildings included in this documentation were designed by the author and supervised by Willi Bielser.

113. **Gutschow, Niels.** The restoration of the Cyaslim Mandap in Bhaktapur. *Kailash : a Journal of Himalayan Studies*, vol. 4, no. 3 (1976), pp. 227-235. bibliog.

Cyāsliṃ Maṇḍap (pronounced "chashin" in Newari, meaning "eight-cornered"; maṇḍap in Sanskrit means "pedestal"), was located on the Yahsiṃkhel near Chupin ghāt, at Bhaktapur and was restored by a private association, the Vereniging Nederland-Nepal. The maṇḍap is a freestanding one-storied building on a two-stepped pedestal (2.40 m. above ground level). This maṇḍap is utilized only during Bisket jātrā (the New year festival in April) for worshipping Bhairava. In this article, the author has described structural and functional importance of the *Cyāsliṃ Maṇḍap*, process of restoration, and costs of restoration. The project was started in February 1975 and completed in October 1975. Includes illustrations.

114. **Helffer, Mireille,** Fanfares villageoises au Népal. *Objects et mondes*, tome 9, fasc. 1 (1969), pp. 51-58.

The author has described the musical instruments which are played in Nepalese fanfares. He has also clarified the role of musicians, known as Damai in Nepal, and points out their importance in the Nepalese society, The theories concerning the origin of these groups of instrumentalists in Nepal are also highlighted. Includes illustrations.

115. **Helffer, Mireille** and **Macdonald, A.W.** Sur un sârangi de Gâine. *Objects et Mondes*, tome VI, fasc. 2 (1966), pp. 133-142.

This article is in French language and deals with the traditional musical instrument, Sarangi. Includes illustrations.

116. **Höfer, Andras.** On cire perdue casting in Nepal. *Journal of the Nepal Research Centre*, vol. 4 (Humanities) (1980), pp. 32-66. bibliog.

This paper is English translation of the original in German by the author written in 1970. The author has described about the workshop for casting, followed by the technology : modelling the wax-figure, the reproduction process, the casting, and quick water gilding. Includes 14 illustrations.

117. **Joshi, Hari Ram.** Uttaraprācīna kālina mudrā. Kathmandu : Sajha Prakashan, 1976. 237 p.

The coins of Licchavi period are the simplest and of appealing design. The figures of the animals, vase-and-flower motifs, and the vajras on copper coins represent the artistic importance of that time. This book includes details of 61 type of coins with size and weights. Out of these 45 coins are illustrated by photographs. Some of these coins are described for the first time. In Nepali.

118. **Joshi, Satya Mohan.** Nepālī rāshtriya mudrā. Lalitpur, Nepal : Jagdamba Prakashan, 1962 or 63. 182 p., 31 p. of illus. bibliog. (Jagdamba Prakashan mala ; 24).

This is a numismatic study of Nepal. This is the first work of its kind by a modern scholar of Nepal based on firsthand investigation in the representative types of coins from Lacchavi period to the present age, arranged chronologically. The study is systematic in all aspects of the coins, namely the metal, minting technique, measurement, weight, etc. The study of the Malla coins included in this volume is consider as a pioneer attempt. In Nepali.

119. **Khatri, Tek Bahadur.** The postage stamp of Nepal. Kathmandu : Sharada Kumari K.C., 1973. 2nd ed. 176 p.

This is the study of postage stamps of Nepal with historical background.

120. **Kirkpatrick, William.** An account of the Kingdom of Nepal, the substance of observations made during a mission to that country in the year 1793.

For full entry refer to History—General section.

121. **Kooij, Karel Rijk van.** The iconography of the Buddhist wood-carving in a Newar Monastery in Kathmandu (Chuṣya-Bāhā). *Journal of the Nepal Research Centre*, vol. 1 (Humanities) (1977), pp. 39-82.

An iconographical study of the Buddhist deities in wood-carvings has some advantages over the better known stone sculptures, although these are older and sometimes more impressive. In this article, the author has studied the complete iconography of one sacred building, Newar Monastry (Chuṣya-Bāhā *or* Guṇākarmahāvihāra) in Kathmandu. This has given a better understanding of the meaning of the series of images represented in wood-carving of the struts and the tympanums. Includes illustrations of deities.

122. **Korn, Wolfgang**. Traditional architecture of the Kathmandu Valley. Kathmandu : Ratna Pustak Bhandar, 1976. 125 p. (Bibliotheca Himalayica; series III, volume 11).

Kathmandu Valley is well known for the richness, exuberance, and exoticism of traditional architecture. This is a book on high culture traditional Nepali architecture written and drawn by professionals. This book is arranged in chapters on the main types of buildings and the general descriptions of these type provide adequate background to any person who wishes to visit the Kathmandu Valley and can have the understanding of what will be seen there. Location of the buildings it discusses is not clear on the city map, even then the graphic and written information in this book is really valuable. Includes 61 line drawings, 12 sketches, and one photo.

123. **Landon, Perceval.** Nepal.

For full entry refer to History—General section.

124. **March, Kathryn S.** The iconography of Chiwong Gomba. *Contributions to Nepalese Studies*, vol. 5, no. 1 (Dec. 1977), pp. 85-92.

Chiwong Gomba is very active monastery of southern Solu region. In this paper, the author has given a brief description of the monastery, its setting and surrounding, and the paintings of the monastery.

125. **NAFA Art Magazine.** Kathmandu : Nepal Association of Fine Arts.

An annual publication which publishes scholarly articles on arts of Nepal. Till 1970, this was issued in English and now being issued in Nepali.

126. **Nepalese Art.** Department of Archaeology, Nepal. Kathmandu : The Department, 1966. 85 p.

A catalogue of the art objects exhibited in Paris during the state visit of King Mahendra Bir Bikram Shah Deva and Queen Ratna Rajya Lakshmi Devi Shah to France in October 1966. Includes thirty-six plates of illustrations and 'An introduction to Nepalese art' by N. R. Banerjee.

127. **Nepalese art in a nutshell.** National Museum of Nepal. Kathmandu : The Museum, 1975. 46 p. bibliog.

This book is intended to present the salient features of Nepalese art, so that foreign visitors may have the necessary background within a small compass to have a better appreciation of the objects they see. Includes nineteen leaves of plates carrying forty illustrations.

128. **Pal, Pratapaditya.** The arts of Nepal. Part I : Sculpture with 300 plates. Leiden/Köln : E.J. Brill, 1974. vol. 1. (186 p., 300 plates) bibliog. (Handbuch der orientalistik. Siebente. abteilung. III. Band, 3. Abschnitt, 2. Lieferung. I)

This is volume one of three-volumes work. The second volume is devoted to painting and third to architecture. This book has grown out of Ph. D. thesis on the *Sculpture and painting of Nepal,* submitted to the University of Cambridge in 1965. This book brings together, for the first time, three hundred examples of Nepali sculpture and traces their history from about the third century until the eighteenth. The author attempts not only to put the sculpture of Nepal in its proper historical perspective, but also explores its relationship with the Indian traditions. The book also clearly establishes that although Nepali artists were always aware of the major artistic movements on the Indian subcontinent, nonetheless, their aesthetic genius was never over-whelmed by imported ideas. On the contrary, the book makes clear the remarkable vitality of the Nepali aesthetic tradition for well over a millennium.

129. **Pal, Pratapaditya.** Vaisnava iconology in Nepal. Calcutta : Asiatic Society, 1970?

Vaishnavism has had an important place in the religious life of Nepal from at least 14th century A.D. This book is not only a specialized discussion of Vaishnava iconography as it is found in Nepal but an attempt as well at an historical reconstruction of the religion there through the investigation of its art. The study reveals that without a thorough examination of Vaishnavism and its relations with Shivaism and Buddhism, no one can understand religion in Nepal and also that Vaishnavism was influenced by tantrism more in Nepal than in India. Includes illustrations.

130. **Pal, Pratapaditya** and **Bhattacharya, Dipak Chandra.** The astral divinities of Nepal. Varanasi, India : Prithvi Prakashan, 1969. 82 p. bibliog. (Indian civilization series ; no. 9)

This is a study of the icons of astral divinities in Nepal. The author has based this study from sculptures and literary texts. The Nepalese art and religion evolved through centuries with Hindu and Buddhist traditions are discussed in detail. Includes illustrations.

131. **Pandey, Ram Niwas.** The art of Kapilavastu. *Journal of the Tribhuvan University*, vol. 8, no. 1 (1973), pp. 9-52.

This article refers to descriptions of the images and paintings at Kapilavastu by the Chinese travellers Fahien and Huien Tsiang. Objects of art, both Hindu and Buddhist, yielded by the excavations of Tilaurakot are discussed and described in detail. The article also refers to a recent excavation at Piparahawa near Tilaurakot. Includes sixteen plates of photographs.

132. **Pradhan, Mrigendra Singh** [et al.]. Nṛtyakalā. Kathmandu : Sajha Prakashan, 1980. 198 p.

Describes classical Indian and various Nepali folk dances. Chapters on Nepali folk dances are well written. Not much has been written on this subject so far and this book serves a very useful purpose. In Nepali.

133. **Rajaure, D.P.** Tattooing among the Tharus of Dang Deokhuri, par western Nepal. *Contributions to Nepalese Studies*, vol. 2, no. 1 (Feb. 1975), pp. 91-98.

In this article the author has described tattooing and the material needed for tattooing, preparation, time and place for tattooing, aims and objective, parts of division of tattooing, and order of tattooing work. Includes illustrations.

134. **Rau, Heimo.** On the origin of the pagoda style in Nepal. *Journal of the Nepal Research Centre*, vol. 4 (Humanities) (1980), pp. 223-232.

The author states clearly that the pagoda-type towers in the valley of Kathmandu originated indigenously in Nepal as an essential part of the wooden architecture prevailing in a country which was covered with dense forests in earlier times. Includes illustrations.

135. **Riccardi, Theodore, Jr.** A note on a Nepalese image of Surya-Narayana. *Kailash*, vol. 1, no. 1 (Mar. 1973), pp. 89-90.

The author has presented an image of the sun god—Surya-Narayan—which he found in Patan and has discussed that the image falls in part anthropomorphic and in part symbolic which is different from the various known images of the sun god in India.

136. **Ridley, Michael.** Oriental art : India, Nepal, and Tibet—for pleasure and investment. London : Gifford, 1970. 195 p. bibliog.

A brief account of oriental art up to the 19th century. Includes material on the mythology, painting, sculpture, and bronzes of India, Nepal, and Tibet. The volume contains illustrations and a glossary.

137. **Rimal, Pradip.** Karṇālī loka saṃskṛti. Vol. 5 : Sāhitya, saṅgīta, kalā.

For full entry refer to Literature—Folklore section.

138. **Row Dayal, Leela.** Bhaktapura ratnam = Jewel of Bhaktapur : its architecture and sculpture. New Delhi : Arnold-Heinemann, 1980. 30 p., 48 p. of illustrations. (UNESCO collection of representative works : Indian series)

Bhaktapur (formerly known as Bhadgaon) was founded by King Ananda in the 9th century and was one of the Newar kingdoms of the Kathmandu Valley. The Newars were excellent craftsmen and artistic gems are still to be found in Bhaktapur in happy though scattered profusion. This book describes architecture and sculpture in this visual description of the town. The author has revealed the architecture of the magnificent ancient temples and palaces. The illustrations are of various temples, statues, palaces, animals, etc.

139. **Roy, Amita.** Art of Nepal. New Delhi : Indian Council for Cultural Relations, 1973. 158 p.

This is a study, in depth, of the artistic heritage of Nepal. The author has described architecture; sculpture and bronzes; wood-carvings and terracottas; paintings; religion and pantheons of gods and goddesses. Includes eighty pages of illustrations, some coloured.

140. **Sharma, Prayag Raj.** Preliminary study of the art and architecture of the Karnali Basin, West Nepal. Paris : Centre National de la Recherche Scientifique, 1972. 96 p. 3 maps. bibliog.

Dr. Prayag Raj Sharma is a pioneer in the field of research in the art, architecture, and sculpture of the Karnali region. This book is based on his observations of the wooden shrines housing gods of diverse cults, locally described as *thans* or *madus*, the temples generally called *devals*, and miscellaneous structures of stonemasonry such as a large water reservoir at Dullu, a rest house at Vyauli, and an open Hypostyle hall, called *mandap*, at Bayalkantiya. The book is illustrated with thirty-four black and white photographs of temples. Translation in French is supervised by Marc Gaborieau.

141. **Sharma, Yagya Raj.** Svara tāla paricaya. Kathmandu Royal Nepal Academy, 1979 or 80. 120 p.

This is a handbook of meter, rhythm, and tune in Hindustani classical music by an eminent musician of Nepal.

142. **Singh, Madanjeet.** Himalayan art : wall-painting and sculpture in Ladakah, Lahaul, and Spiti, the Siwalik Ranges, Nepal, Sikkim, and Bhutan. London : MacMillan, 1971. 287 p. bibliog. 1 map. (UNESCO art book series)

The Nepal portion deals with a study of Nepalese art from 300 B.C. to 18th century. The author has also discussed the development of art with changing historical and cultural scene. Includes illustrations.

143. **Talwar, Kay** and **Krishna, Kalyan.** Indian pigment paintings on cloth. Ahmedabad, India : Calico Museum of Textiles, 1979. 166 p. bibliog. (Historic textiles of India at the Calico Museum; v. 3)

On the temple hangings of the Vallabhacharya sect, Jain patas, phadas, and panchangas of western India, Orissa patachitras, cloth paintings of Nepal, and other regional styles. Includes an annotated catalog of the Museum's collection and an index. Also includes 58 leaves of plates (illustrative matter), some coloured.

144. **Toba, Ingrid.** Folk art and culture change as observed in a Khaling village. *Kailash : a Journal of Himalayan Studies*, vol. 5, no. 1 (1977), pp. 13-27. bibliog.

This study concerns Khastap Village having 75 houses of Khalings, a group of Tibeto-Burman language stock. In this article, the author has tried to enumerate and describe those items of Khaling material culture which are to date made by hand of materials provided by the natural surroundings of Khaling villages. These items are rapidly decreasing as raw materials, especially hemp, bamboo, and wood are getting scarce now and people are prefering for manufactured items. This has resulted in linguistic change and a change in people's thinking and in their attitude towards market-bought items.

145. **Tuladhar, Buddha Ratna**. Saṅgīta-sādhana. Kirtipur, Nepal : Syllabus Development Centre, Tribhuvan University, 1979. 2 vols. bibliog.

The author is a professor of music at Padam Kanya Campus. In this work he has described the Indian classical music, Hindustani school, as practiced in Nepal. Includes songs with music in letter notation.

146. **Van der Wee, L.P**. Notes on a Nepalese thanka. *Kailash : a Journal of Himalayan Studies*, vol. 7, no. 1 (1979), pp. 27-33.

In this article the author has given the description of Vajravārāhi-paubha, a Nepalese painting. Also given text of the inscription in romanized form. Vajravārāhi is a very prominent Buddhist deity and very popular in Nepal and Tibet. This deity belongs to Hevajracycle having white or a red complexion and in her red appearance usually holds a chopper.

147. **Walsh, E.H**. The coinage of Nepal. Delhi : Indological Book House, 1973. 92 p.

Discusses in brief about the coins of the Malla dynasty of Newar kings and Gorkha coinage. Includes lists of Licchavi and Thakuri dynasties' coins. Includes seven plates of coins.

148. **Wiehler-Schneider, Sigrun** and **Wiehler, Hartmut**. A classification of the traditional musical instruments of the Nevars. *Journal of the Nepal Research Centre*, vol. 4 (Humanities) (1980), pp. 67-132.

The traditional musical instruments of the Nevars can still be observed in active use in many places and in a wide variety of circumstances for religious devotions, processions, ceremonies, etc. These are either purely instrumental or a mixed vocal-instrumental ensemble. In this article, the authors have classified and discussed the traditional musical instruments of the Nevars. These are Idiophones; Membranophones; Chordophones; Aerophones. Includes illustrations.

5

BIBLIOGRAPHIES

149. **Bernier, Ronald M.** A bibliography of Nepalese art. Kathmandu : Voice of Nepal, 1970. 46 p. Distributor : Educational Enterprise.

This is bibliography of selected books and periodical articles on Nepalese art but also includes Indian, Tibetan, Bhutanese, and Sikkimese art.

150. **Boulnois, L.** and **Millot, H.** Bibliographie du Népal. Paris : Centre National de la recherche scientifique, 1969- vols. (Cahiers népalais, 1).

This bibliography is in French language. Vol. 1 : Sciences humaines ; references en langues europeennes.

151. **Chandra, Jagdish.** Bibliography of Nepalese art. New Delhi : Delhi Printers Prakashan, 1980. 152 p. bibliog.

This bibliography exclusively deals with the various branches of plastic and visual art : stone-sculpture, bronzes and metal images, terracotta, ivory figures, wood-carvings, miniature paintings, and thankas. It also encompasses a wide field of allied subject like archaeology, cultural history, historical geography, and cultural relations of Nepal with other countries. Includes a list of 'Important collections of Nepalese art (museums and personal collections) from Nepal, India, America, and Europe with collectors' names and addresses'. Also includes a list of 'Illustrated manuscripts and the name of person or museum possessing these'.

152. **Credit.** Agricultural Documentation Centre (Nepal). Kathmandu : Agricultural Documentation Centre, Agricultural Projects Services Centre, 1979. 20 leaves. (Occasional bibliography / Agricultural Documentation Centre ; no. 4)

This is a bibliography on agricultural credit in Nepal, and includes a selection of publication from and about other areas of the world. Mimeographed.

153. **Dixit, Hemang.** Medical bibliography of Nepal. Kathmandu : Tribhuvan University, Institute of Medicine, Research & Review Division, 1978. 62 p.

This is comprehensive listing of books, articles, and reports that cover a wide range of medical topics on Nepal. Apart from medical science, it also covers traditional medical beliefs, health care systems, and health education. Includes WHO assignment reports and some unpublished articles also.

154. **Doctoral dissertation on Asia** : an annotated bibliographical journal of current international research. Ann Arbor, Michigan : Association for Asian Studies, Inc., 1974 ?- semiannual.

This is an occasional compilation designed to provide both comprehensive and accurate information for recently accepted and inprogress dissertations dealing with Asia, from Afghanistan in the west to Japan and the Philippines in the east, and Siberia in the north to Indonesia and Sri Lanka in the south. This covers research not only in the humanities and the social sciences but also in the natural sciences.

155. **Erhard, Franz-Karl.** Tibetan texts in the National Archives, Kathmandu. *Journal of the Nepal Research Centre*, vol. 4 (Humanities) (1980), pp. 233-250.

Several Tibetan works were microfilmed by the Nepal-German Manuscript Preservation Project during the years 1973/74. These are available on 340 microfilm reels (no. A 635-836 and B 543-628), copies of these are kept both in the National Archives, Kathmandu and in the Staatsbibliothek Preussischer Kulturbesitz, Berlin. A provisional catalogue of the texts contained on these reels was prepared by the author and this list is only an abstract of that. The list is meant for practical rather than for scientific purposes.

156. **FAO; Nepal.** Agricultural Documentation Centre. (Nepal). Kathmandu : Agricultural Documentation Centre, Agricultural Projects Services Centre, 1981. 35 p. (Occasional bibliography / Agricultural Documentation Centre : no. 8).

This is a bibliography of FAO publications on agricultural development in Nepal. The FAO being one of Nepal's oldest development partners has produced a significant amount of literature, which taken as a whole, reflects agricultural development efforts and priorities in Nepal over the last thirty years.

157. **Gupta, Raj Kumar**. Bibliography of the Himalayas. Gurgaon, India : Indian Documentation Service, 1981. 373 p.

Himalayas are divided in the following regions : The Kashmir Himalayas; The Himalayas of Himachal Pradesh; The Grahwal and Kumaon Himalayas (Uttar Pradesh); The Nepal Himalayas; The Eastern Himalayas including Sikkim and Bhutan. This bibliography is an exhaustive compendium of references on various aspects of resources and regional development.

158. **Hugoniot, Richard D.**, ed. A bibliographical index of the lesser known languages and dialects of India and Nepal. Kathmandu : Summer Institute of Linguistics, India-Nepal, 1970. 312 p.

This publication is a reference bibliography of the lesser known languages and dialects of India and Nepal. Many of the languages and dialects are known by different names or by different spellings of a common name. All languages and dialects including their alternate names are listed alphabetically with the main entries being cross-referenced to the bibliographical index by number.

159. **Husain, Asad**. Bibliography of Nepal. Kathmandu : His Majesty's Government of Nepal, Ministry of Information and Broadcasting, Department of Information, 1966- vol. 1-

Vol. one of this bibliography deals with historical and political publications.

160. **Integrated rural development**. Agricultural Documentation Centre. (Nepal). Kathmandu : The Centre, 1978.

12 leaves. (Occasional bibliography / Agricultural Documentation Centre ; no. 2).

Agricultural Documentation Centre is publishing a series of occasional bibliographies. This is bibliography on Integrated rural development in Nepal and is an important bibliography. Mimeographed.

161. **Irrigation**. Agricultural Documentation Centre (Nepal). Kathmandu : The Centre, 1978. 19 leaves. (Occasional bibliography / Agricultural Documentation Centre ; no. 1)

Agricultural Documentation Centre is publishing a series of occasional bibliographies. This bibliography, on irrigation, compiled from documents in the Centre, represents a component of the Centre's programme to disseminate information for the agricultural development of Nepal. Mimeographed.

162. **Madana Puraskara Pustakalaya.** Madana-gaurava : Madana Puraskāra Pustakālayako patrikā-sūcī. Lalitapur, Nepal : Madana Puraskara Pustakalaya, 1979 or 80. 135 p.

Madana Puraskara Pustakalaya, Lalitpur, is a well known library in Nepal. This is bibliography of serials available in this library.

163. **Malla, Kamal Prakash**. Nepāla bhāshāya dhvānā saphūyā dhalaḥ, Ne. sam. 1020-97 = Bibliography of Nepal Bhasha, 1900-77. Kathmandu : Chvasapasa, 1979. 44, 104 p.

This is a bibliography of Newari books. Entries are arranged alphabetically and include information regarding the subjects also. In introduction (44 p.), the author has given information about Newars, trends in Newari literature from medieval age, and also discusses the future of Newari language and literature.

164. **Malla, Khadga Man**, comp. and ed. Bibliography of Nepal = Nepālako granthasūcī. Kathmandu : Royal Nepal Academy, 1975. 529 p.

Under the Programme of producing source materials on Nepal, the Royal Nepal Academy included in its Five Year Plan (1969-1973) the compilation of *Bibliography of Nepal* as a supplement. It is divided into two parts: (1) the list of books and articles written in foreign languages on Nepal; (2) that of similar things written exclusively in Nepali language. The Royal Nepal Academy gave priority to the compilation of the list of the first category of books and decided to include in it a short account in Nepali as well, along with that in foreign languages. The present volume is the result of the compilation made in that way, and contains accounts of the materials available upto 1972. Arranged by subject and includes: Alphabetical index of anonymous works; Alphabetical index of authors; and List of titles of periodicals cited into the bibliography.

165. **Manandhar, Thakurlal**, comp. Works on Nepal in the Kaiser Library. Supervisor: Saket B. Thakur ; Editor: Lindsay C. Friedman. Kirtipur, Nepal; Institute of Nepal and Asian Studies, Tribhuvan University, 1974. 119 p.

An annotated bibliography, reproduced from Union Catalogue being established at Institute of Nepal and Asian Studies.

166. **Manandhar, Thakurlal**, comp. Works on Nepal in the National Library : an annotated bibliography. Kirtipur, Nepal : Institute of Nepal and Asian Studies, Tribhuvan University, 1975. 57, 75 leaves.

This mimeographed publication is divided into two parts. First part includes English publications and second part includes Nepali publications. The entries are arranged by subjects and under each subject section, books available in the National Library are listed.

167. **Marketing**. Agricultural Documentation Centre (Nepal). Kathmandu: Agricultural Documentation Centre, Agricultural Projects Services Centre, 1979. 25 leaves. (Occasional bibliography / Agricultural Documentation Centre ; no. 3)

This is a bibliography of agricultural marketing in Nepal. Agricultural marketing comprises all the operations involved in the movement of food and raw materials from farm to final consumer. In Nepal, agricultural products constitute more than 66% of total national production. Mimeographed.

168. **Mitra, Rajendra Lal**. The Sanskrit Buddhist literature of Nepal. Reprinted. Calcutta : Sanskrit Pustak Bhandar, 1971. 341 p.

Descriptive catalog of selected Sanskrit manuscripts presented to the Asiatic Society of Bengal by Brian Houghton Hodgson, 1800-1894, British Resident in Nepal. The work is very useful to the scholars of Buddhism and allied subejcts. Includes an introduction by Dr. Alok Ray. First published in 1882 by Asiatic Society of Bengal, Calcutta. Includes illustrations.

169. **Rajvanshi, Shankarman**, ed. Bhaktapura śilālekha sūcī. Kathmandu : His Majesty's Government, Department of Archives and Culture, 1963. 169 p. bibliog. (Purātattva-prakāśanamālā ; 12).

Bhaktapur (formerly known as Bhadgoan) was a capital during the time of Malla Kings. Inscriptions were quite common in Nepal at that time. These are generally found in temples. This book is a bibliography of 390 inscriptions of Bhaktapur arranged chronologically. These cover the period 329 A.D. to 1929 A.D. This bibliography gives location, date, occasion, size, no. of lines, and script of the inscriptions. The scripts of the inscriptions are Lachhavi (Gupta), Newari, and Devanagari. There is a geographical index at the end. These inscriptions are very useful for scholars to do the scientific study of the history of Nepal.

170. **Regmi, Jagadish Chandra**, comp. A comprehensive bibliography on the ethnology and anthropology of Nepal, including Sikkim, Darjeeling, and Kumaon. Kathmandu : Office of the Nepal-Antiquary, 1976. 36 leaves. 1 map. (Bibliographical series of the Nepal-Antiquary ; no. 1)

171. **Regmi Jagadish Chandra**, comp. and ed. A concise dictionary of Himalayan people : bibliographical. Assistant editor : Sheshraj Shiwakoti. Kathmandu : Office of Nepal-Antiquary, 1979. 250 leaves. 1 map.

This is no. 15, Aug. 1979 issue of *Nepal-antiquary*; *journal of socio-historical research & digest*. This is in fact a bibliographical projection of the subject and is only a preliminary stage of their programme in presenting a grand dictionary of Nepalese people in the form of original and comparative research in the near future. The study covers 404 topics on various tribes and races of Nepal describing their history, diet, origin, religion, marriage customs, language, socio-economic status, etc. Includes a map of Nepal depicting the location of various tribes and races of Nepal.

172. **Regmi, Jagadish Chandra**, comp. and ed. The Newars. Kathmandu : Office of the Nepal-Antiquary, 1978. 49

leaves. (Nepal Antiquary ; no. 8 : Subject bibliography ; no. 1) Distributors : Ratna Pustak Bhandar, Kathmandu.

A subject bibliography, classified extract from *An account of the Kingdom of Nepal* by Francis Hamilton Buchanan, 1762-1829; *An account of the Kingdom of Nepal*, by William Kirkpatrick, 1754-1812; and *Vaṁśavali* (Buddhist recension), translated by Pandit Gunanand, on the social life and customs of the Newar community of Nepal.

173. **Shafer, Robert**, ed. Bibliography of Sino-Tibetan languages. Associate editor: Pentti Aalto and others. Wiesbaden : O. Harrassowitz, 1957- vols.

Some of the languages of Sino Tibetan family spoken in Nepal are included in this publication.

174. **Sharma, Buddhi Sagar**, ed. Nepālarājakīya-Vīrapustakālayasthahastalikhitasamastapustakānaṃ saṅkṣiptasūcīpatram. Kathmandu : Bir Pustakalya, 1963. 171 p. (Purātattvaprakāśanamālā ; 18)

An index to the titles of the manuscripts stocked in the Bir Pustakalaya, Kathmandu.

175. **Shreshtha, Bhagavati Prasad**. Nepāla bhāshā patra-patrikāyā jātaḥ. Kathmandu : Nepal Bhasha Parishad, 1981. 58 p. (Nepal Bhasha Parishada saphy gū ; 39)

This bibliography is in Newari language and is a useful reference tool of Newari periodicals. Includes a brief history of journalism. The author is an enthusiastic Newari and has collected almost all Newari periodicals so far published.

176. **Shrestha, Indira**. Annotated bibliography on women in Nepal. Kathmandu : Centre for Economic Development and Administration, Tribhuvan University, 1979. 69 p. (The status of women in Nepal : vol. 1: Background report, pt. 4);

This annotated bibliography is not a comprehensive bibliography but still it is a valuable tool for understanding the problems of integrating women in development in Nepal or for those wishing to generate new approaches for solving these problems. This bibliography has been included as part of the project on *The status of women in Nepal.*

177. **Singh, Tulsi,** comp. Nepāla (ṛtu-pau) yā cvasu-dhalaḥ = Bibliography of Nepal. Edited by Kashinath Tamota. Kathmandu : Gyan Bahadur Maharaja, 1978. 47 p.

This is a bibliography in Newari of poems, essays, short stories, etc., published in *Nepāla*, a Newari language bimonthly.

178. **Small farmer development.** Agricultural Documentation Centre (Nepal). Kathmandu : Agricultural Documentation Centre, Agricultural Projects Services Centre, 1980. 27 leaves. (Occasional bibliography / Agricultural Documentation Centre ; no. 6)

This is a bibliography, chiefly on agricultural development in Nepal. This has 23 major sections which are arranged alphabetically. This bibliography will be of help to assimilate necessary information needed on agricultural and rural development regarding the small farmer. Mimeographed.

179. **Soil, Nepal.** Agricultural Documentation Centre (Nepal). Kathmandu : Agricultural Documentation Centre, Agricultural Projects Services Centre, 1980. 14 p. (Occasional bibliography / Agricultural Documentation Centre ; no. 7)

Bibliography on soil research and classification.

180. **Thakur, S.B.** comp. Panchayat : an annotated bibliography. Kirtipur, Nepal : Institute of Nepal and Asian Studies, Tribhuvan University, 1974 or 75. 8 v. in 11.

These volumes are reproduced from the union catalogue being established by Institute of Nepal and Asian Studies. The contents are: v. 1: Books and articles; v. 2: Speeches and addresses; v. 3: National Panchayat, selective news, views, and editorials; v. 4: Books (in Nepali); v. 5: Articles (in Nepali); v. 6: Royal addresses, speeches on panchayat (in Nepali); v. 7: Speeches (in Nepali); v. 8: Editorials and debates in the National Panchayat (in Nepali), Panchayat news (in Nepali).

181. **Union book list on science and technology.** National Council for Science and Technology, Library Sub-Committee (Nepal). Kathmandu : The Sub-Committee, 1980. 395 p.

In Nepal, there is a communication gap between the users and the suppliers in libraries. In order to fill this gap, the Library Sub-Committee of National Council for Science and Technology is extending facilities through dessiminating information on science and technology to research, planning personnels, etc. This List indicates major sources of scientific and technological information. 7000 entries have been included in the List from 16 various libraries of Kathmandu. Mimeographed.

182. **Wagley, Surendra Prasad** [et al.], comp. Nepal documentation. Kathmandu : Documentation Centre, Centre for Economic Development and Administration, 1973. 82 p. (CEDA occasional bibliography ; no. 4).

This is a bibliography of selected current books, reports, official documents, and periodicals articles available in the library of CEDA and covers documents related to contemporary socio-political-economic-administrative aspects of Nepal. Material included is in English and Nepali languages. Mimeographed.

183. **Wood, Hugh Bernard**. Nepal bibliography. Kathmandu : Bureau of Publication, College of Education, 1959. 108 p.

This bibliography is the first of a series of studies to be sponsored by the Central Library, which was established through the cooperative efforts of the Ministry of Education of His Majesty's Government of Nepal and the University of Oregon, acting for the United States Operations Mission.

6

CONSTITUTION AND LAW

CONTEMPORARY

184. **Agrawal, Hem Narayan.** Nepal, a study in constitutional change. New Delhi : Oxford and IBH, 1980. 218 p. bibliog.

A study of constitutional changes in Nepal between 1948-62 in the context of the patterns of the political interaction among power groups and institutions. Based on archival and documentary evidence, field work, interviews in Nepal, and an extensive tour of zone and district headquarters, this work is a detailed and objective examination and exposition of the constitutional—political process in change. It also discusses the first and the second amendments to the 1962 Constitution in January 1967 and December 1975 and how political development in Nepal has gradually led to the consolidation of power under the king. The final chapter presents the conclusions. The author believes that the Nepalese monarchy must either evolve toward constitutional monarchy and transfer power to the people or it will be violently overthrown.

185. **Bahadur, Kaisher, K.C.** The judicial customs of Nepal. 2nd rev. and enl. ed. Kathmandu : Ratna Pustak Bhandar, 1971- , vol. 1- folded maps, illus.

As well as the indigenous groups, several tribes and clans have migrated from India, Tibet, and China to Nepal. The Nepalese have their own judicial customs and many of the emigrant tribes and clans brought judicial customs with them. This study of the judicial customs of all the tribes and clans of Nepal is intended to be the first in a series.

186. **Bajracharya, Maniklal.** Constitutional development in Nepal. Kathmandu : Chandra Prasad & Bros. [1974?]. 117 p.

Describes constitutional development in Nepal with historical background.

187. **Bennett, Lynn.** Tradition and change in the legal status of Nepalese women. With assistance from Shilu Singh. Kathmandu : Centre for Economic Development and Administration, Tribhuvan University, 1979. 107 p. bibliog. (Status of women in Nepal. Vol. 1: Background report, pt. 2)

This monograph is a review of the legal status of women, with special emphasis on property ownership and inheritance, marriage, divorce, and other family laws as well as laws affecting women's ability to enter into business contracts, obtain employment, etc.

188. **Company Act, 1964.** Ministry of Law and Justice, Nepal. Kathmandu : The Ministry [1964?].

The official translation of the *Company Ain*, 2021, first issued in Nepali.

189. **The Constitution of Nepal.** Kathmandu : His Majesty's Government of Nepal, Ministry of Law and Justice, Law Books Management Committee, 1976. 68 p.

The constitution, incorporating the first and second amendments.

190. **The Constitution of Nepal** : English translation. Ministry of Law and Justice, Nepal. Kathmandu : The Ministry, 1963. 64 p.

The official translation of the Constitution, issued originally in Nepali.

191. **Foreign Exchange (Regulation) Act, 1962.** Ministry of Law & Justice, Nepal. Kathmandu : The Ministry, [1962]. 11 p.

The official translation of the act, originally issued in Nepali.

192. **Gyawali, S.P.** Towards better legal order. Kathmandu : Voice of Nepal, 1969. 52 p.

A collection of articles, some previously published in various periodicals: 'The role of substantive criminal law in the protection of human rights and the purposes and legitimate limits of penal sanctions'; 'Legal aspects of the problem of disarmament', 'Some thoughts on judicial administration'; and 'Legal aspects of industry'.

193. **Gyawali, S.P.** Towards rule of law. Kathmandu : Department of Information, His Majesty's Government of Nepal, 1969. 83 p. illus.

A collection of articles originally written in Nepali: 'Contributions of King Mahendra in the protection of justice'; 'Criminal investigation under different legal systems'; 'The role of the legal profession'; 'King Mahendra and the rule of law'; and 'Human rights and their protection in Nepal'.

194. **Khanal, Revati Raman.** Nepālamā kānūnī masaudā, siddhānta, ra vyavahāra. Kathmandu : Sajha Prakashan, 1978. 2 vols.

Discusses the drafting, principles, and application of certain legal documents. In Nepali.

195. **Muluki Aina** : sātauṃ saṃśodhanasameta milāieko rūpamā. Kathmandu : His Majesty's Government of Nepal, Ministry of Law and Justice, Law Books Management Commtttee, 1979. 242 p.

The *Muluki Ain* (civil code) of Nepal, including all the amendments and additions upto 1978.

196. **Nepal Income Tax Act, 2019** [**1962 A.D.**]. Law Books Management Committee, Ministry of Law & Justice, Nepal. Kathmandu : The Committee, [1963?]. 12 p.

The official translation of *Nepal Ayaker Ain* 2019, first published in Nepali in the *Nepal Extraordinary Gazette.*

197. **Nepal Miscellaneous Series.** Kathmandu : Regmi Research (Private) Ltd., 1977- irregular.

This journal includes translation of the Nepalese legislation. Earlier this was published by Nepal Press Digest, Kathmandu and was a monthly publication. This journal supersedes *Nepal law translation series.*

198. **Poudyal, Niranjan Bhakta.** The history of constitutional development in Nepal, 1948-1980. Lalitpur, Nepal : The Author, 1981. 148 p. biblog.

A history of constitutional development in Nepal from 1948 onwards, with a brief historical background to give readers a historical perspective. The book is intended for students of history and political science at the tertiary level. The author has divided the work into separate sections in order to aid easy comprehension of the topic.

199. **Pradhan, Prachand Prasad.** A guide to the Constitution of Nepal. Kathmandu : Sagar Prasad Mishra [196- ?]. 170 p.

A useful guidebook to the Constitution of Nepal.

200. **Press and Publication Act, 1962.** Ministry of Law and Justice, Nepal. Kathmandu : The Ministry [1963?]. 12 p.

The official translation of the act, originally issued in Nepali.

201. **Shreshtha, Prem Nand.** Rājanaitika sujhāvamālā. Virendra Nagar, Nepal : Laxmi Narayan Shreshtha, 1980. 98 p.

The author presents suggestions for the revision of the Nepalese constitution. In the course of the analysis, he critically, and with great sympathy and clarity of vision, reviews the social, political, and economic conditions of Nepal.

202. **Third amendment, background and main feature.** Ministry of Communication, Department of Information, Nepal. Kathmandu : The Department, 1981. 33 p.

This booklet reviews the historical role of the Nepalese monarchy, the Referendum Proclamation, and the main features of the constitution, highlighting the third amendment. This presents the background, salient features, and relevant provisions of the third amendment in some detail.

203. **Tuladhar, Tirth Raj.** The Constitution of Nepal. Kathmandu : The Author, 1966. 124 p.

A historical account of the Constitution of Nepal.

HISTORY

204. **Adhikari, Krishna Kant.** A brief survey of the organization and structure of Nepali law courts during the third quarter of the nineteenth century. *Contributions to Nepalese Studies*, vol. 6, no. 2 (June 1979), pp. 11-20.

It was Jung Bahadur who created more judicial courts, both in the hills and the Terai. This study is divided into two main sections: 'Centre' and 'Districts'. The section on the Centre is further divided into headings for the *Kausal* (State Council) and the *Sadar* Courts. District courts are examined both before 1850 (i.e. before the introduction of the legal code) and after 1850. The author describes the functions and jurisdiction of the courts: *addas* and *adalats* (district-level judicial courts), *amals* and *kachacharis* (village-level courts having original jurisdiction).

205. **Adhikari, Krishna Kant.** Criminal cases and their punishments before and during the period of Jang Bahadur. *Contributions to Nepalese Studies*, vol. 3, no. 1 (Jan. 1976), pp. 105-116.

The first influencial proponent of judicial law in Nepal was Jayasthiti Malla, whose laws were generally based on the Shastras (religious scriptures). Jung Bahadur (Prime Minister 1846-77) occupies a unique position in the legal history of Nepal. In 1854, he laid down the first legal code (*Ain*) which covered civil and criminal cases and applied to whole of Nepal. It was later on known as the *Muluki Ain*. Several amendments were made from 1854 to 1955 and finally a new *Muluki Ain* was introduced in 1962. In this study the author compares the provisions of the *Ain* with earlier criminal laws, keeping in view the official orders issued before 1846 as well as the published and unpublished papers of B. H. Hodgson. He also analyses cases which led to reforms in the legal code prior to 1854.

206. **Hofer, Andras.** The caste hierarchy and the state in Nepal : a study of the Muluki Ain of 1845. Khumbu Himal, emgebnisse des forschungsunternehmens Nepal Himalaya. Innsbruck, Austria : Universitätsverlag Wagner, 1979. 240 p. bibliog.

A scholarly study which examines the state-caste relationship in detail, probing certain crucial issues within the setting of Nepal. The work is a useful tool for anthropological studies of caste, because of its consideration of the *Muluki Ain*, a historical-legal document of the mid-19th century. The main enquiry is into the caste hierarchy of Nepal and some of its bases and ramifications, the correlation between caste and status, the dimensions of status, and finally, the role of the state in the management of intra-caste and inter-caste relationships. Information on individual subjects dealt with in the *Muluki Ain* is presented with descriptive texts and tables. Brief mention is made of the theoretical formulation of each problem, further supported by ethnographic data from published sources.

207. Nepala Kanuna Paricarca = Nepal Law Review.

For full entry refer to Professional periodicals section.

208. Riccardi, Theodore, Jr. The royal edicts of the King Rama Shah of Gorkha. *Kailash : a Journal of Himalayan Studies*, vol. 5, no. 1 (1977), pp. 29-65.

King Rama Shah played a major role in strengthing the Kingdom of Gorkha. He was the son of King Purandara Shah and ruled from 1606 to about 1633. King Rama Shah was skilled in foreign relations and also known as a law-giver in west and central Nepal. The Nepali legal code reflects the influence of the Nepali-speaking peoples of western and central Nepal and their rulers, the Shahs and later the Ranas. The author says that it is difficult to fully discuss the *Muluki Ain* (Law of the Realm) in this paper, but that one of the most important contributions to its development can be found in the edicts of King Rama Shah.

209. Sri 5 Surendra Vikrama Sahadevaka sasanakalama baneko : mulkī ena. Ministry of Law and Justice, Nepal. Kathmandu : Law Books Management Committee, Ministry of Law and Justice, His Majesty's Government of Nepal, 1955. 712 p.

Prior to the unification of Nepal by Prithvi Narayan Shah, there were no written law codes, and legal disputes were judged on the basis of Hindu dharma Shastras. Prithvi Narayan Shah laid down the principles for civil legal codes, but could not complete the work. During the reign of Surendra Vikram Shah Deva (ruled 1847-81), however, a commission was appointed to compile the legal codes, which were issued in 1863. These codes were subsequently revised in 1864-67. The compilers of these legal codes took into consideration all the professions, rights, castes and *varnas* in the social setting, age-old social customs, inter-caste marriage, suttee, social evils like rape and forcible conversion, and economic offences like cheating, forgery, etc. These code were written in 19th century Nepali, which is not now easy to understand. The codes are not in force today, but they have historical importance as legal and social source material. They are bound and preserved in the Royal Nepal Archives and presented in this book in their original form. During the regime of the Ranas under the Gorkha kings, some of the codes were repealled and some were added, and these changes are given in the appendixes of this book.

7

COUNTRY AND ITS PEOPLE

210. **Bühler, Jean.** Nepal. Lausanne, Switzerland : Editions, Rencontre, 1964. 214 p. maps. bibliog. illus. (L'Atlas des Voyages, 25).

A detailed description of Nepal.

211. **Etherton, P.T.** The last strongholds. London : Jarrold 1934. 297 p. illus.

A detailed description of Nepal.

212. **Facts about Nepal.** Kathmandu : Department of Information, Ministry of Information & Broadcasting, 1970. 53 p.

A book in question-and-answer form, giving replies to 119 questions on history, the panchayat (village council) system, foreign affairs, economy, and education, as well as on more general matters.

213. **Frank, Dietmar.** Trumland Nepal. Munich, GFR : Suddeutscher Verlag, 1974. 192 p. maps. illus.

A description of Nepal in German, based on the author's experiences while trekking with Sherpa companions. The book has a short text, 196 colour illustrations, a block-print on orange cloth of a Buddhist prayer flag, graphs, and a separate guidebook (24 pages) in a pocket on the inside cover. The account is authoritative, but glosses over the hardships of Nepalese life.

214. **Gordon, Eugene.** Nepal, Sikkim, and Bhutan (Himalayan kingdoms) in pictures. New Delhi ; Oxford, England :

IBH Publishing, 1972. 64 p. illus. (Visual geography series).

Photographs by the author depicting the land, history, government, people, and economy of the Himalayan kingdoms.

215. **Gurung, Harka.** Vignettes of Nepal. Kathmandu : Sajha Prakashan, 1980. 435 p. 19 maps. bibliog. illus.

The author, a geographer and mountaineer, has made numerous treks across the country, and this book provides unexpected insights into the scenic grandeur of Nepal. In addition to the topographic descriptions, it contains informative anecdotes on local history and lore, festivals, the economy, and the culture of diverse ethnic groups. There are also vivid accounts of geology, flora, fauna, and history, and subtle observations on the changes taking place in rural Nepal. The chapters are arranged geographically from the west to east, and for trekkers, the book prove to be an encyclopaedic guide to the various trekking areas.

216. **Hagen, Toni** [et al.]. Mount Everest : formation, population, and exploration of the Everest region.

For full entry refer to Geography—General section.

217. **Hedric, Basil C.** and **Hedrick, Anne K.** Historical and cultural dictionary of Nepal. Metuchen, New Jersey : Scarecrow Press, 1972. 198 p. bibliog. (Historical and cultural dictionaries of Asia series, no. 2).

Provides information on persons, places, events, geographical and political divisions, contemporary and past governmental information, etc.

218. **Hodgson, Brian H.** Essays on the languages, literature, and religion of Nepal and Tibet. New Delhi : Manjusri Publishing House, 1972. 145, 124 p. illus. (Bibliotheca Himalayica, series II, vol. 7)

The author was Assistant Resident of Nepal in 1825 and was Resident of Nepal, 1833-42. First published in 1874, this publication reflects his thorough and wide ranging knowledge of the country. Part one contains articles on the languages, literature, and religions of Nepal and Tibet and includes a list of Buddhist works, and notes on Buddhist cosmology and philosophy. Part two deals with the physical geography of the Himalaya, the aborigines of the Himalaya, the military tribes of Nepal, the Chepang and

Kusunda tribes, Nayakoti and its tribes, the tribes of northern Tibet (Horyeul and Sokyeul) and Sifau, the colonization of the Himalaya by Europeans, and the commerce of Nepal. The work is illustrated with contemporary engravings.

219. **Hosken, Fran P.** The Kathmandu Valley towns; a record of life and changes in Nepal. New York : Weatherhill, 1974. 327 p. 9 maps. illus.

Until the 1950s, when political changes opened it to the outside world, Nepal was a mysterious and practically inaccessible kingdom; today it stands on the verge of a transformation that may rob it of its unique cultural heritage. This richly illustrated book (505 illustrations) is both a tribute to the remarkable civilization of Nepal's Kathmandu Valley and a warning against the type of development that threatens to destroy it. It is also a record of that civilization, designed to capture and explain the present-day life and culture.

220. **Jest, Corneille.** Tarap, une vallée dans l'Himalaya. Paris : Seuil, 1974. 157 p. bibliog. illus.

Tarap is one of the four valleys in the Dolpa region in northwest Nepal. The author has lived with the people of Dolpa long enough to be their anthropological witness, and in addition has travelled extensively in other parts of Himalayas, so that he is able to distinguish the characteristics peculiar to the Tarap region. In this book he describes the Tarap valley and the way of life of the population. Stories from the author's main informant, Kagar Rinpoche, as well as a fourteen page essay on the Tibetan cultural background of the region are also included. The book is very richly illustrated.

221. **Kailash** : a Journal of Himalayan Studies. Kathmandu : Ratna Pustak Bhandar, 1973- quarterly.

An independent, interdisciplinary journal of Himalayan studies, very useful for scholars. Generally in English but includes some articles in Hindi and Tibetan also.

222. **Lall, J.S.** and **Moddie, A.D.** ed. The Himalaya : aspects of change. New Delhi : India International Centre, 1981. 481 p. 3 maps. illus. (Distributed by Oxford University Press, Delhi, London, New York)

Contributions on the physical, political, and ecological aspects of the Himalayas. This collection falls into three parts on nature, man, and their inter-relationships.

223. **Landor, A. Henry Savage.** Tibet and Nepal : political, cultural, geographical & historical. Reprint. New Delhi : Light & Life Publisher, 1975. 233 p. illus.

An interesting guidebook, first published by A. & C. Black of London in 1905, Includes 75 leaves of illustrations.

224. **Mahila karmacari nirdesika**.

For full entry refer to Encyclopaedias, directories, and who's who section.

225. **Majupuria, Trilok Chandra** and **Majupuria, Indra**. Peerless Nepal : covering broad spectrum of the Nepalese life in its right perspective. Gwalior, India : M. Devi, 1979. 271 p. bibliog. illus.

The authors' travels abroad encouraged them to produce works on the Nepalese people, their culture, traditions, customs, etc., for foreigners interested in the cultural and natural ecology of Nepal. In this monograph the authors present detailed descriptions of Nepal and its people. The study is supported by 12 leaves of plates, some coloured, illustrating the Nepalese life.

226. **Nepal** : a profile. Kathmandu : Nepal Council of Applied Economic Research, 1970. 253 p. illus.

A collection of essays, published on the occasion of the marriage of Crown Prince Birendra Bir Bikram Shah Deva and Aishwarya Rajya Laxmi Devi, on Phagun 16, 2026 (February 1970).

227. **Nepal** : an introduction to Nepalese culture. Kathmandu : Sahayogi Press, 1975. 60 p.

A collection of articles: 'Social implications of education' by Mohammad Moshin; 'Language and literature' by Surya Bikram Gewali; 'Nepalese folk songs' by Madhav Prasad Ghimire; 'Nepalese paintings' by Lain Singh Bangdel; 'A glance at Nepalese history' by Bal Chandra Sharma; 'The panchayat system of government' by Kul Shekhar Sharma; 'Environment and heritage' by Richard Greenbough; 'An art that conciliates Gods and men' by Ernest A. Connally; 'The valley of Kathmandu' by Carl Pruscha; 'The crown, the coronation, and the country' by Krishna Raj Aryal.

228. **Nepal : monograph on Nepalese culture**. Department of Information, Nepal. 2nd ed. Kathmandu : The Department, 1968. 80 p. illus.

First published in 1962 by the Ministry of Education, with the assistance of the UNESCO.

229. **Nepal** : the Himalayan kingdom. Kathmandu : His Majesty's Government, Ministry of Communications, Department of Information, 1981. 69 p. illus.

A compilation of essays by eminent writers, each an expert in his field, to commemorate King Birendra's state visit to the Arab Republic of Egypt in February 1981. This publication presents an overall view, though not an exhaustive one, of some of the important aspects of Nepalese life and culture as well as of the development efforts and achievements.

230. **Nepal to-day**. World Health Organization ; photographs by : Gordon Boshell. Bombay : Orient Longmans, 1960. 1 vol. illus.

An introduction in pictures to the kingdom, its people, and their progress towards health and prosperity.

231. **Nepalese culture**. Kirtipur, Nepal : Nepalese History, Culture, and Archaeology Instruction Committee, Tribhuvan University, 1979- annual.

An annual journal of Nepalese History, Culture, and Archaeology Instruction Committee. Publishes scholarly articles in English and Nepali.

232. **Northey, William Brook**. The land of the Gurkhas, or, the Himalayan Kingdom of Nepal. Cambridge, England : W. Heffer, 1937. Reprinted, New York : AMS Press, 1975. 284 p. bibliog.

Information about Nepal and the Gurkhas. Includes a chapter by C. G. Bruce.

233. **Pradhan, Bhuwan Lal**. On the antiquity of Nepalese culture. *Nepalese Culture*, vol. 1 (1979), pp. 1-8.

Describes Nepal's rich cultural heritage. This ancient culture has grown into its present form by absorbing influences that came from outside over a long period. One of the outstanding Nepalese characteristics is religious tolerance which is rarely found in other parts of the world.

234. **Rana, Pashupati Shumshere J.B.** and **Malla, Kamal P.** ed. Nepal in perspective. Kathmandu : Centre for Economic Development and Administration, 1973. 310 p. 2 maps.

A collection of essays by leading Nepalese scholars: Prachanda Pradhan, Yadu Nath Khanal, Rishikesh Shaha, Mahesh Chandra Regmi, Dor Bahadur Bista, Ratna Shumshere J.B. Rana, Pashupati Shumshere J.B. Rana, Yadav Prasad Pant, Prakash C. Lohani, Prayag Raj Sharma, and Kamal P. Malla. The articles cover culture, language, literature, art, history, economics, and politics.

235. **Regmi, Jagadish Chandra,** comp. A comprehensive bibliography on the ethnology and anthropology of Nepal, including Sikkim, Darjeeling, and Kumaon.

For full entry refer to Bibliographies section.

236. **Regmi, Jagadish Chandra,** comp. and ed. A concise dictionary of Himalayan people : bibliographical.

For full entry refer to Bibliographies section.

237. **Regmi, Jagadish Chandra.** comp. and ed. Newars. Assistant editor : Sheshraj Shivakoti. Kathmandu : Office of Nepal-Antiquary, 1980. 372 leaves. bibliog.

This publication, which is in English, Newari, and Sanskrit, is a special issue of the *Nepal-Antiquary : Journal of Socio-historical research and digest and Nepal studies,* no. 21-25 (1 June 1980) on Newar society The contents are: Newars : a socio-historical study; Sanskrit studies; Historical background; Behaviourial Hinduism; Nepal Buddhism; Newari studies; HMG Nepal studies; Nepal foreign affairs; Nepal law studies; Nepal affairs; Himalayan archives; and Nepal bibliography.

238. **Regmi, Jagadish Chandra,** comp. and ed. People of Nepal. Assistant editor: Sheshraj Shivakoti. Kathmandu : Office of the Nepal-Antiquary, 1980. 216 leaves. 1 map.

This mimeographed publication is a special issue of *Nepal-Antiquary : Journal of socio-historical research and digest,* no. 26-30, November 1980. It not only covers the people of Nepal, but other areas also. The contents include: Limbus : orbito-nasal index of Limbus; Mercenary Gurkhas; Nepal foreign affairs; US AID to Nepal, 1951-1972; Nepal law studies; Nuwakot district gazetteer; HMG Nepal studies; Nepal affairs; Nepal minerals; Nepal numismatics; Old Newari literature; US contributions to Oriental studies with special reference to Nepal. In addition, there are illustrations of silver coins of the Patan kings and an appendix on the people of India.

239. **Regmi Research Series.** Kathmandu : Regmi Research (Private) Ltd., 1969- monthly.

Translations of the documents available in the personal collection of Mr. Mahesh C. Regmi on all aspects of Nepal. These documents are really useful for research purposes. Includes some articles on Nepal and try to enlighten government deficiencies from time to time.

240. **Ripley, S. Dillon.** A naturalist's adventure in Nepal : search for the Spiny Babbler.

For full entry refer to Flora & Fauna section.

241. **Rose, Leo E.** and **Scholz, John T.** Nepal : profile of a Himalayan kingdom. Boulder, Colorado : Westview Press, 1980. 144 p. (Nations of contemporary Asia)

A study of the environment, history, political system, society, economy, and international relations of Nepal in the post-1951 period.

242. **Satyal, Yagya Raj**, ed. Nepalese cultural heritage in a nutshell : compiled from lectures in Monumental Guide Course, 1978. Kathmandu : His Majesty's Government, Hotel Management & Tourism Training Centre, 1979. 240 p.

This book, in English and Nepali, is the by-product of series of lectures delivered by the specialists in the Monumental Guide Course, which was designed and planned for professional licenced guides. The information is equally useful for foreign visitors, students, and teachers, since it portrays the country's historical, cultural, and religious heritage. It includes a list of sightseeing places, giving descriptions, comments, and locations.

243. **Scientific results of the Japanese Expedition to Nepal Himalaya, 1952-53.**

For full entry refer to Flora & Fauna section.

244. **Seemann, Heinrich.** Nepal 2029, Gestern noch verbotenes Land. Stuttgart : Verlag Bendell A.B., 1973. 196 p. 3 maps. illus.

This book in German is the result of the author's stay in Kathmandu as a diplomat from 1967-71 and is intended as an introduction to Nepal. The information is primarily on the Kathmandu Valley and most of the illustrations are also of the valley. The author covers geography, climate, the people, religion, history, art, German-Nepalese relations, and mountaineering. Includes 45 coloured plates.

245. **Shaha, Rishikesh.** An introduction to Nepal. Kathmandu: Ratna Pustak Bhandar, 1975. 374 p.

A useful publication which provides detailed information on Nepal.

246. **Sharma, Chandra K.** Nepal and the Nepalese. Kathmandu : Sangeeta Sharma, 1979. 175 p. 20 maps. bibliog.

This book describes the development of the landscape and discusses how to preserve its beauty for future generations. It also discusses the people and their culture. There are some informative chapters intended to help tourists to choose places to visit, depending upon time and money, and the book is also be very useful for Nepalese readers.

247. **Sharma, Nagendra**. Nepal : A to Z. Kathmandu : Nepal Association of Travel Agents, 1978. 270 p. map. bibliog.

A sourcebook which provides glimpses of Nepal's past and present, its people and places, its rich artistic and cultural heritage and other facets of Nepalese life. The main aim is to promote tourism.

248. **Sharma, Nagendra.** This is Nepal. Kathmandu : Sajha Prakashan, 1977. 100 p.

Contains articles on the lore, legends, history, and cultural life of Nepal.

249. **Sharma, P.R.** The Nepalese culture : its historical background. *Nepal Review*, vol. 1, no. 2 (Dec. 1968), pp. 7-15.

A historical interpretation and description of Nepalese culture.

250. **Simha, Teeka**. The royal wedding in Nepal, the Himalayan Kingdom, and Kathmandu. Kathmandu : The Author, [1971?].

A pictorial brochure presenting glimpses of the royal wedding of Birendra Bir Bikram Shah Deva, Maharajadhiraja of Nepal, to Aishwarya Rajya Laxmi Devi. The wedding took place on Phagon 16, 2026 (February 1970).

251. **Souvenir issue on the happy occasion of the silver jubilee of the Council, Feb. 18, 1973.** Nepal Council of World Affairs. Kathmandu : The Council, 1973. 116 p.

A collection of articles on economic, political, and historical aspects of Nepalese society.

252. **Trier, Jesper.** Ancient paper of Nepal ; results of ethno-technological field work on its manufacture, uses, and history—with technical analyses of bast, paper, and manuscripts.

For full entry refer to Industry section.

253. **Upadhyaya, Yogeshraj.** Facts about Nepal. Kathmandu : His Majesty's Government of Nepal, Ministry of Communications, Department of Information, 1980 124 p.

Contains chapters on the land and the people, history, the economy, government and the political system, Nepalese foreign policy, social services, and cultural life.

254. **Waddell, L.A.** Among the Himalayas. 2nd ed. reprint. Kathmandu : Ratna Pustak Bhandar, 1978. 452 p. 4 maps.

This book is divided into eleven chapters. Two chapters are devoted to Nepal. Chapter 9: Along the Nepal frontier towards Everest, etc. to Sandook-Phu and Faloot. Chapter 11: The Kang Pass for the western glaciers of Kanchen-Junga and for Jannu-Nepalese jealous exclusiveness. These chapters discuss the tribes of Nepal, political position of Nepal, Nepalese marriage customs, Nepalese exorcists, divisions of eastern Nepal, etc.

255. **Who is who—Nepal, 1972-74.**

For full entry refer to Encyclopaedias, directories, and who's who section.

256. **Who is who—Nepal, 1975-1977.**

For full entry refer to Encyclopaedias, directories, and who's who section.

257. **Who's who in Indo-Nepal, 1980.**

For full entry refer to Encyclopaedias, directories, and who's who section,

258. **Yatri, Purna Prakash Nepal.** Setīañcala digdarśana : vividha anusandhānātmaka vishayasamanvita.

For full entry refer to Geography—General section.

8

ECONOMY

DEVELOPMENT PLANNING

259. **Agrawal, Govind Ram.** Management in Nepal. Kathmandu : Curriculum Centre, Tribhuvan University, 1980. 292 p. bibliog.

The author is a well known economist of Nepal. This book is an attempt to facilitate understanding the role of Management for accelerating the pace of development in the complex and dynamic environment of Nepal. The practical applications of concepts to the Nepalese situation have been provided for in a number of experiential consisting of case studies, incidents, and simulation exercises.. This seems to be an exhaustive work on the status of and objectives of management in Nepal.

260. **Agrawal, Govind Ram.** Mobilization of resources for a basic needs oriented public sector programme in Nepal. Kathmandu : Centre for Economic Development and Administration, Tribhuvan University, 1979. 88 p. bibliog. (CEDA occasional papers).

Meeting basic needs is a challenge which needs to be converted into meaningful opportunities and resource constraints are the major stumbling block in the fulfillment of basic needs. The author concludes that if the government makes a concerted effort to mobilize additional resources from domestic sources, if the local people attempt to fulfill their basic needs from local sources on a self-sustaining basis, and if foreign aid can supplement these resources, then the process of fulfilling basic needs can be accelerated, if not completed, over the coming plan periods.

261. **Agrawal Govind Ram.** Resource mobilization in Nepal. Kirtipur, Nepal : Centre for Economic Development and Administration, Tribhuvan University, 1980. 251 p. bibliog.

Nepal still faces the challenge of meeting basic minimum needs releated to food, drinking water, health, education, housing, and communication. This challenge, however, cannot be met unless adequate financial resources are mobilized from both domestic and external sources. With this in mind, the Centre for Economic Development and Administration (CEDA) undertook a research project, and this book is the outcome of that study, given final shape by Dr. Govind Ram Agrawal, Executive Director of CEDA. Emphasis is placed on the mobilization of resources from domestic sources, especially through the reform of income tax.

262. **Basic principles of the Sixth Plan, 1980-1985.** National Planning Commission. Kathmandu : National Planning Commission Secretariat, Government of Nepal, 1979. 72 p.

A recommedation for fundamental changes, not only in the contents of the plan, but also in the methods of plan-formulation and implementation, so that it can respond to the basic needs of the people and enlist their active participation in a more meaningful manner than in the past.

263. **Bhooshan, B.S.** The development experience of Nepal. New Delhi : Concept, 1979. 195 p. 3 maps. bibliog.

Along with his colleague, R.N. Achyutha, the author went to Nepal in November 1977 in connection with a project on habitat. They collected several pamphlets, made notes on interviews, recorded tapes, obtained statistics, and official publications, etc., regarding the progress of the project. As they had enough material to give a comprehensive picture of Nepal's development programmes, they decided to bring out this book combining all those bits and pieces of information, together with their own impressions.

264. **Chand, Diwakar.** Recent trends of economic development in Nepal. Kathmandu : Printed by Shree Mahalaxmi Mudranalaya, 1978. 126 p. illus. bibliog.

A summary of the significant economic developments in Nepal. Each chapter is an independent essay, impartially evaluating contemporary economic trends. Some of the chapters have appeared previously as articles in the national papers.

265. **Evaluation of USAID—Village Development Project in Nepal, 1954-1962** : submitted to USAID, Kathmandu, Nepal. Himalayan Studies Centre (Nepal). Kathmandu : The Centre, 1981. 199 leaves. map.

The Village Development Project was initially started as a joint venture between the Government of Nepal and the United States Operation Mission, now called the United States Agency for International Development (USAID). The project was later joined by the Ford Foundation and the Government of India. The main aim of this study was to evaluate rural development of Nepal under this Project during 1954-1962, The study was undertaken at the request of USAID. Mimeographed.

266. **Jain, Sharad Chandra**. Poverty to prosperity in Nepal. Indore, India : Development Publishers, with the International Development Agency, Bonn, 1981. 114 p.

Like other low-income developing countries, Nepal's poverty is not visible. This book highlights the poverty problem in Nepal and suggests long-term policies and programmes to alleviate it. The author suggests that the low standard of living could become an advantage and bring prosperity to the individual as well as to the nation if selective programmes of income generation through asset creation and production are launched for the poor by the banking sector. Credit programmes to encourage efficient cropping among poor farmers are recommended. The author also considers the annual level of investment required for the elimination of poverty.

267. **The Journal of Development and Administrative Studies.**
For full entry refer to Professionals periodicals section.

268. **Kansakar, Vidya Bir Singh**. Effectiveness of planned resettlement programme in Nepal. Kirtipur, Nepal : Centre for Economic Development and Administration, Tribhuvan University, 1979. 2 vols. 3 maps. bibliog.

This mimeographed research report is one of the multi-country studies by the Resettlement and Transmigration Programme, sponsored and financed by the International Development Research Centre, Canada. The study was conducted with the twin objectives of evaluating the aims and policies of the planned resettlement programme in Nepal and of suggesting some policies for its success. On the basis of its findings, the study makes pragmatic recommendations for the successful implementation of current and future resettlement programmes. These suggestions will provide a valuable basis for government plans for resettlement and population problems.

269. **Lohani, Prakash Chandra**. Economic plans and economic planning in Nepal. Kathmandu : Centre for Economic Development and Administration, Tribhuvan University, 1979. 87 p. (CEDA occasional paper. International Relations Group series, no. 2).

This mimeograph publication makes a useful contribution to the understanding of Nepal's experiences in economic planning so far and the problems to be faced in the future. The work will help to focus attention on some of the major issues confronting the nation during the 1980s.

270. **Lohani, Prakash Chandra**. People's participation in development. Kathmandu : Centre for Economic Development and Administration, Tribhuvan University, 1980. 107 p.

Deals mainly with the conceptual aspects of public participation in development. The author makes a critical and comparative survey of the ways and means of people's participation in China, India, Sri Lanka, and Nepal. The emphasis is placed on the importance of identifying development programmes with the needs and aspirations of the people.

271. **Pant, Yadav Prasad**. Planning for prosperity : a study in Nepal's experiences. Kathmandu : Navayuga Sahitya Mandir, 1962. 152 p.

Discusses various aspects of planning in Nepal and the problems faced by the country as it strives for development.

272. **Pant, Yadav Prasad** and **Jain, Sharad Chandra**. Rural problems and rural development in Nepal : a search for new strategy. Indore, India : Development Publishers, with the International Development Agency, Bonn, 1980. 88 p.

Part one of this work deals with problems of rural households and rural communities; part two lays out an integrated rural development strategy, giving programmes for solving rural problems and frameworks for the administration of integrated rural development. The book is a useful reference source for individuals and organizations seeking imformation on rural development in Nepal.

273. **Pokhrel, Durga,** ed. Birendra ra bikas : birthday souvenir, development special. Kathmandu : The Editor, 1977. 108 p.

A special publication on the development of Nepal, issued on the occasion of the thirty-third birthday of Bir Bikram Shah Deva, Maharajadhiraja of Nepal.

274. **Pre-project planning of industrial districts in the Kingdom of Nepal.** Battelle Institut. Kathmandu : Nepal Industrial Development Corporation, 1966. 204 p.

This report was prepared for the Nepal Industrial Development Corporation and the Industrial Promotion and Productivity Centre (Private) Limited. Includes folded illustrations and maps.

275. **Rana, Pashupati Shumshere J.B.** Nepal's Fourth Plan : a critique. Kathmandu : Yeti Pocket Books, 1971. 71p. (Yeti Pocket Books, E.T. 29)

Contains three essays: The objective and investment programmes of the Fourth plan; Problems of implementation in Nepalese planning; The Fourth Plan : a drama manque.

276. **Report of Seminar/Workshop on People's Participation in Rural Development in Nepal, July 24-26, 1978, Kathmandu, Nepal.** Organized by the Ministry of Home Panchayat, His Majesty's Government of Nepal & Agricultural Projects Services Centre. Kathmandu : Agricultural Projects Services Centre, 1978. 104 p.

His Majesty's government of Nepal and various international donors have felt the need for greater public involvement in all phases of development planning, decision-making, and implementatian, as well as in the benefits. This seminar was organized to explore the meaning and importance of people's participation in Nepal's development efforts.

277. **Report of the Expert Group Meeting on Development Planning at District Level, 1980.** Lalitpur, Nepal : Central Panchayat Training Institute, 1980. 130 leaves.

These are papers and recommendations from the meeting which was convened by the German Foundation for International Development in collaboration with the Central Panchayat Training Institute, Lalitpur, and was held in Kathmandu on 24-31 October 1980. The objectives were: to take stock of the present state of local-level planning and development in the countries of South Asia in particular and elsewhere in general; to prepare guidelines for a training programme on local-level planning and development; and to prepare a curriculum for and a methodological approach to a training programme on development planning at district level in Nepal.

278. **Rural area development, Rapti Zone : project paper.** Kathmandu : USAID, Nepal, 1980. 1 vol.

A mimeographed project report on a programme intended to improve crucial aspects of the quality of life, including income, productivity, employment, nutrition, family size, and education, in the five districts of the Rapti Zone. This is USAID, Nepal, project no. 367-0129.

279. **Seminar-cum-Workshop on Development Planning : selected papers.** Kirtipur, Nepal : Centre for Economic Development and Administration [1971?]. 251 p.

Presents papers from a seminar conducted with special reference to economic planning in Nepal.

280. **Short Term Course on Plan Implementation and Project Analysis, November 8-December 8, 1970 :** selected papers. Kathmandu : Centre for Economic Development and Administration [1971?]. 2 vols.

Contains papers relating to the course.

281. **Shreshtha, Bhumi N.** and **Beyer, John.** Resource mobilization for development of Nepal, Jan. 18, 1973-Jan. 20, 1973. Kathmandu : Centre for Economic Development and Administration, 1973. 53 leaves, 42, 30 p.

This is the report of the Seminar on Resource Mobilization for Development of Nepal, held in January 1973. The seminar was sponsored by the National Planning Commission and the Ministry of Finance, and organized by Centre for Economic Development and Administration.

282. **Strategic elements of rural development in Nepal.** Kathmandu : Centre for Economic Development and Administration, Tribhuvan University, 1980. 218 p. 3 maps.

A collection of papers presented at a seminar-cum-workshop organized by the Centre for Economic Development and Administration on elements of rural development for Nepal's Sixth Plan. Mimeographed.

283. **A substantial new programme of action for accelerated development of Nepal.** National Planning Commission ; preface by Ratna Shumshere J. B. Rana. Kathmandu : His Majesty's Government, 1981. 2 vols. map.

This publication is intended to describe Nepal's development problems and to promote better understanding of Nepal by the international community. It presents: an assessment of development potentials, bottlenecks and assistance requirements for the 1980s; an inventory of projects and programmes now requiring finance and those identified as likely to be ready for financing during the 1980s; and a review of modalities of assistance as they have operated, including the problem of aid co-ordination and administration, and the questions of local costs, recurring costs, and programme financing. Mimeographed.

284. **Thapa, Govind.** Nepālako grāmīna kshetra ra tyasakā vikāsa. Pokhara, Nepal : The Author, 1980. 74 p.

Briefly describes various development programmes undertaken for rural areas of Nepal.

285. **Wildavsky, Aaron.** Why planning fails in Nepal. *Administrative Science Quarterly* (Dec. 1972), pp. 508-527.

Explores the various factors which create problems in implementing and achieving the targets of Nepalese plans. Among other reasons, the author emphasizes that the failure of planning is mainly due to the limited capacity to administer development projects and the formulation of poor project proposals.

GENERAL STUDIES

286. **Bahadur, Ram, K.C.** A general study on land reform, land administration, and socio-economic activities. Kathmandu : Lands Department, Ministry of Land Reform, 1972. 157 p.

Contains articles on land reform, land administration, cooperative and compulsory saving, and socio-economic programmes.

287. **Bajracharya, Bhuban Bajra.** A review of the cooperative development in Nepal. Kathmandu : Centre for Economic Development and Administration, Tribhuvan University, 1980. 197, 95 p. bibliog.

Co-operative societies are important institutional vehicles for improving the quality of life of the rural poor in Nepal; such societies serve as the kingpins of the rural marketing systems. This mimeographed study examines the development of the co-operative movement in Nepal from a historical perspective. The major problems are identified and recommendations are made for consolidating and revitalizing this movement. The arguements are supported by ninety-five pages of statistics tables.

288. **Banskota, Mahesh**. Indicators in the context of Nepal's Sixth Plan, 1980-1986. Kathmandu : Centre for Economic Development and Administration, 1980. 46 p.

This mimeographed study essentially deals with poverty, destitution, and unemployment in a regional context. The conceptual framework applied by the author is a valuable basis for selecting and quntifying an appropriate set of indicators. Such indicators should be useful in the process of finalizing the Sixth Plan. This study should also be relevant for designing policies to reduce inter and intra-regional inequalities in Nepal.

289. **Basic needs and government services** : an area study of Bhaktapur, Nepal. Kathmandu : Centre for Economic Development and Administration, Tribhuvan University, 1980. 315 p. 2 maps. bibliog.

Theoretical knowledge about basic needs has been multiplying in economic literature; however, very few empirical studies are available about practical applications. This research study is the first attempt to look at the empirical aspects of basic needs of Nepal. The study was jointly funded by the Centre and the International Labour Organisation. This mimeographed report includes several charts and appendixes.

290. **Blaikie, Piers** [et al.]. Nepal in crisis : growth and stagnation at the periphery. Delhi : Oxford University Press, 1980. 311 p. 2 maps. bibliog.

This book arose out of research project financed by the British Ministry of Overseas Development. The authors are members of the School of Development Studies at the University of East Anglia. The core of the book is the socio-economic study of west-central Nepal, with special reference to the effects of road construction. However, the authors generalize from this to give a picture of the situation in Nepal as a whole and to draw conclusions about dependency relationships between different countries and between different elements within an individual country.

291. **Dhungana, Bhavani**. Nepal's special situation in economic inter-dependence. Kathmandu : Centre for Economic Development and Administration, Tribhuvan University, 1980. 29 leaves. bibliog. (CEDA occassional paper series)

A brief discussion of the interdependence of Nepal in the context of trade, aid, and energy.

292. **The Economic Journal of Nepal.** Kirtipur, Nepal : Economics Instruction Committee, Tribhuvan University.

This is a quarterly academic publication of the Faculty of Economics, Tribhuvan University.

293. **The Economic Monthly**. Kirtipur, Nepal : Economic Instruction Committee, Tribhuvan University.

An academic publication of the Faculty of Economics, Tribhuvan University.

294. **Facts about American aid to Nepal, FY 1952-1969.** U.S. AID Mission to Nepal. Kathmandu : The Mission, 1969. 32 p.

A detailed study of American aid to Nepal.

295. **Gurung, Nareshwar Jang**. An introduction to the socio-economic structure of Manang District.

For full entry refer to Geography—General section.

296. **Jilla paricaya**.

For full entry refer to Geography—General section.

297. **Lohani, Prakash C**. Nepal in 1974.

For full entry refer to Politics section.

298. **Mihaly, Eugene Bramer**. Foreign aid and politics in Nepal : a case study. London : Oxford University Press, 1965. 202 p. map. bibliog.

Nepal, where eighty-five percent of the population is employed in the agricultural sector, has been receiving foreign aid to promote economic development. This work is a case-study of the aid programmes and their effects on Nepal's economy. The author concludes that foreign aid has harmed rather than helped Nepal's development and political stability.

299. **Mountain environment and development.**

For full entry refer to Geography—General section.

300. **Nath, Tribhuvan.** The Nepalese dilema, 1960-74. New Delhi : Sterling, 1975. 528 p.

The author was a correspondent for *The Times of India* during 1962-71. In this book he describes the economic and political changes in Nepal since 1950.

301. **Nepal Recorder.** Kathmandu : Nepal Press Digest (Private) Ltd., 1977- irregular.

This is translation of basic documents on the government and economy of Nepal. This supersedes *Nepal gazette.*

302. **Rana, Madhukar S. J. B.** Organizational manual, CEDA as an institution. Kirtipur, Nepal : Centre for Economic Development and Administration, Tribhuvan University, 1978. 132 p.

This mimeographed publication is an organizational manual for the Centre for Economic Development and Administration, (CEDA), which is a part of Tribhuvan University and was established on 15 May 1969. This Centre's primary purpose is to identify the problems relating to poverty, distribution (of income, wealth and power), and employment and to undertake studies on these issues. CEDA has made many contributions to research, consultancy, documentation and executive development programmes.

303. **Regmi, Mahesh Chandra.** A study in Nepali economic history, 1768-1846. New Delhi : Manjusri Publishing House, 1971. 235 p. map. bibliog. illus. (Bibliotheca Himalayica, series I, vol. 14).

A study of the economic and social effects of Nepal's territorial unification by the Gorkha rulers. The structure and function of Gorkhali rule from 1768 to 1846 are described.

304. **Regmi, Mahesh Chandra.** Thatched huts and stucco palaces : peasants and landlords in 19th-century Nepal. New Delhi : Vikas, 1978. 173 p. bibliog.

The study is of Nepal economic history during 19th century and approaches history as 'a dialogue between past and present'.

Economic development is presently the leading national concern in Nepal, and this work attempts to explore some of the historical and institutional constraints facing such development. The book concentrates on relations between the state and the land owning elites on the one hand and the peasants on the other, in order to identify the form and nature of their share in agricultural production. This book also helps to explain how the Ranas were able to sustain their family rule for over a century, and why efforts towards agrarian reform in Nepal since the 1950s have not had the desired measure of success.

305. **Reports of the National Seminar on Land Reform.** Kathmandu : National Seminar on Land Reform, 1971. 181 p. illus.

A report of the seminar held in 1970 at Kathmandu, sponsored by His Majesty's Government of Nepal in co-operation with the John C. Lincoln Institute and the Food and Agriculture Organisation of the United Nations.

306. **Shrestha, Amritman.** Problems of Nepalese economy. 2nd ed. Kathmandu : Gayetri Shrestha, 1967. 263 p.

A useful reference book describing problems in various aspects of Nepal's economy.

307. **Shrestha. B. P.** An introduction to Nepalese economy. 4th ed. Kathmandu : Ratna Pustak Bhandar, 1981. 274 p.

This book is a by-product of research work on the Nepalese economy carried by the author for a Ph. D. degree in economics. This covers almost all aspects of the Nepalese economy. The author takes an original approach to the economic problems and makes a critical appraisal of current government policies on economic matters.

308. **Shrestha, B.P.** Monetary policy in an emerging economy : a case study of Nepal. Kathmandu : Ratna Pustak Bhandar, 1965. 89 p. bibliog.

In Nepal, as in the rest of the world, prices are rising and the money supply is being increased. In this publication. the author considers the factors responsible for the rise in prices in Nepal and also discusses the increase in the money supply.

309. **Shrestha, Ratna Lall.** Impact of Kathmandu Raxaul Highway (Tribhuban Rajmarg) on Nepalese economy, 1956-1975. Kathmandu : G. S. Agrawal, 1980. 222 p. 7 maps. bibliog.

This work was originally the author's Ph. D. thesis in Economics, submitted to the Institute of Humanities and Social Sciences, Tribhuvan University. Tribhuvan Rajmarga, the first road linking the Terai with Kathmandu, has been in existence from 1956. The study shows that the road has played a significant role in the promotion of different sectors of the Nepalese economy, e.g. : foreign trade, tourism, industry, employment, agriculture, revenue, etc. However, its most important contribution has been the reduction of transport costs, affecting in turn price levels in the Kathmandu Valley. It has facilitated several development projects of national importance in and nearby the Kathmandu Valley.

310. **Verma, Yugeshwar P.** Nepal : progress and problems, 1972-80.

For full entry refer to Politics section.

311. **Zaman, M. A.** Evaluation of land reform in Nepal. Kathmandu : Ministry of Land Reforms, 1973. 124 p.

A very useful reference on land reform. The author is Land Reform Evaluation Adviser, and the publication is jointly sponsored by His Majesty's Government of Nepal and the Food and Agriculture Organization.

REGIONAL DEVELOPMENT

312. **Bajracharya, Chakra Mehar,** ed. Small Area Development Programme : a survey and action program for Khandbari. Jawalakhel, Nepal : Central Panchayat Training Institute [1976?]. 22, 76 leaves. maps.

This mimeographed publication is in three parts: the first explains the Small Area Development Programme concept; the second briefly presents a general survey of Khandbari SADP area; and the third part comprises the plan of action and the proposed organizational and administrative structures for implementing the programme. Maps illustrate the principal areas and topics under discussion.

313. **Banskota, Mahesh,** ed. Some issues on regional planning in Nepal : approaches to regional development : proceedings of the Seminar on Regional Planning. Kathmandu : Centre for Economic Development and Administration, Institute of Business Administration, Commerce, and Public Administration, Tribhuvan University, 1974. 82 p.

The proceedings of a seminar held in Kathmandu in 1974. The seminar was jointly sponsored by the National Planning Commission, His Majesty's Government of Nepal and the Centre for Economic Development and Administration.

314. **Chitwan Valley Development Project, Nepal.** Asian Development Bank and His Majesty's Government of Nepal. Essen, GFR : Agrar-Und Hydrotechnic GMBH, 1972. [various pagination]. illus.

A detailed plan for the development of the Chitwan Valley, with primary emphasis on agriculture and livestock development. The study also covers project organization and management, the implementation schedule, total costs, and the economic impact of the Project.

315. **Elder, Joseph W.** [et al.]. Planned resettlement in Nepal's Terai : a social analysis of the Khajura/Bardia Punarvas Project. Kathmandu : Institure of Nepal and Asian Studies, Tribhuvan University ; Madison, Wisconsin : Department of Sociology, University of Wisconsin, 1970. 307 p. maps. bibliog.

This project was sponsored by the Institute of Nepal and Asian Studies; the Centre for Economic Development and Administration, Tribhuvan University; and the Department of Sociology, University of Wisconsin.

316. **Feasibility study of Rapti Zone Integrated Rural Development Project.** Prepared for the Government of Nepal & United States Agency for International Development by Agricultural Projects Services Centre. Kathmandu : Agricultural Projects Services Centre, 1980. 5 vols.

This multi-sectoral rural development project attempts to combine increased production, administrative support, physical plant development and social services into a functioning whole. The project is intended to encourage growth at village, district, and zonal levels in the Rapti Anchal. It supports government programmes to improve agricultural production, livestock production, horticulture production, renewable resource management, small rural works, irrigation and drinking water facilities, health services, education of the rural poor and institutional development, especially at the local level. Mimeographed.

317. **Fleming, W.M.** Phewa Tal Watershed Management proposals. Kathmandu : Department of Soil and Water Conservation, 1978. 90 leaves. 7 maps. (Phewa Tal technical report, no. 5).

Makes the following proposals : 1. to ensure sound land-use practices so that the needs of local people are met, especially in forestry and agriculture; 2. to implement a conservation programme to maintain erosion losses of soil nutrients within defined 'tolerable' limits, including the protection of downstream investments such as hydroelectric facilities and fisheries from excessive sedimentation; 3. to manage resources for the maximum rate of production and economic return but consistent with conservation objectives; 4. to develop a methodology for integrating the land-use activities of various government departments and international agencies. Mimeographed.

318. **Goldstein, Melvyn C.** A report on Limi Panchayat, Humla District, Karnali Zone. *Conrtibution to Nepalese Studies*, vol. 2, no. 2 (June 1975), pp. 89-101.

This report discusses the adaptation of the inhabitants of Limi Panchayat and assesses the potential for development in the area. Based on field-work carried out from March to September 1974, the article provides a corpus of basic ethnographic-ecological data which can be used by planners in the Nepalese Government to develop this and similar high-mountain econsystems throughout northern Nepal and also presents some tentative but specific suggestions concerning areas for implementing development.

319. **Gurung, Sant B.** Regional development planning and administration in Nepal. Kathmandu : Centre for Economic Development and Administration, Tribhuvan University, 1978. 52 p. 2 maps. bibliog.

The success of any regional development strategy depends to a large extent on the structure and responsiveness of the administration implementing the plan. This study reviews the planning process and the administration of Nepal in the context of regional planning. The concept of regional planning has been questioned in recent years and the information and the suggestions in this report will be useful for formulating future development policies and programmes in Nepal. Mimeographed.

320. **Gurung, Sant B.** and **Buchmann, H.** Causes and impact of migration (preliminary survey in Surkhet region). Kathmandu : Centre of Economic Development and Administration, 1973. 116 p. maps. bibliog.

This joint study by the Centre for Economic Development and Administration and the Swiss Federal Institute of Technology, Zurich, analyses the causes of migration and its impact on the migrants themselves and on the economy of the Surkhet District. Tables provide useful information for further study on the region. Mimeographed.

321. **Kraayenhagen, J.** Work programme, integrated watershed planning and development at Phewa Tal : report. Prepared for the Integrated Watershed Management Project. Pokhara, Nepal : Food and Agricultural Organisation of the United Nations, 1979. 18 leaves. (Phewa Tal technical report, no. 8).

The object of this project is to demonstrate, through planning and partial implementation, the benefits of integrated watershed management and land development in Phewa Tal Watershed Catchment. The plan provides for appropriate watershed management, water storage components, bench terracing, flood control, range development, farm management, fish farming, irrigation, and fostering farmers' associations. This paper deals with the work programme necessary for a comprehensive integrated development study. Mimeographed.

322. **Land inventory Karnali-Mahakali watersheds** : a basic inventory for general assessment of land degradation. Department of Soil and Water Conservation, Nepal. Kathmandu : Ministry of Forest, Department of Soil and Water Conservation, Integrated Watershed Management, Torrent Control, and Land Use Development Project, 1977. 37 leaves. bibliog.

This land inventory of the Karnali-Mahakali watersheds, western Nepal, is a part of the Integrated Watershed Management, Torrent Control, and Land Use Development Project. The objectives of this study were: to investigate the unique characteristics of Landsat imagery as an aid in recognizing major land-unit boundaries; to explore the use of Landsat imagery for low-intensity land resources surveys; and to investigate the use of Landsat imagery as a base map for thematic land-resource maps which could provide basic watershed information needed for land-use planning. Mimeographed.

323. **Lumbini Development Project**. Lumbini Development Committee (Nepal). Kathmandu : The Committee, 1979. 31 p. illus.

Lumbini is situated in the western Terai of Nepal and is the birthplace of Gautama Buddha. The Government of Nepal appointed the Lumbini Development Committee to look after the development of the area and this report deals with the Committee's activities.

324. **Management plan for the integrated development of Phewa Watershed, 1980-1985.** Ministry of Forest, Nepal. Kathmandu : Department of Soil Conservation and Watershed Management [and] Integrated Watershed Management, Torrent Control, and Land Use Development Project, 1980. 140 leaves. maps. (Phewa Tal technical report, no. 12).

This plan was prepared to assist with the development planning of the Phewa Watershed project. Mimeographed.

325. **Okada, Ferdinand E.** Preliminary report on regional development areas in Nepal. Kathmandu : National Planning Commission, His Majesty's Government, 1970. 125 p. bibliog. 5 maps.

This report is the product of extensive field surveys and documen tary research undertaken by an interdisciplinary team supported by the National Planning Commission. The work designates the Kosi Metropolitan, Gandaki, and Karnali sectors as the focus of a comprehensive development effort, starting in the Fourth Plan period. Brief descriptions of each sector are given, followed by some suggestions for development schemes within an integrated regional framework.

326. **Pandey, Sher Bahadur** [et al.]. Identification of fuel problem and its solution in Kathmandu Valley. Kathmandu : National Planning Commission Secretariat, 1974. 114 p.

The report of the study team of a project sponsored by the National Planning Commission in 1973.

327. **Pant, Yadav Prasad** and **Jain, Sharad Chandra.** Regional imbalances and process of regional development in Nepal. Delhi : Development Publishers, with the International Development Agency, Bonn, 1980. 72 p.

An interesting analysis of regional imbalances, the process of regional development in the past, and regional development strategy and programmes for the years ahead.

328. **Pradhan, Prachanda,** ed. A new dimension in Nepal's development : the regional approach in planning and people oriented development strategy. Kathmandu : Centre for Economic Development and Administration, 1973. 106 p. map.

Describes the implications of the introduction of the new dimension in Nepal's development, outlining the necessary policy adjustments. This collection contains articles by renowned planners and administrators. Includes tables.

329. **Rana, Ratna S. J. B.** An economic study of the area around the alignment of the Dhanagadi-Dandeldhura Road, Nepal. Kathmandu : Centre for Economic Development and Administration, 1971. 163 p. maps. (CEDA study series, no. 1)

This study was undertaken for the National Planning Commission Secretariat of His Majesty's Government of Nepal. The area discussed is in the Mahakali Zone.

330. **Regional Development Study, Nepal.** Centre for Economic Development and Administration. Kirtipur, Nepal : Centre for Economic Development and Administration, Institute of Business Administration, Commerce, and Public Administration, Tribhuvan University, 1975. 5 vols.

This regional development study relates to the Far Western Development Region and the Kosi Zone. It presents background information on regional development and recommends a rural development package programme.

331. **Sainju, Mohan Man** [et al.]. Revisit to Budhbare. Kirtipur, Nepal : Centre for Economic Development and Administration, 1973. 107 p.

A study measuring the effects of the comprehensive land-reform programme in a village in the Jhapa District of Mechi Zone during 1963-73.

332. **Seeland, Klaus T.** The use of bamboo in a Rai Village in the Upper Arun Valley : an example of a traditional technology. *Journal of the Nepal Research Centre*, vol. 4 (Humanities) (1980), pp. 175-187. illus.

This study was done in Hedangna, a Rai village in the remote parts of the Upper Arun Valley in northeastern Nepal. The author describes Rai land ownership and discusses the use of bamboo for household items; agricultural, hunting, and fishing implements; means of transport; tools, toys and musical instruments; and other types of equipment. After commenting on the technical and ecological advantages of bamboo, the author concludes that a return to traditional and pre-colonial modes of production is more real development than the introduction of Western technologies.

333. **Shrestha, B. P.** and **Jain, S. C.** Regional development in Nepal : an exercise in reality. New Delhi : Development Publishers, 1978. 160 p.

Analyses the regional disparities in social services and agricultural and industrial development, showing that remote areas are more backward. The authors present a plan to narrow these differences.

334. **Shrestha, Bihari K.** and **Choudhari, Gayatri.** Some socio-economic aspects of Sainbu-Bhainsepati Village Panchayat. Lalitpur, Nepal : Women's Affairs Training & Extension Centre and Home Panchayat Ministry, Training Material Production Centre, Nepal, 1971. 37 leaves. (Publication — Home Panchayat Ministry, Training Material Production Centre, Nepal, no. 15)

A survey of socio-economic conditions in Sainbu-Bhainsepati Village, undertaken to help in the formulation of an effective rural development policy. It serves as the basis of the programmes in the pilot project launched in the Village by the Women's Affairs Training and Extension Centre at Jaulakhel, Lalitpur. Mimeographed.

335. **Small Area Development Programme** : a survey report on area delimitation in Parbat Districts. Tulsi Narayan Shrestha [et al.]. Kathmandu: His Majesty's Government, Panchayat Ministry, Research Section, 1975. 57 p. map.

This survey conducted in the Parbat District highlights several areas for potential development and recommends that the region be selected for the SADP. The study concentrates on area delimitation rather undertaking an in-depth examination of development potential and recommendations. The authors suggest that, in order to have proper co-ordination and co-operation, an administrative office should be set up at the district headquarters in Kusma. Mimeographed.

336. **Some characteristics of the agrani trainees from remote regions of eastern Nepal.** Jaulakhel, Nepal : Home Panchyat Ministry, Training Material Production Centre, 1971. 18 p. (T.M.P.C.S., no. 14)

Studies the socio-economic characteristics of official and non-official workers in rural development programmes undergoing training at the Panchayat Training Centre, Jhapa, Nepal.

9

EDUCATION

337. **Agrawal, Govind Ram.** Higher education for business in developing nations : a proposed model for Nepal. Kathmandu : Centre for Economic Development and Administration, 1974. 262 p. bibliog.

This study uses a systematic approach to assess the need and design a formative model for higher education in Nepal. The work was submitted to the Graduate Faculty of Texas Technical University, USA in partial fulfilment of the requirements for the degree of doctor of business administration.

338. **Agrawal, Govind Ram.** Management of individual differences : the essence of qualitative improvements in Nepalese education. Kirtipur, Nepal : Centre for Economic Development and Administration, Tribhuvan University, 1978. 20 leaves. (CEDA occasional paper. Human resources series, no. 2)

The individual differences of students have remained a largely neglected aspect of Nepalese education. Proper consideration of individual differences, however, is essential for bringing about qualitative improvements in the Nepalese education system. Individual differences must be managed through appropriate administrative as well as instructional provisions. This study deals with the various aspects of the management of the individual differences of students. Mimeographed.

339. **Avaja = The Voice.** Bombay : Nepali Students' Association, 1967- annual.

An annual publication in Nepali and English giving information about the Nepalese students in India.

340. **Baral, Ishwar** [et al.]. National Education Plan as they see it. Kathmandu : National Education Committee Office, 1972. 82 p.

The National Education Plan of Nepal was introduced in 1971. This publication presents comments on the plan, made by various authorities in the field of education. Some of the interviews were published earlier in ***Rising Nepal,*** a daily from Kathmandu. Includes illustrations.

341. **Basnet, Prabha.** Female education in Nepal : a study. *Nepal Digest*, (1977), pp. 71-77.

A study of female education in Nepal.

342. **Chand, Geeta** [et al.]. Studies in bilingualism in Nepal.

For full entry refer to Languages & Dialects—Linguistic studies section.

343. **Colloquium report of the fifteenth anniversary of International Bureau of Education, 8 July 1979.** National Education Committee, Centre for Educational Research, Innovation & Development. Kathmandu : The Committee, 1979. 19 leaves.

Nepal, as a member country, celebrated the 50th anniversary of International Bureau of Education on July 8, 1979 in the form of a colloquium. This is the report of this colloquium. The objective of the colloquium was to disseminate information on the International Bureau of Education's role in the development of education, and its contribution to the development of the national system of education of each of the member countries.

344. **Development of low-cost/simple educational materials** : a report of national workshop, 25 September-1 October, 1978. Kathmandu : National Education Committee, Centre for Educational Research, Innovation, and Development, 1978. 48 p.

This is a report of the seminar. Twenty-six participants comprising teachers, supervisors, and specialists from various educational institutions took part in the seminar. The purpose of the seminar was to popularize the concept of the development and use of low-cost/simple educational materials, to design and to produce samples of low-cost/simple materials, and to display low-cost/simple materials and toys produced within the country. Mimeographed.

345. **Education and development.** Kathmandu : National Education Committee, Centre for Educational Research, Innovation, and Development. annual.

A publication on education in Nepal. This is a modest attempt at bringing together an assortment of ideas, reflections, and experiences of people that education is key to development.

346. **Education Quarterly**. Kirtipur, Nepal : Tribhuvan University, Institute of Education, 1957-

An aeademic journal publishes articles on education. This publication was published for sometime by the College of Education and was suspended during 1974.

347. **Educational research and innovation in Nepal** : national seminar, 22 June-27 June 1977, Pokhara, Nepal : a report. Organised by the Centre for Educational Research, Innovation, and Development. Kathmandu : National Education Committee, Centre for Educational Research, Innovaticn, and Development, 1977. 116 leaves.

The objectives of the seminar were : to examine, review, and synthesise activities in educational research and innovation in Nepal; to explore possible areas of collaboration and sharing of experiences in educational research and innovation; and to formulate areas of priorities in educational research and innovation and guidelines for future activities in Nepal. Mimeographed.

348. **Equal access of women to education programme in Nepal** : an evaluation study. Sponsored by UNICEF. Kathmandu : National Education Committee, Centre for Educational Research, Innovation, and Development, 1978. 50 p.

To propagate and expedite female education in Nepal, His Majesty's Government, Ministry of Education undertook this project with the cooperation of UNICEF. This report represents a study of the effectiveness of the programme which had been in operation for eight years in three development regions, the Eastern, Western, and Far-Western. One of the notable conclusion of this study is that the appointment of female teachers, especially in remote and very backward areas, serves as a great incentive to the increase of girls' enrollment at school. The data and findings given in this report may help to formulate further strategies for the well planned development of education in Nepal, particularly with reference to female education. Mimeographed.

349. **Financing of education in Nepal** : a report of national seminar, 9-13 January 1978. Organised by the Centre for Educational Research, Innovation, and Development. Kathmandu : National Education Committee, Centre for Educational Research, Innovation, and Development, 1978. 230 p.

The aim of the seminar was to assess the present system of financing of education in Nepal, to point out the problems which were then being faced and to make some practical suggestions for improving the existing financial management of Nepal's educational system. Mimeographed.

350. **A hand book of general information and academic programmes.** Institute of Law, Tribhuvan University. Kathmaudu : The Institute, 1975. 42 p.

Gives information regarding the University ; the Institute; application and admission; financial information; student services, and facilities; courses & regulations; examinatton & degree; courses offered, and course descriptions.

351. **INAS handbook**. Institute of Nepal and Asian Studies. Kirtipur, Nepal; The Institute, 1973 or 74. 22 p. bibliog.

The Institute of Nepal and Asian Studies (INAS) is a research institute devoted to scholarship concerning Nepal and its Asian setting within the disciplines of the social sciences. It is primarily concerned with promoting socially relevant research and making this available to society at large through its publications. This booklet provides information on INAS' establishment, its aims, coordination with other institutes, etc. Also discusses the shortage of staff and the lack of academic research equipment at INAS.

352. **Journal (Tribhnvan University)** Kirtipur, Nepal; Tribhuvan University, 1965- semiannual.

An academic journal of Tribhuvan University. Publishes articles in English and Nepali.

353. **Kankalli, M.S.** The odds are changing for women in Nepal. *UNICEF* News, vol. 76 (1973), pp. 18-22.

A very general report on training programmes for female teachers in Pokhara, Gandaki Zone, designed with the help of UNICEF and UNESCO. It describes the aims and achievements of the programme entitled "Experimental project for equal access for girls and women to education".

354. **Kasaju, Prem Kumar** and **Pradhan, Gaja Sundar**, ed. Education and development: trends and issues. Kathmandu : Centre for Educational Research, Innovation, and Development, 1979. 218 p.

Contains abridged reports of important research projects and of major seminars and workshops undertaken or organized by the Centre. These reports cover several research works and innovative projects, both completed and continuing, in various aspects of education, ranging from primary to higher education, within the framework of national education as a whole in Nepal. This book throws light on the major trends and issues appearing currently in the education sector of Nepal.

355. **Kasaju, Prem Kumar** [et al.], ed. Education for rural development, National Seminar, Dhunche, Rasuwa, 17-25 December 1979. Kathmandu : Tribhuvan University, Research Centre for Educational Innovation and Development, 1980. 117 p.

A report of the Seminar organized by the Research Centre for Educational Innovation and Development with the collaboration of UNESCO, Paris. Papers were presented by Dr. Nicholas Bennett, Dr. Suresh Raj Sharma, Dr. Prem Kasaju, and Sri Ram Lamichhane. The aims of the Seminar were to review and examine the implications and viability of formal and non-formal educational programmes which focus on rural development in Nepal, and to formulate strategies and guidelines for stimulating the expansion of educational programmes emphasizing rural development.

356. **Kasaju, Prem Kumar** [et al.]. Studies in cognition and perception (children of age 4-8). Kathmandu : National Educational Committee, Centre for Educational Research. Innovation, and Development, 1977. 23 p.

These studies were undertaken with reference to Nepalese children.

357. **Malla, Kamal Prakash.** The road to nowhere : a selection of writings, 1966-1977.

For full entry refer to Literature—Texts section.

358. **Maskay, Bishwa Keshar.** Higher education in Nepal : perspective and retrospective. Kathmandu : Tribhuvan University, Institute of Education, 1980. 19 leaves. bibliog.

Studies of the state of affairs, delimitations, the development of higher education in Nepal, task forces for the planning of education in Nepal, the National education system plan, National development service, trends of development: quantitive expansion. Mimeographed.

359. **MIllion, Steven K.** Rote learning in Nepalese public schools. *Contributions to Nepalese Studies*, vol. 5, no. 1 (Dec. 1977), pp. 55-70.

Rote learning is the most used system in many Nepalese schools. Research into rote learning and related topics has been extensive, but this study is unusual in that, it is limited to the Nepalese application of the technique. This article attempts to cite studies yielding information which is transferable to the Nepalese situation, and restricts the scope of concern to studies of educational psychology, pragmatic philosophy, and analytic philosophy.

366. **Mohsin, Mohammad** and **Kasaju, Prem Kumar**, ed. Education and development. Kathmandu : National Education Committee, 1975. 174 p.

A collection of articles by eminent figures on the National Education System Plan introduced in Nepal in 1971. Includes illustrations and an index.

361. **Mohsin, Mohammad** and **Kasaju, Prem Kumar**, e'. On education in Nepal. Kathmandu : National Education Committee, 1974. 93 p.

This compilation is an attempt to bring into focus the many aspects of educational change that are taking place at the conceptual and action level, to provide a critical assessment of reforms and innovations, and to provide new perspectives for the future development of education in Nepal.

362. **National Seminar on Education Today and Tomorrow : a** report. Centre for Educational Research, Innovation and Development. Kathmandu : National Education Committee, Centre for Educational Research, Innovation & Development, 1977. 56 leaves.

The seminar, which was held from 5 to 7 January 1977, discussed the important features of the report *Learning to be* within the overall context of the National Education System Plan of Nepal. The aim of the seminar was to provide ideas for the planning of educational schemes in Nepal in the future. Has cover title: National Seminar on Learning to be. Mimeographed.

363. **National Seminar on Women's Decade, 27-30 May 1979 : proceedings.**

For full entry refer to Employment & Manpower section.

364. **Pant, Mahes Raj.** On Sanskrit education. Kathmandu : The Author, 1979. 202 p. bibliog.

A brief and lucid description of both the traditional approach and the western critical and analytical approach to the study of Sanskrit language and literature. It ends with a fervent plea that neither be neglected in Nepal. Includes a bibliography of Sanskrit manuscripts edited by Nepali scholars.

365. **Pradhan Ratna Man.** In-service teacher education in Nepal. *Education Quarterly*, vol. 16, no. 1 (Jan.-March 1973). pp. 1-19.

The author highlights the ongoing in-service teacher education in Nepal with an emphasis on creating professional confidence among the teachers.

366. **A Profile of Centre for Educational** Research, **Innovation, and Development.** Centre for Educational Research, Innovation, and Development. Kathmandu : National Education Committee, Centre for Educational Research, Innovation, and Development, 1978. 13 p.

This pamphlet gives information regarding the nature of the Centre's work and activities, its administrative set up, projects in operation, publications, and objectives. The cover title is *Centre for Educational Research, Innovation & Development.*

367. **Ragsdale, Tod.** Patterns of education and literacy in a village panchayat of central Nepal. *Contributions to Nepalese Studies*, vol. 2, no. 1 (Feb. 1975), pp. 19-38.

The author studied a village panchayat having a 63% Gurung population, which lies approximately six miles north east of Pokhara town in Kaski District. The author conducted, with the help of panchayat ward members, a census of literacy of Gurung and non-Gurung population at the beginning of 1974. The figures in this paper, being the results of an on-going project, cannot be taken as final. The study proves that the Gurung population has a high literacy rate of 72% among males and 29% among females aged between 6 and 19. Similarly, the percentage of literacy at other ages is also very high in comparison with that of non-Gurungs in the village.

368. **Reed, Horace B.** and **Jane, Mary**. Nepal in transition : educational innovation. Pittsburgh, Pennsylvania : University of Pittsburgh Press, 1968. 215 p. bibliog.

A case study of educational development in Nepal, which also provides information on the country as a whole. Includes illustrations and appendixes.

369. **Roberts, Katya**. Guidelines for pre-school centres operated by the Nepal Children's Organisation. Kathmandu : Tribhuvan University Press, 1975. ca. 100 p.

This publication contains the results of a study conducted under the auspices of UNICEF between 1972 and 1975.

370. **Sakya, Thakur M.** and **Kasaju, Prem Kumar**, ed. Education and development. Kathmandu : Centre for Educational Research, Innovation, and Development, National Education Committee, 1977. 104 p.

A collection of articles on education in Nepal. This is a modest attempt at bringing together an assortment of the ideas, reflections, and experiences of people engaged in various educational tasks and reflects a growing consensus that education is the key to development.

371. **Sharma, Gopi Nath.** School curriculum in Nepal. Kathmandu : Him Kumari Sharma, 1980. 89 p. bibliog.

Deals with approaches adopted at different times towards linking education with the needs of the country. The book covers different system of education such as classical Sanskrit education, Buddhist education of the Gompa type, Muslim education of the Madarasa type, basic education of the Gandhian type, and modern English education. It also elaborates the policy of His Majesty's Government towards the adoption of the most appropriate type of education. The author gives an extensive account of attempts which have been made to blend academic education with work based vocational education.

372. **Shrestha**, **Bihari K.** and **Gurung**, **Sant B.** Equality of access of women to education in Pokhara (a sociological survey). Kathmandu : Centre for Economic Development and Administration, 1973. 116 p map. bibliog.

This study undertaken for UNESCO, Paris, presents the sociological factors governing the equality of access of women to education, teacher training, and teaching careers in Pokhara. The school going behaviour of the male and female children of various ethnic groups in Pokhara has also been studied from a socio-economic viewpoint. Mimeographed.

373. **Shrestha**, **Kedar N.** Educational management in Nepal. Bhaktapur, Nepal : Tribhuvan University, Institute of Education, 1980. 123 p. bibliog.

The main purpose of this publication is to trace the historical development of educational administration in Nepal, in the context of the socio-political milieu of the Nepalese school system.

374. **Shrestha**, **Kedar N.** Educational planning and the new education plan. *Education Quarterly*, vol. 16, no. 1 (Jan.-March 1973), pp. 1-19.

This article discusses various steps undertaken to formulate an educational policy and relates these to the new education plan, along with an account of the concept of educational planning in developing countries.

375. **Shrestha**, **Ramesh**. Adult literacy in Nepal : a report. Kathmandu : Institute of Nepal and Asian Studies, Tribhuvan University, 1977. 144 leaves. bibliog.

This report deals with the past achievements, the current programme, problems, and future prospects for the spread of literacy as a result of adult education in Nepal. The aim was to collect information on the work of all the agencies which were significantly active in the field of literacy through adult education in Nepal, both in a historical and a synchronic perspective, and to evaluate their contributions. The main focus was on the Adult Education Section of His Majesty's Government. Mimeographed.

376. **Shrestha, Rudra,** ed. Toran : selected research oriented articles. Kathmandu : Laxman Kayastha, 1977. 104 p. map.

A collection of articles in English and Nepali on education in Nepal.

377. **Subba, Subhadra.** The medium question in Nepalese higher education. *Contributions to Nepalese Studies*, vol. 7, no. 1/2 (Dec. 1979/June 1980), pp. 71-95. bibliog.

The purpose of the survey was to provide a clear picture of the language medium currently used in classes and examinations in order to help planners to establish Nepali as the exclusive medium in higher education in Nepal by 1983.

378. **Tribhuvan University newsletter.**

For full entry refer to Professional periodicals section.

379. **Tuladhar, Nirmal M.** and **Tuladhar, Sumon K.** Testing Nepali as a second language. *Contributions to Nepalese Studies*, vol. 6, no. 2 (June 1979), pp. 21-26. bibliog.

This paper is a preliminary attempt. Describes the competence in the learning of Nepali at the primary school level.

380. **Verma, Yugeshwar P.** Nepal : progress and problems, 1972-80.

For full entry refer to Politics section.

10

EMPLOYMENT & MANPOWER

381. **Acharya, K.B.** [et al.], comp. Census of His Majesty's Government employees. Kathmandu : His Majesty's Government of Nepal, National Planning Commission Secretariat, Central Bureau of Statistics, 1974. 141 p.

A census of His Majesty's Government employees, first of its kind, was undertaken by the Central Bureau of Statistics with the reference date 15th July 1971. Results presented in this study do not include the employees of Ministries and Departments. The study covers a total of 1910 establishments and covers all the returns received up to 31st January 1974. Information is presented on the number of employees by various categories classified by status, sex, age, and academic qualification. The information is arranged by districts. Chiefly tables.

382. **Dixon, Ruth B.** Rural women at work : strategies for development in South Asia. Baltimore : Published for Resources for the Future by John Hopkins Press, 1978. 227 p. bibliog.

Based on the author's intensive interviews with personnel from international agencies, governments, population institutes, family planning clinics, and rural community development programmes in Nepal, India, Pakistan, and Bangladesh, the study focuses on ways of improving women's status in rural areas.

383. **Employment of graduates in Nepal.** National Planning Commission. Kathmandu : National Planning Commission, 1968. 2 vols. in 1.

This study covers the period 1964-66. Vol. 1 deals with master level and vol. 2 deals with bachelor level.

384. **Hitchcock, John T.** A Nepalese hill village and Indian employment. *Asian Survey*, vol. 1, no. 9 (1961), pp. 15-20.

Explain the meaning of Indian employment and the employment of the Magras of Banyan Hill, Nepal in army service.

385. **National Seminar on Women's Decade, 27-30 May 1979 :** proceedings. Editor : Padma Shrestha; associated editors: Shanta Aryal, Dilli Raman Acharya. Lalitpur, Nepal : Central Panchayat Training Institute [1980?], 83 p.

Three papers were presented in this Seminar: 1. Women and employment, by Hon'ble Dr. Mohan Man Sainju; 2. Women's education in Nepal, by Dr. Narsingh Narayan Singh; 3. Women and health, by Dr. Rita Thapa. These papers were presented in Nepali and translated into English.

386. **Schroeder, Robert** and **Schroeder, Elaine.** Women in Nepali agriculture : all work and no power. *The Journal of Development and Administrative Studies*, vol. 1, no. 2 (1978), pp. 172-192.

Based on data collected in the village of Batulechaur in Pokhara, the paper analyses the importance of the female labour forces in the agricultural production in Nepal. The authors criticize the policy of giving agricultural training only to boys who tend to go ultimately for non-agricultural occupations. They point out the possible changes that may come from extension programmes designed to reach women agriculturists.

387. **Technical and vocational training in Nepal, 1966-67.** Ministry of Economic Planning, His Majesty's Government of Nepal. Kathmandu : The Ministry, 1968. 80 p.

This is the result of the first manpower survey conducted in Nepal in different sectors.

11

ENCYCLOPAEDIAS, DIRECTORIES & WHO IS WHO

388. **Bajracharya, Manik Lal.** Nepal, 1972-73 : trade and information directory.

For full entry refer to Trade section.

389. **Dhakhwa, Dev Ratna.** Exclusive encyclopaedia of Nepal. Kathmandu : Sahayogi Prakashan, 1974. 309 p.

A very useful publication for general information.

390. **Directory of foreigners in Nepal.** Prepared by the staff of the American Embassy. Kathmandu : American Embassy, 1972. 76. leaves.

391. **Directory of foreigners in Nepal.** Kathmandu : Kathmandu Jaycees Publication, 1975. 28 p.

392. **Export promotion directory of Nepal.** Compiled by: Office of the Economic Trends. Katamandu : Amrit Man Shrestha, 1972- vol. 1.

Economic Trends is a quarterly publication in Nepali and English brought out from Kathmandu. They have compiled this directory for export promotion.

393. **Henberger, H.** and **Hofer, A.** Deutsche forschung in Nepal, 1950-1975. Heidelberg, W. Germany : Andras Hofer, South Asian Institute, University of Heidelberg, 1976. 61 p.

This publication is a summary of German research in Nepal and divided into three parts. Part one relates to a brief historical description of research by West German scholars in Nepal during the past 25 years; part two is a subjectwise list of scholars with some biographical and research data, and a list of German institutions sponsoring work in Nepal; part three contains authorwise bibliography with a subject index of persons and institutions.

394. **Jonchhe, Sushila**, comp. Research directory. Kathmandu: Research Division, Tribhuvan University, 1976. 56 p.

Listing of research done in Nepali and English, chiefly during the period, 1970-76.

395. **Kathamadaum upatyakako udyoga karyalayako nama-suci.**

For full entry refer to Industry section.

396. **Karki, Yuvaraj Singh.** Viśva-paricaya : viśva-kośako laghurupa = Vishwa parichaya : mini encyclopedia. Vill. Chuplu Dhanda, Dist. Okhaladhunga, Nepal : The Author, 1977. vol. 1 (594 p.) 1 map.

A very useful encyclopedia of Nepal in Nepali language. The author has plan to issue this work in two volumes. This volume deals with Nepal on the whole. Includes illustrations.

397. **List of personnel of the United Nations Organisation and its specialized agencies in Nepal.** Kathmandu : United Nations Development Programme, 1979. 34 leaves.

This list gives information regarding (1) Offices of the United Nations and Specialised Agencies Projects and Project Personnel ; UNTCD, UNDP, ILO, FAO, ITU, ICAO, UNESCO, UNIDO, IBRD, ITC, UNICEF, WHO; Sub-contractors: EPDC, Nippon Koei, Tahal; (2) Useful telephone numbers; (3) Alphabetical list of personnel giving name and nationality, designation and date of arrival, and addresses. Mimeographed.

398. **Mahila karmacari nirdesika** = Directory of working women. International Women's Year Committee. Kathmandu : The Committee, Nepal, 1975. 88 p.

This Nepali publication is a directory of working women in Nepal.

399. **Mantri-patro** : 2007 sāla Phāguna 7 gate prajātantra bhaepachi Rāṇā-Kāṅgresa-mantrīmaṇḍalamā Śrī 3 Mahārāja Mohana Śamaśera Ja. Ba. Rā. Prāimaminishṭara ra Pararāshtra Mantrī bhaedekhi ājasammako : Gorakhāpatra, Nepala gajeṭa. Kathmandu : Bibliographical Research Centre, 1979. 40 p.

Directory of ministers in various cabinets in Nepal, February 17, 1951 through June 1979. A very useful reference tool. Also gives information regarding issue of the Nepal gazette, in which the information has appeared for the first time.

400. **Nepal trade directory**. Compiled, checked, and edited by Intertrade Publications (India) Private Limited. Calcutta : Intertrade Publications (India) Private Limited, 1979? 316 p.

Identifying principal business and industrial units trading from and with Nepal. Gives information regarding: Business enterprises in Nepal; Royal Nepalese diplomatic missions; Foreign diplomatic corps; Travel agencies; Libraries; Royal Government Undertakings; Export houses.

401. **Tandulkar, Shyam.** comp. and ed. Nepāla pustakālaya nirdeśikā. Kathmandu : National Council for Science and Technology, Library Sub-Committee, 1980. 58 p.

Directory of libraries of Nepal ; includes glossary of library terms, English-Nepali. Mimeographed.

402. **Trade and industrial directory of Nepal.**

For full entry refer to Trade section.

403. **Who is Who—Nepal, 1972-74.** Edited by Deepak Kumar Aryal [et al.]. Kathmandu : Kathmandu School of Journalism, 1974. 392 p. 1 map.

A biographical dictionary of the distinguished Nepali personalities. The book includes almost 400 personalities who have earned their name or fame in social, political, economic, administrative, scientific, and other important fields. Includes the new generation of emerging personalities in different fields, whose names may still be unknown to many people in Nepal.

404. **Who is Who—Nepal, 1975-77.** Edited by Deepak Kumar Aryal [et al.]. 2nd ed., improved and enl., and rev. Kathmandu : Kathmandu School of Journalism, 1977. 378 p.

A biographical dictionary of distinguished Nepali personalities. Includes illustrations.

405. **Who's Who in Indo-Nepal, 1980.** Edited by Tanu Gupta. New Delhi : Demco Press International, 1980. 348 p.

India and Nepal are together in a number of ways on international map. This work attempts to stimulate understanding and cooperation among the people of India and Nepal. This includes nearly 1200 biographical notes in brief, crisp, and personal sketches of India and Nepal. A useful reference work, though selective, is completely unbiased and independent. Includes an index and list of abbreviations used.

12

ENVIRONMENT

406. **Banskota, Mahesh**. Environment, management, rural development, and project planning. Kathmandu : Centre for Economic Development and Administration, Tribhuvan University, 1980. 43 p. (CEDA occassional paper series. Rural Development Group).

This paper discusses some of the major issues involved in environmental management, rural development, and project planning. This mimeographed paper will prove to be very useful to policy-makers, researchers, and those concerned with the management of Nepalese environment.

407. **Bhatt, Dibya Deo** and **Shrestha, Tej Kumar.** The environment of Sukia Phanta : A study report sponsored by the National Planning Commission of Nepal.

For full entry refer to Flora & Fauna section.

408. **Bishop, Barry** C. A cultural-ecological analysis of Karnali Zone in the western Nepal Himalaya : with emphasis on the movements of people, animals and goods, seasonality, and recent change : a preliminary report Kathmandu : The Author, 1970. 48 leaves. map.

409. **Gelder, A. von.** Comments on erosion control activities of the Department of Soil and Water Conservation. Edited by Eric P. Rusten. Kathmandu : Ministry of Forest, Department of Soil & Conservation, Integrated

Watershed Management, Torrent Control & Land Use Development Project, 1978. 34 leaves.

This report reviews the activities of the Department of Soil and Water Conservation (DSWC). With the review of the past activities, the author has discussed current trends within the DSWC. One of the major trends is the involvement of local people and the use of inexpensive alternative methods in dealing with soil and water conservation problems. Finally, the author discusses the future plan of DSWC. Mimeographed.

410. **Gelder, A. von.** The Integrated Watershed Management approach for erosion control project formulation. Kathmandu : Ministry of Forest, Department of Soil and Water Conservation, Integrated Watershed Management, Torrent Control, and Land Use Development Project, 1978. 37 leaves. map.

The main conclusions of the author's paper *Review of DSWC erosion control activities* were that the erosion control projects would be more successful if they were more systematic in project selection and planning; they were better integrated with agencies having similar objectives and if there were greater participation by the people. This paper presents a method of overcoming these short comings.

411. **Gurung, Ram Bahadur.** Local conservation needs and attitudes in the Phewa Tal Catchment. Edited by Eric P. Rusten. Kathmandu : Department of Soil and Water Conservation, Integrated Watershed Management, Torrent Control and Land Use Development Project, Food and Agriculture Organization of the United Nations, 1978. 15 leaves. (Phewa Tal technical report, no. 3)

The author conducted a series of meetings in twenty villages within the Phewa Tal Catchment area. He met with the local people and held discussions on the Soil and Water Conservation Project in the Phewa Tal Catchment area and recorded detailed information regarding the forests, landslides, water sources, agricultural activities, and inhabitants. This booklet presents his results and recommendations. Mimeographed.

412. **Household beseline study resource conservation and utilization project.**

For full entry refer to Society and Social structure section.

413. **Kandel, G. P.** Report on suspended sediment measurement in Kathmandu Valley. Kathmandu : Integrated Watershed Management Project (FAO), Department of Soil & Water Conservation, His Majesty's Government, 1978. 17 leaves. maps.

To carry out the study six streams around Kathmandu Valley were selected and their catchment vary mainly in landuse, topography, soils, geology, rainfall, etc. The following six catchments were studied for this report: 1. Bagmati Khola near Sundarizal reservoir; 2. Nagmati Khola near Sundarizal reservior; 3. Godawari Khola at the dam site near Godawari Botanical Garden; 4. Bishnumati Khola near Budhanilkantha School building; 5. Manumati Khola near the joining point of Manohara in Sankhu: 6. Mahadev Khola at the iron bridge near Balaju. Mimeographed.

414. **Kathmandu Valley** : the preservation of physical environment and cultural heritage ; a protective inventory. Prepared by His Majesty's Government of Nepal in collaboration with the United Nations and UNESCO. Coordination and production by Dr. Carl Pruscha; description of individual monuments by Dr. Prayag Raj Sharma; field surveys by A. Tuladhar, R. R. Bajracharya, K. K. Joshi, H. R. Sakya, K. Lamichane; photography by G. M. Chitrakar, S. D. Manandhar; airphotography by E. Schneider, F. Grifoni; editorial and clerical assistance by J. Oates, B. P. Shrestha, D. Durkee Miller; special UNESCO consultants : Dr. Eduard Sekler, Dr. F. R. Allchin. Vienna : Anton Schroll, 1975. 2 vols. maps. bibliog.

These fully illustrated volumes are a useful reference tool for those who are interested in knowing about Kathmandu Valley with its rich heritage and for those who are interested to conserve and improve it.

415. **Laban, Peter.** Landslide occurrence in Nepal. Kathmandu: Ministry of Forest, Department of Soil and Water Conservation, Integrated Watershed Management, Torrent Control, and Land Use Development Project, 1979. 27 leaves. bibliog.

This report presents the findings of a study on the occurrence of landslides in Nepal, based on accounts of landslide from aircraft.

416. **Mulder, R. P.** Erosion plot measurement in Phewa Tal Catchment. Place and publisher not known, 1978. 10 leaves. bibliog. (Phewa Tal technical report, no. 6)

The Phewa Tal Catchment is situated in the middle mountains in the western region of Nepal. The figures presented in this paper are only representative of the Phewa Tal Catchment. The paper also includes description of the author's experiences with plot monitoring which may be used as a guideline for further plot experiments in Nepal. Mimeographed.

417. **Report on Rapati Baseline Survey.**

For full entry refer to Society and Social structure section.

418. **Sjoholm, H.** [et al.]. Towards a soil and water conservation education program for Nepal. Rev. ed. Kathmandu : Ministry of Forest, Department of Soil Conservation and Watershed Management, Integrated Watershed Management, Torrent Control, and Land Use Development Project, 1980. 34 leaves.

The objectives of this work are to increase knowledge of soil and water conservation and to foster and improve soil and water conservation action by various groups of people. Mimeographed. Includes illustrations.

419. **Zollinger, F.** The Sapt Kosi unsolved problems of flood control in the Nepalese Terai. Kathmandu : Ministry of Forest, Department of Soil and Water Conservation, Integrated Watershed Management, Torrent Control, and Land Use Development Project, 1979. 94 leaves. 3 maps. bibliog.

The main objective of this study is to assist the engineering staff of the Department of Soil and Water Conservation in developing a programme of protection for the Kosi River and avoiding floods. Mimeographed. Includes illustrations.

13

FINANCE & BANKING

420. **Agrawal, Govind Ram** and **Bista, Bal Govind**. Government accounting in Nepal. Kathmandu : Centre for Economic Development & Administration, Tribhuvan University, 1981. 43 p. bibliog.

This is a case study presented at the National Workshop on Planning, Budgeting, Accounting, and Auditing, jointly sponsored by the Asian and Pacific Development Centre, Malaysia, Financial Comptroller General's Office, Ministry of Finance, His Majesty's Government of Nepal, and the Centre for Economic Development and Administration, Tribhuvan University, Kathmandu. The case study has been prepared exclusively for teaching purposes. Mimeographed.

421. **Banskota, Mahesh**. Sectoral allocation of development and its productivity. Kirtipur, Nepal : Centre for Economic Development and Administration, Tribhuvan University, 1980. 63 p. bibliog.

This is an attempt to examine the productivity of previous investment efforts. In the study, the author also examines the problems encountered in a research of this type. The report would prove to be useful to plan future investment allocations. Mimeographed. Has cover title: Sectoral allocation of investment and its productivity.

422. **Bulletin (Nepal Bank Limited)**. Kathmandu : Nepal Bank Limited, 1968- monthly.

Articles on banks and banking in Nepal in English and Nepali.

423. **Devakota, Bharat.** Government expenditure on road transport in Nepal. Kathmandu : Centre for Economic Development and Administration, Tribhuvan University, 1980. 83 p. bibliog.

An analysis of government expenditure on roads and bridges in Nepal, 1966-78. It also investigates the extent of capital formation through road transport. A novel aspect of this study is its attempt to identify the causes of the demand for roads in the country. The study shows that due to lack of supplementary investment, the impact of roads on the transformation of the economy has not been pronounced in Nepal. Mimeographed.

424. **Devakota, Bharat.** Nepālamā śaharī ghara jaggā kara : eka viśleshana. Kathmandu : Centre for Economic Development and Administration, Tribhuvan University, 1980. 44 p.

This publication studies urban property tax in Nepal, supported by statistics. Mimeographed. In Nepali.

425. **Dhungana, Bhavani.** Financial resource mobilization in Nepal during the nineteen eighties. Kathmandu : Centre for Economic Development and Administration, Tribhuvan University, 1980. 71 p. bibliog. (CEDA occasional paper series)

This paper highlights the problems of resource mobilization in Nepal. The author rightly points out that the financial resources may come as a major constraint in the effective implementation of development plans during the current decade. The measure suggested to deal with the resource mobilization problem are worth the consideration of Nepalese policymakers. Mimeographed.

426. **Dhungana, Bhavani.** Indirect taxation in Nepal. Kathmandu : Centre for Economic Development and Administration, Tribhuvan University, 1980. 153 p. bibliog.

Examines the problems and prospects of various indirect taxes such as customs duties, excise tax, and sales tax. Since indirect taxes generate most of the tax revenue in Nepal, rationalization and reforms of these taxes are overdue. This has become more urgent in view of the rapidly growing gap between government income and expenditure. This should be useful to policy-makers, researchers, and students of Nepalese public finance. Mimeographed.

427. **Dhungana, Bhavani** and **Kayastha, Narendra**, ed. Studies on prices, Nepal. Kirtipur, Nepal : Centre for Economic Development and Administration, Tribhuvan University, 1977. 176 p. bibliog.

Collection of articles on prices in Nepal. Dr. B. Pradhan deals with monetary policy and inflation; Dr. H. Pant examines the macro aspects of Nepalese inflation; Dr. P. Mathema considers agricultural prices and their effects on the general price level; P. Rana looks at fiscal policy and its effect on general prices; H. Giri discusses the general price problem and the role of private sector; and B. Dhungana and N. Kayastha analyse the prices of basic commodities in different regions of the country. Mimeographed.

428. **Dhungana, Bhavani** and **Ojha, Durga P.** Price analysis. Kirtipur, Nepal : Centre for Economic Development and Administration, 1972. 99, 23 p.

Comprises the main papers and the proceedings of the Seminar on Price Policy, 10-12 September 1972, sponsored by Centre for Economic Development and Administration and Federation of Nepalese Chamber of Commerce and Industry.

429. **Dhungana, Bhavani** [et al.]. An analysis of tax structure of Nepal. Kirtipur, Nepal : Centre for Economic Development and Administration, 1979. 130 p. bibliog.

The study reveals that Nepal's existing taxation policy has had only marginal effect on the country's development and that a new policy will have to be designed, not merely for maximization of revenue but also for meeting other development objectives. This publication will be very useful to anyone seeking information on the Nepalese tax structure. Mimeographed.

430. **Investing in Nepal**. Investment Promotion and Publicity Division, Nepal Industrial Development Corporation. 3rd ed. Kathmandu : Investment Promotion and Publicity Division, Nepal Industrial Development Corporation, 1971. 149 p.

A resume of Nepalese laws and regulations governing the establishment and operation of an industrial enterprise.

431. **Jha, Kumar Kant.** Agricultural finance in Nepal : an analytical study. New Delhi : Heritage Publishers, 1978. 241 p. bibliog.

This is revision of the author's thesis completed at the University of Bombay in 1975. The field work for the study was done in 1969 for 142 farmers in 6 villages of eastern Terai. The author discusses both the demand for and supply of agricultural finance in Nepal. On the demand side, he concentrates on the demand for credit, indebtedness, investment, and disinvestment among various groups of farmers classified by the size of their land holdings. On the supply side, money lenders, debt legislation, cooperatives, and compulsory savings are discussed.

432. **Khanal, Mohan Prasad**, ed. Sainika dravyakosha. Sundhara, Nepal : Karmachari Sanchaya Kosha, 1978. 604 p.

This is a collection of historical documents related to the Provident Fund for armymen of Nepal. In Nepali.

433. **Mahat, R. S.** Capital market, financial flows, and industrial finance in Nepal. Lalitpur, Nepal : Sajha Prakashan, 1981. 350 p. bibliog.

The author has made a very competent study of the problem of industrial finance in Nepal by presenting a critical examination of all the aspects related to the problem. It is informative and analytical. Despite its focus on industrial finance, the analysis has significant bearing on the problem of financing Nepal's economic development process itself.

434. **Malla, Kamal Prakash** and **Kanaskar, Tej R.**, ed. Occasional papers in the humanities and social sciences.

For full entry refer to Languages & Dialects—Linguistic studies section.

435. **National accounts of Nepal, public corporations.** Central Bureau of Statistics, Nepal. Kathmandu : The Bureau, 1971. 39 leaves.

This study is a modest beginning in the direction of compilation of accounts according to the recommendations of the UN and presents the Production account, Income and outlay account, and Capital finance account in respect of Public corporations in

Nepal. The study is restricted to one year, i.e. 1967/68, the period for which the accounts of a larger number of corporations have become available. The accounts presented here are illustrative rather than exhaustive. Mimeographed.

436. **National Accounts Project.** National Planning Commission Secretariat. Kathmandu : Central Bureau of Statistics, His Majesty's Government of Nepal, 1978-79. 3 vols.

Volume one covers agriculture; volume two covers mining, quarrying and manufacturing, finance, insurance, real estate, and business services, public sector accounts : government agencies, private non-profit making institutions, 1976-77; volume three covers electricity, construction, wholesale and retail trade, restaurants and hotels, transport, storage, and communication, community, social and personal services. Mimeographed. Vol. 3 has title: Gross domestic product of Nepal, 1976/77.

437. **Nepalese Economic Journal.**

For full entry refer to Professional periodicals section.

438. **Pant, Hari Dhoj.** Incidence and effects of excise taxation in Nepal. Kathmandu : The Author [1978?]. 265 p.

This study is mainly concerned with the role of excise taxes in mobilizing domestic resources. Specifically, this study investigates: the place of excise taxes in the revenue structure of Nepal; the role of excise taxes in development finance; the effect of excise taxes on selective industry; and the effect of excise taxes on prices of excisable commodities. Mimeographed.

439. **Pant, Yadav Prasad.** Banking and development. Kathmandu : Nepal Rastra Bank, 1971. 99 p.

A collection of speeches by the Governor of the Nepal Rastra Bank on banking and economic development in Nepal.

440. **Regmi, Mahesh Chandra.** Land tenure and taxation in Nepal. 2nd ed. Kathmandu : Ratna Pustak Bhandar, 1978. 895 p. bibliog. (Bibliotheca Himalayica, series I, vol. 26)

A description of the legal and administrative framework within which land tenure and taxation systems have evolved during the past two centuries. It is a reprint of a four-volume work originally published by the Institute of International Studies, University of California, 1963-68.

441. **Seminar-cum-Workshop on Financial Management, March 30-April 21, 1971.** Kathmandu : Centre for Economic Development Administration, 1978. 1 vol.

Collection of papers read at the seminar. Includes case studies of some Nepalese establishments. Has title on spine: Financial management.

442. **Seminar-cum-Workshop on Program Budgeting, 1971.** Kathmandu : Centre for Economic Development & Administration, 1971. 1 vol.

Collection of papers read at the seminar. The papers pay special attention to budget preparation and implementation in Nepal. Spine title: Program budgeting, 1971. In English and Nepali.

443. **Singh, S.K.** The fiscal system of Nepal. Kathmandu : Ratna Pustak Bhandar, 1977. 268 p. bibliog.

Discusses public finance, fiscal policy and the taxation system of Nepal.

444. **Study of Rastriya Banjiya Bank, Kathmandu an undertaking of HMG/N, May-Sept. 1974.** Consultancy services: Centre for Economic Development and Administration, Institute of Business Administration, Commerce, and Public Administration, Tribhuvan University. Kirtipur, Nepal : Centre for Economic Development and Administration, 1974. 318 p.

This study concerns with the working of the Rastriya Banjiya Bank, a commercial bank in Nepal. Mimeographed.

14

FLORA & FAUNA

445. **Bajracharya, Mana Bajra**. Ayurvedic medicinal plants and general treatment. Kathmandu : Piyusavarsi Ausadhalaya, 1979. 230 p.

The compiler is a famous practising ayurvedic doctor and is Chairman of Nepal Ayurveda Association. Here he describes the medicinal herbs and plants commonly used in Ayurvedic medicine, explaining their properties and applications.

446. **Bark allowance table for Nepal, 1979**. Forest Survey and Research Office, Department of Forests, Nepal. Kathmandu : The Office [1980?]. 8 leaves. (Forest Survey and Research Office publication, no. 31)

Presents bark-thickness and bark-allowance estimating tables for the four most important indigenous trees; Sal (Shorea robusta); Asna (Terminalia sp.); Semal (Bombax ceiba); Karma (Adina cordifolia).

447. **Bhatt, Dibya Deo** and **Shrestha, Tej Kumar**. The environment of Sukla Phanta : a study report sponsored by the National Planning Commission of Nepal. Kathmandu : Curriculum Development Centre, Tribhuvan University, 1977. 80 p. maps. illus.

Contains information on wildlife conservation in the reserve forest of Sukla Phanta in the Kanchanpur District., Nepal.

448. **Bue, Erberto Lo.** The use of officinal plants among the Lama people of Yol-Mo. *Kailash : a Journal of Himalayan Studies*, vol. 8, no. 1-2 (1981), pp. 89-108.

A preliminary report to ascertain how and to what extent Tibetan traditional medicine survives in one culturally Tibetan area of Helambu (or Yol-Mo). The report is based on fieldwork carried out during October-November 1975 which surveyed the use of officinal plants among the local population.

449. **Fleming, Robert L., Jr.** The general ecology, flora, and fauna of Midland Nepal. Kathmandu : United States Agency for International Development, 1973. 105 p. illus.

The first chapter explains the meaning of ecology, and the second describes the common plants and animals of a typical subtropical forest in Nepal. The third chapter discusses the plants, birds and animals of the mixed or twilight belt. The fourth chapter mentions a few examples of aquatic ecosystems in Nepal. The last chapter is entitled 'Man living with nature : the Kathmandu Valley'. Includes an appendix of scientific names.

450. **Fleming, Robert L., Sr.** [et al.]. Birds of Nepal : with reference to Kashmir and Sikkim. Illustrated by Hem Poudyal, et al. 2nd ed. Kathmandu : Avalok Publishers, 1979. 358 p. 3 maps. bibliog., illus.

In Nepal there are 800 species of birds and they form an important part of Nepal's natural history. This study of birds includes colour illustrations, two appendixes: Kashmir birds and Sikkim birds, an index to scientific names and an index and checklist of English names.

451. **Gjaerum, Halvor B.** and **Steineger, Erik**. Some interesting Nepalese rust fungi. *Kailash : a Journal of Himalayan Studies*, vol. 6, no. 1 (1978), pp. 37-43. bibliog.

The fungi of Nepal is not well known and few papers have been published on the subject. Mr. Steineger visited Rolwaling Valley in east Nepal in 1973 and collected some specimens which are now preserved at the Botanical Museum, Oslo. This article includes descriptions of ten specimens collected by Mr. Steineger.

442. **Keys to the Dicot genera in Nepal**. Kathmandu : Department of Medicinal Plants, His Majesty's Government of Nepal, 1967- vols. 1-2.

Volume 1 covers polypetalae, and volume 2 contains gamopetalae and monochlamydeae.

453. **Kiauta, B.** On a small dragonfly collection from Nepal. *Kailash : a Journal of Himalayan Studies*, vol. 3, no. 3, (1975), pp. 259-294.

During a post-monsoon mission to Humla and western Tarai in 1972, Professor H. Franz of Hochschule fur Bodenkultur, Vienna, collected some odonate material and passed it on to the author for identification. He collected thirty-two adult specimens of twelve species from nine genera. In this article the author identifies these specimens and presents them in an annotated list. Since hardly anything is known about the odonate fauna of the Terai region and Humla, this collection is very useful.

454. **Kirkpatrick, William.** An account of the Kingdom of Nepal, the substance of observations made during a mission to that country in the year 1793.

For full entry refer to History—General section.

455. **Lamichhaney, B.P.** and **Joshi, R.B.** Distribution seeding and method of propagation of forest trees of Nepal. Kathmandu : Forest Survey and Research Office, Department of Forestry, His Majesty's Government, 1980. 19 leaves. bibliog. (Forest Survey and Research Office publication, no. 32)

A booklet containing information collected from numerous sources. Mimeographed.

456. **Landon, Perceval.** Nepal.

For full entry refer to History—General section.

457. **Malla, S.M., ed.** Flora of Langtang and cross section vegetation survey central zone. Kathmandu: His Majesty's Government of Nepal, Ministry of Forests, Department of Medicinal Plants, 1976. 269 p. maps. bibliog. (Bulletin of the Department of Medicinal Plants, Nepal, no. 6)

The entry for each plant gives its scientific name, together with any synonyms or literary references associated with it. In addition, each entry lists the place and date of collection, with the state of the specimen (whether flowering or fruiting), the name of the collector, and the collection number of the specimen. All of the plants are kept in the Herbarium of Nepal at Godawari. The book includes two indexes, one listing the Latin names and one the local names of the plants. This will help botanists identify plants with the local names with the help of local persons. This book is a part of a bigger work, *Flora of Nepal.*

458. **Majupuria, Trilok Chandra, ed.** Wild is beautiful : introduction to the magnificent, rich, and varied fauna and wildlife of Nepal : a compendium during trekking and visiting wildlife observatories. Gwalior : S. Devi, 1981-82. 507 p. 12 maps. bibliog. illus.

Nepal has a rich variety of fauna because of its diversified climate and vegetation. This is a collection of articles on the fauna and wildlife of Nepal, written by an expert in the field . The articles cover many aspects of fauna and wildlife, e.g. zoogeography, systematics, ecology, conservation, etc. Includes 59 colour, 45 black-and-white, and 321 line drawings.

459. **Manandhar, N.P.** Medicinal plants of Nepal Himalaya. Kathmandu : Ratna Pustak Bhandar, 1980. 85 p. bibliog. illus.

Medicinal properties are ascribed to a number of Himalayan plants, and the recent revival of interest in traditional medicine has created an interest in the flora of Nepal. This book is a contribution to the knowledge of medicinal plants in Nepal and their properties. It includes illustrations of the plants, an index to scientific names and an index to the vernacular names.

460. **Medicinal plants of Nepal.** Kathmandu : Department of Medicinal Plants, His Majesty's Government of Nepal, 1970. 153 p. (Its Bulletin no. 3)

A handbook of medicinal plants, arranged alphabetically by Nepali names, with local synonyms, botanical names, description, distribution, and medicinal uses in English.

461. **Mierow, Dorothy** and **Shrestha, Tirtha Bahadur.** Himalayan flowers and trees. Kathmandu : Sahayogi Press, 1978. 204 p. 2 maps. illus.

Illustrates a large number of Himalayan trees and flowers and also shows their diverse environments and tells something about the inter-relationships of the plants with the local people. The first part of this book is devoted to the important plant families; the second part consists of over 400 colour pictures of flowers, trees, settings and people along with small maps. The third part contains notes and explanations on the illustrations; these provide much information on the natural history and ecology of Himalayan plants. Trekkers will find it convenient to carry, since it is divided into sections corresponding to the major treks.

462. **Mishra, Hemant R.** and **Mierew, Dorothy.** Nepālakā jaṅgalī jantu = Wild animals of Nepal. Kathmandu : Ratna Pustak Bhandar, 1976. 82 p. bibliog.

An introduction to some of the wild mammals of Nepal, including mammals that live near the country's border or are familiar to the Nepalese because of cultural, religious or historical traditions. Reptiles and birds are not included. The text is in English and Nepali, with scientific names in English only. Common names are given both English and Nepali.

463. **The Nepal Journal of Forestry.** Kathmandu : Nepa Forestry Association, 1975- semiannual.

Publishes scholarly articles on forestry in Nepal.

464. **Newseletter (Nepal Nature Conservation Society).**

For full enyrt refer to Professional periodicals section.

465. **Rand, Austin Loomer** and **Fleming, Robert L.** Birds from Nepal. Chicago : Chicago Natural History Museum, 1957. 218 p. maps. bibliog. (Chicago Natural History Museum publication, 826)

466. **Regional Seminar on the Ecology and Tropical Highlands 8-16 April 1968.** Kathmandu, 1968- vols. 1-3.

The seminar was jointly organized by the Government of Nepal and UNESCO. To date three reports from the seminar have been issued: vol. 1: *The faunal studies of Nepal; including zoogeography, fisheries, amphibia, reptilia, birds, and mammalia* by S. S. Singh and others; vol. 2: *The physical aspects of the Kingdom of Nepal* by J. B. S. Burathokey and U.M. Malla; vol. 3: *Report on a few hill-stream fishes of Nepal* by Rohit Bahadur Thapa and K.G. Rajbanshi.

467. **Ripley S. Dillion.** A naturalist's adventure in Nepal : search for the Spiny Babbler. Reprint. Kathmandu : Ratna Pustak Bhandar, 1978. 301 p. map. bibliog. (Bibliotheca Himalayica, series I, vol. 27)

This book was first published in 1952. Ripley visited Nepal in 1948 to collect birds for the Smithsonian Institute, Washington, and this is a vivid account of his travels with his team to Kathmandu Valley and to eastern and western Nepal.

468. **Sacherer. Janice.** The high altitude ethnobotany of the Rolwaling Sherpas. *Contributions to Nepalese Studies*, vol. 6, no. 2 (June 1979), pp. 45-64. bibliog.

Rolwaling is an east-west running valley, parallel with the Chinese border. Some 297 different species of plants were identified in this altitude zone, although the local Sherpas had names for only 150. The author explains about edible plants and mushrooms, medicinal plants and poisons, incense plants, natural dyes, and plants with special uses and has classified plants found in Rolwaling Valley within those categories.

469. **Scientific results of the Japanese expedition to Nepal Himalaya, 1952-53.** Flora and Fauna Society. Kyoto, Japan : University of Kyoto Press, 1955-57. 3 vols.

Vol. 1 Fauna and flora of Nepal Himalaya; vol. 2 : Land and crops of Nepal Himalaya; vol. 3; Peoples of Nepal Himalaya, by J. Kawakita.

470. **Shah, Birendra B.** National parks and wildlife conservation in the Kingdom of Nepal : an introduction. Kathmandu : National Parks and Wildlife Conservation Office, Government of Nepal, 1978. 15 p. map.

Gives information on geography, climate, population, flora and fauna, conservation in the past, the National Parks and Wildlife Conservation Programme, legislation, parks and reserves, conservation education and publicity, research, and international cooperation.

471. **Shrestha, Keshab.** Nepali name for plants. Kathmandu : Natural History Museum, 1979. 38 p. bibliog.

The author is an assistant research officer at the Natural History Museum, Institute of Science, Tribhuvan Unlversity. This booklet contains more than 800 Nepali plant names, together with their scientific names. It will be useful to naturalists, forest researchers, collectors, students, etc. since it identifies plants with local names.

472. **Singh, S. C.** Some wild plants of food value in Nepal. *Journal of the Tribhuvan University*, vol. 4, no. 1 (June 1968), pp. 50-56.

Describes the plants and their food value for a common man.

473. **Toba, Sueyoshi.** Plant names in Khaling : a study in ethnobotany and village economy. *Kailash : a Journal of Himalayan Studies*, vol. 3, no. 2 (1975), pp. 145-169.

Khaling is one of the Rai languages spoken in Solu Khumbu, Sagarmatha Zone. Lists some of the plant names recorded as a by product of linguistic studies conducted during January-May 1974. All of the plants discussed grow at altitudes of 1300-3500m. above sea-level, and this paper includes only those plants which are specifically useful to the inhabitants of the area. The list is arranged alphabetically by Khaling name of the plant, followed by its Latin name, Nepali name, and the usage. The work is divided into three parts: the utilization of natural resources; bartering and trading; and plant names.

474. **Trier, Jesper.** Ancient paper of Nepal; results of ethno-technological field work on its manufacture, uses, and history—with technical analyses of bast, paper, and manuscript.

For full entry refer to Industry section.

15

FOREIGN RELATIONS

475. **Banskota, Narrottam Prasad.** Indo-Nepal trade and economic relations. Delhi : B.R. Publishing, 1981. 267 p. bibliog.

An in depth analysis of economic relations between India and Nepal. It identifies the areas of mutual co-operation, defining the role of established countries in promoting the economic development of poor land-locked countries and in bringing about regional co-operation for mutual benefit. A detailed analysis of trade and economic flows between the two countries is presented to highlight the importance of mutually beneficial inter-dependence.

476. **Basnet, Lal Bahadur.** Sikkim : a short political history. New Delhi : S. Chand, 1974. 21 p. bibliog.

Chapters six and eight of this book contain historical information on relations between Nepal and Sikkim.

477. **Bhasin, A.S., ed.** Documents on Nepal's relations with India and China, 1949-66. New Delhi : Academic Books, 1970. 295 p.

A collection of documents which throw light on Nepal's political and economic relations with India and China.

478. **Bhatt, Dibya Deo.** Nepal and non-alignment. 4th rev. ed. Lalitpur, Nepal : C.K. Bhatt, 1980. 45 p.

Discusses the topic under the following headings : 'Genesis of the non-aligned movement', 'Nepal and non-alignment', 'Validity of the non-aligned movement', 'Non-alignment and Nepal's zone of peace proposal' and 'International economic order'.

479. **Bhattacharya, G.P.** India and politics of modern Nepal. Calcutta : Minerva Associates, 1970. 244 p. bibliog.

A detailed study of Indo-Nepalese relations since 1947. The author also covers the growth of Chinese influence on Nepal, the role of Pakistan in Nepal's politics, and the changes in Nepal's foreign policy.

480. **Birendra Bir Bikram Shah Deva, King.** His Majesty King Birendra speaks on foreign policy. 2nd ed. Kathmandu : Ministry of Communications, Department of Information, 1976. 20 p.

The foreign policy of King Birendra Bir Bikram Shah Deva, the ruler of Nepal.

481. **Birendra Bir Bikram Shaha Deva, King.** King Birendra and foreign affairs. Kathmandu : Centre for Nepal Foreign Affairs Studies, 1975. 167 p.

Contains biographical sketches and selected speeches of King Birendra Bir Bikram Shah Deva and queen Aishwarya Rajya Laxmi Devi Shah. Messages and articles by various persons are also included.

482. **Birendra Bir Bikram Shah Deva, King.** Peace and progress. Edited by Ram Krishna Karmacharya. Kathmandu : Goreto [1976?]. 87 p.

Some of the speeches and press extracts of King Birendra Bir Bikram Shah Deva, the ruler of Nepal. This collection was published on the occasion of the king's visit to the Soviet Union in 1976.

483. **Dhanalaxmi, Ravuri.** British attitude to Nepal's relations with Tibet and China, 1814-1914. Chandigarh, India : Bahri Publications, 1981. 182 p. bibliog.

Nepal's relations with Tibet and China very often had an important impact on British policy towards Nepal. It was not unusual for Nepal to make the fullest use of its traditional relations with Tibet and China, either to save itself from British pressure or to further its own ambition at cost to its northern neighbours. This tangled skein of interrelations in the Himalayan states is analytically treated in this monograph. The work is based on a vast mass of original material, mostly unpublished and first-hand. In understanding the roots of many contemporary problems in the relations between India and Nepal, this work should prove very useful.

484. **Directory of foreigners in Nepal**. 1972.

For full entry refer to Encyclopaedias, directories, and who's who section.

485. **Directory of foreigners in Nepal**. 1975.

For full entry refer to Encyclopaedias, directories, and who's who section.

486. **Foreign policy and development** : report of the seminar, Jan. 15-17, 1973. Kathmandu : Centre for Economic Development and Administration, 1973. [various pagings].

A seminar organized by the Government of Nepal for foreign service officers and others in related areas. Includes papers and discussions on various aspects of Nepal's foreign policy, mainly the political, economic, and organizational aspects. Mimeographed.

487. **Husain, Asad**. British India's relation with the Kingdom of Nepal, 1857-1947 : a diplomatic history of Nepal. London : Allen & Unwin, 1970. 480 p. maps. bibliog.

This work was originally the author's Ph.D. disseratation, submitted to the University of Minnesota, Department of International Relations. The author refers to much unpublished material, and deals with treaties and other documents concerning Nepal and her diplomatic relations with British India. Includes a very useful bibliography and appendices.

488. **Husain, Asad** and **Anwar, Asifa**. Conflict in Asia : a case study of Nepal. New Delhi : Classical Publications, 1979. 88 p. map.

Describes the diplomatic history of Nepal, 1947-1978; chiefly relations with India and China.

489. **Jain, R. K.**, ed. China South Asian relations, 1947-1980. New Delhi : Radiant Publishers, 1981. 2 vols.

This is the most comprehensive documentary history so far of Chinese policy towards South Asia in the post-war period. It traces the evolution, nature, and objectives of Chinese policy, and considers the methods (including economic and cultural diplomacy and military aid) adopted to implement the policy in the context of changes both in the international environment and in Chinese perspectives and strategy in the region.

490. **Jha, Shree Krishna**. Uneasy partners—India and Nepal in the post-colonial era. New Delhi : Manas Publications, 1975. 344 p.

A detailed analysis of the changing relationship between India and Nepal.

491. **Journal of the Council of World Affairs : commemorative issue, 24th February 1975**. Kathmandu : Nepal Council of World Affairs, 1975. 78 p.

Articles on Napal's foreign relations, comprising the texts and speeches of various dignitaries. This publication was issued to commemorate the coronation of King Birendra Bir Bikram Shah Deva, the King of Nepal.

492. **Khanal, Yadunath**. Reflections on Nepal-India relations. New Delhi : The Author, 1964. 96 p.

A collection of speeches delivered on various occasions. They record the author's impressions of the state of Indo-Nepalese relations during 1963-1964.

493. **Lohani, Prakash C**. Nepal in 1974.

For full entry refer to Politics section.

494. **Mahendra Bir Bikram Shah Deva, King**. Statement of principles : major foreign policy speeches. 2nd ed. Kathmandu : Department of Publicity, Ministry of Panchayat Affairs, 1964. 44 p.

A collection of speeches on foreign policy by Mahendra Bir Bikram Shah Deva, Maharajadhiraja of Nepal, 1920-1972.

495. **Mojumdar, Kanchanmoy**. Anglo-Nepalese relations in the nineteenth century. Calcutta : Firma K.L. Mukhopadhyay, 1973. 195 p. map. bibliog.

Discusses the factors which influenced and at times dominated India's relations with Nepal in the 19th century.

496. **Mojumdar, Kanchanmoy.** Political relations between India and Nepal: 1877-1923. New Delhi : Munshiram Manoharlal, 1973. 331 p. map. bibliog.

Discusses Anglo-Nepalese relations during the period.

497. **Muni, S. D.** Foreign policy of Nepal. Delhi : National Publishing House, 1973. 320 p. bibliog.

A revised version of the author's Ph.D. dissertation. The work surveys and highlights Nepal's foreign policy, with accounts of its role as a small nation in international politics since the early 1950s.

498. **Narayan, Shriman.** India and Nepal : an exercise in open diplomacy. Bombay : Popular Prakashan, 1970. 172 p. bibliog. illus.

India and Nepal not only have a common border, but they also share much of their culture and religion. The author, who was an Indian ambassador in Nepal, describes cultural and religious relations between India and Nepal and recommends 'diplomacy of truth' between the countries.

499. **Nepal Council of World Affairs presents a souvenir issue on the happy occasion of the fifty first birthday celebration of His Majesty King Mahendra, June 12, 1970.** Kathmandu : Nepal Council of World Affairs, 1970. 106 p.

Contains five articles : 'Nepal, Tibet and China' by R. Shaha; 'The United States and Asia in' 70's by C. C. Laise; 'The British monarchical tradition' by T.J. 'Brien; 'A century of change' by H. Kira; and 'A decade of economic development', by K.D. Shrestha.

500. **The Nepal Council of World Affairs presents a souvenir issue on the happy occasion of the thirty first birthday celebration of His Majesty King Birendra Bir Bikram Shah Dev.** Edited by Prayag Raj Sharma, et al. Kathmandu : Nepal Council of World Affairs, 1975. 83 p.

A collection of articles on foreign relations and Nepal's political situation.

501. **The Nepal Council of World Affairs presents a souvenir issue on the happy occasion of the thirty second birth day celebration of His Majesty King Birendra Bir Bikram Shah Dev, 1976.** Kathmandu : Nepal Council of World Affairs, 1976. 55 p.

Contains articles on Nepal's foreign policy.

502. **Nepal treaty series, 1972-1974.** His Majesty's Government of Nepal, Ministry of Law and Justice. Kathmandu : The Ministry, 1981. 454 p.

A collection of bilateral and multilateral treaties and agreements between Nepal and other countries or organizations, e.g. the People's Republic of China, the USSR, Japan, the World Wildlife Fund, the International Development Association, the Asian Development Bank, etc.

503. **Raj, Prakash A.** Roads to the Chinese border.

For full entry refer to Geography—General section.

504. **Rana, Bhola Bikram,** ed. Documents on Nepalese foreign policy, 1973-July 1979. Kathmandu : Foreign Affairs Journal, 1979. 68 p.

A collection of documents on Nepalese foreign policy first published in the regular issues of *Foreign Affairs Journal*, an English Language periodical.

505. **Regmi, Jagadish Chandra,** comp. and ed. Nepal—Tibet—China. Assisted by : Sheshraj Shivakoti. Kathmandu : Office of the Nepal-Antiquary, 1980. 355 leaves. bibliog.

A special issues of *Nepal-Antiquary* : *Journal of Socio-historical Research and Digest*, no. 17-20 (1 Jan. 1980). The contents are: Nepal—Tibet—China affairs; Nepal foreign affairs; Nepal Buddhism; Minor Sanskrit texts; Nepal law studies; Studies in HMG, Nepal; Social glimpses; Nepal documents; Nepal bibliography (listing important titles on Nepal); and Behavioural Hinduism. Mimeographed.

506. **Shah, Rishikesh.** Nepal and the world. 2nd ed. Kathmandu : Nepali Congress, 1955. 54 p.

A discussion of Nepali nationalism in its various aspects. The author deals with Nepal's foreign policy and its relations with other countries, especially with India, China, and Tibet.

507. **Shrestha, Sita.** Nepal and the United Nations. New Delhi : Sindhu Publications, 1974. 218 p. bibliog. (Studies in Asian History and Politics, 3)

Following the opening chapter which covers the historical background of Nepal, the remaining six chapters deal with Nepal's political behaviour in the United Nations, Nepal's stand on colonialism and racialism, major political and security issues, the problems of land-locked countries. The text throws light on Nepal's foreign policy, with accounts of its role in international politics since the early 1950s. This work was originally submitted as the author's Ph.D. thesis to Jawaharlal Nehru University, New Delhi.

508. **Silver jubilee souvenir, presented on the happy occasion of the silver jubilee of the Nepal Council of World Affairs, Feb. 18, 1973.** Kathmandu : Nepal Council of World Affairs, 1973. 116 p.

A collection of articles, chiefly on international relations.

509. **Tyagi, Sushila.** Indo-Nepalese relations, 1858-1914. Delhi : D.K. Publishing House, 1974. 283 p. map.

Political relations between India and Nepal are briefly discussed for the period 1858-1914.

16

GEOGRAPHY

GENERAL

510. **Amatya, S.L.** and **Shrestha, B.G.** Economic geography of Nepal. Kathmandu : B.P. Amatya, 1967. 149 p. bibliog.

A useful textbook.

511. **Bennett-Campbell, Lynn.** Two water case studies. Kathmandu : Department of Local Development, Government of Nepal and UNICEF, 1973. 20 leaves. (Research-cum-Action Project Paper—Department of Local Development, His Majesty's Government of Nepal/UNICEF, no. 5).

This publication has two papers. The first paper is called 'Narakot : a case study of motivations for self-instigated water projects with a survey of water sources and some notes on practical water use'. Narakot is a village situated on the edge of the Kathmandu Valley with a good natural water supply. The second paper examines rivers, springs, and wells and includes a study of the ritual use of water among Hindu Nepalis. Mimeographed.

512. **Climatological records of Nepal.** Kathmandu : Department of Irrigation, Hydrology and Meteorology, Ministry of Food, Agriculture, and Irrigation, 1977. 3 vols. 10 maps.

Vol. 1 includes monthly and annual precipitation, temperature, and humidity data for all the stations in Nepal from 1971-75.

It is a revised version of previous issues and has been expanded to include ten year temperature and precipitation averages for the period 1961-70 based upon the available data. Vol. 2 contains weather statistics for Kathmandu since 1921, including fifteen year means. Vol. 3 presents sunshine, wind, evaporation, and soil temperature data for selected stations from 1967-75.

513. **Freshfield, Douglas W.** Round Kangchenjunga : a narrative of mountain travel and exploration. With a new introduction by Harka B. Gurung. Reprint. Kathmandu : Ratna Pustak Bhandar, 1979. 373 p. 2 maps. bibliog. illus. (Bibliotheca Himalayica Series I, vol. 25).

First published in London by E. Arnold in 1903, this work remains a classic of Himalayan literature. The author, a distinguished explorer, aroused much academic discussion with his views on mountain glaciation and he contributed greatly to the furtherance of geography as a scientific discipline. In 1899 he visited India and the eastern Himalayas and his travels are the subject of this book. It is not merely a superb travelogue: its details of the extent of the glaciers could form the basis for scientific studies of their processes through time. The glaciers have definitely receded, but the political climate of the Kangchenjunga area has not yet been conducive to systematic exploration and research. For this reason the book still retains much of its initial value. It includes forty pages of plates giving various views of Kangchenjunga.

514. **Geographical Journal of Nepal.**

For full entry refer to Professional periodicals section.

515. **Gurung, Nareshwar Jang.** An introduction to the socio-economic structure of Manang District. *Kailash : a Journal of Himalayan Studies*, vol. 4, no. 3 (1976), pp. 295-308. map. illus.

Manang District is situated in the north-central part of Nepal, and is borderd in the south by Lamjung and Kaski districts, in the north by Tibet, in the west by Mustang, and in the east by the Gorkha districts. The district is surrounded by Himalayas. In this article, the author first describes the physical characteristics of the area, followed by an account of its economic structure.

516. **Hagen, Toni** [et al.]. Mount Everest : formation, population, and exploration of the Everest region. Translated by : E. N. Bowman. London : Oxford University Press, 1963. 195 p. illus.

The contents of this publication are: 'The evolution of the highest mountain in the world' by T. Hagen; 'The mountain exploration of the Everest Massif' by G.O. Dyhrenfurth; 'The Sherpas of the Khumbu region' by Christoph von Furer Haimendorf.

517. **The Himalayan review.**

For full entry refer to Professional periodicals section.

518. **Jilla paricaya**. Kathmandu : Ministry of Home Panchayat, Planning Division, Publicity Sub-Division [1965/66-1978/79]. 36 vols. maps.

Gives brief accounts of the geographical features and economic conditions of various districts in Nepal. The series was supposed to be completed in seventy-five volumes but only thirty-six volumes were published before the project was abandoned. These are the only publications dealing with individual districts. Each volume has a map of the district. The districts covered are: Achham, Arghakhachi, Baitadi, Bajhang, Banke, Bardia, Bhaktapur, Chitwan, Dailekh, Darchula, Dolpa, Humla, Jumla, Kailali, Kanchanpur, Kapilvastu, Kabhre Palanchok, Kaski, Lalitpur, Lamjung, Mugu, Nawal Parasi, Nuwakot, Okhaldhunga, Palpa, Panchthar, Pyuthan, Rukum, Rupandehi, Sallyan, Sarlahi, Sirha, Surkhet, Tanhun, Tarhthum, Udaipur.

519. **Karan, Pradyuman Prasad**. Nepal, a cultural and physical geography. In collaboration with William M. Jenkins. Lexington, Kentucky : University of Kentucky Press, 1960. 100 p. 36 maps. bibliog.

In addition to much geographical information, the author provides a good overview of many aspects of Nepalese history and culture. Includes illustrations and portraits.

520. **Kathmandu Valley** : the preservation of physical environment and cultural heritage; a protective inventory .

For full entry refer to Environment section.

521. **Khule, Matthias.** Settlements on the southern slope of the Dhaula-Himal. Kathmandu : Nepal Research Centre, 1979. 13-22 p. bibliog. illus. (Miscellaneous Papers, Nepal Research Centre, no. 33).

A contribution to the settlement geography of the Nepalese Himalayas, with 22 illustrations.

522. **Manandhar, Mangal Sidhi**. Geopolitical basis of Nepal's existence. *Himalayan Review*, vol. 6 (1973-74), pp. 40-49.

Investigates the geographical and political basis for the continued existence of Nepal as a district political unit.

523. **Mountain environment and development** : a collection of papers published on the occasion of the 20th anniversary of the Swiss Association for Technical Assistance in Nepal (SATA). Kathmandu : University Press, Tribhuvan University, 1976. 214 p.

Papers on the geography and economic conditions of the Nepalese hills.

524. **Raj, Prakash A.** Roads to the Chinese border. Kathmandu : Foreign Affairs Journal Publication, 1978. 77 p.

This publication describes the physical, political, strategic, and economic aspects of the road from Kathmandu to the Chinese border.

525. **Regmi, Jagadish Chandra**, comp. and ed. Himalaya special. Kathmandu : Office of the Nepal-Antiquary, 1979. 37 leaves.

A special issue of the *Nepal-antiquary : Journal of Socio-historical Research and Digest*. The contents are: Synonymical names of Himalaya; Mythologies and legends; Himalaya ranges; A list of important Himalaya peaks; Himalayas; New rules in Himalaya Mountaineering; Publications on Himalayas; 47 Himalayan peaks declared open; Nepali speakers in United Provinces of India; Kathmandu Valley. This publication will be of great use to students and research scholars; the author has filled a long-felt gap in publications on this field.

526. **Shah, Birendra B.** National parks and wildlife conservation in the Kingdom of Nepal : an introduction.

For full entry refer to Flora & Fauna section.

527. **Sharma, Chandra**. Natural resources of Pokhara Valley. Kathmandu : S. Sharma, 1977. 106 p. bibliog. illus.

The Pokhara Valley is in central Nepal, ninety miles west-northwest of Kathmandu, and is a popular tourist centre. In this publication the author describes the natural resources and geography of the Valley.

528. **Sharma, R.P.** Nepal : a detailed geographical account. Kathmandu : Pustak Sansar, 1974. 116 p. 18 maps.

The author, Headmaster at the J.P. High School in Kathmandu, presents a general review of Nepal's geography. The latest facts and figures and current place names are included. The book is very simple and will be of great use to school students and those interested learning about Nepal's geography. It includes a table which gives the male and female populations of each zone and district in 1971, according to figures from the Central Bureau of Statistics. The work also contains a map of each zone.

529. **Singh, Sthira Jang Bahadur.** Karṇālī loka saṃskṛti. vol. 2: Bhaugolika dṛshtikoṇa. Kathmandu : Royal Nepal Academy, 1971. 297 p. 8 maps. bibliog. illus.

The Karnali zone is a hilly area and little is known about its natural resources and people. This series attempts to throw some light on the civilization, economic and social conditions, history, geography, etc. of the zone, and volume 2 deals with the geography of Karnali zone.

530. **Thapa, N.B.** and **Thapa, D.P.** Geography of Nepal. New Delhi : Orient Longmans, 1969. 205 p. bibliog. illus.

Describes the physical, economic, cultural, and regional geography of Nepal.

531. **Yatri, Purna Prakash Nepal.** Setīañcala digdarśana : vividha anusandhānātmaka vishayasamanvita. Biratnagar, Nepal : Himali Saugata Prakashan [1978?]. 639 p. map. (Nepāladarśana ra vāṅmaya paridarśanakālāgi upayogī svadeśadarśana pushpahāra, 3) (Setīañcala-digdarśana : khaṇḍa 2).

The second in a series to be completed in five volumes, this is a geographical and cultural account of the Seti Zone of Nepal. It includes biographical sketches and photographs of eminent people in the area. The contents are: Geographical account; Society and people; Historical outline; Genealogy; Religion and culture; Politics; Tourism development.

MAPS, ATLASES & GAZETTEERS

532. **Annapurna and Dhaulagiri: Himal.** Kathmandu : national Graphic Art, 1968.

A map of 40 by 53 cm., on a scale of 1:250,000. The map is based on the map provided in Harka Gurung's *Annapurna to Dhaulagiri*.

533. **Dobremez, Jean-Francois** [et al.]. Carte ecologique du Nepal. Paris: Centre national de la recherche scientifique, 1975. 161 p. 4 maps.

This publication comprises of 'Carte ecologique du Nepal. Annapurna-Dhaulagiri' by J. F. Dobremez and C. Jest; 'Carte ecologique du Nepal, Jiri-Thodung' by J. F. Dobremez, C. Jest, J. Stebler, P. Valeix; 'Les gymnospermes du Nepal' by T. B. Shrestha; 'Carte ecologique du Nepal, Kathmandu-Everest' by J. F. Dobremez, C. Jest, G. Toffiin, M. C. Vartanian, F. Vigny; and 'Carte ecologique du Nepal, Region Terai central'. This publication also contains four colourful ecological maps and one well-illustrated essay on gymnosperms of Nepal. It has valuable information for scientists, development planners, trekkers, etc.

534. **Khumbu Himal (Nepal)**. Forschungsunternehmen Nepal Himalaya. Vienna, Austria : Kartographische Anstalt Freytag-Berndt und Artaria [1965 ?].

A colour map in German and English on a scale of 1:50,000 or 1 inch to 0.78 mile, measuring 84 by 115 cm. It shows contours and includes an inset map of east Nepal on a scale of 1:3,000,000.

535. **Nepal** : development districts and their headquarters. Kathmandu : Ratna Pustak Bhandar [1970].

A map measuring 50 by 75.5 cm., on a scale of 1:1,140,480, or 18 miles to the inch. It includes two inset maps on a reduced scale: one showing the physical features and a political map giving the zones and their headquarters.

536. **Nepal in maps**. Kathmandu : Ministry of Information and Broadcasting, Department of Publicity, His Majesty's Government of Nepal, 1966. 16 p.

Contains twenty-six colour maps on a scale of 40 miles to 1 inch. All data are based on the five-year plan reports of the Ministry of Economic Planning and the progress reports given by the ministries concerned. The boundaries shown on the maps are not authoritative.

537. **Nepalako naksa : thuma pragnnama janaganana jillaharu**. Kathmandu : Statistics Department, His Majesty's Government of Nepal, 1958. 38 leaves.

Outline maps of all the districts, showing the boundaries of the census areas. Three appendixes are included : 'Relation between census area unit, administrative districts, and zon.s', 'Census areas', 'Notes'.

538. **North of Kathmandu : Langtang, Gosainkung and Helmu.** Kathmandu : International Graphic Art, 1970.

A colour map of 46 by 41 cm., folding to 23 by 13 cm,, on a scale of 1:250,000. It is based on a map provided by Harka Gurung.

539. **Thapa, Netra Bahadur.** Nepal. Kathmandu : Sunita and Ajit Thapa [1969 ?].

A map, in colour, based on the Survey of India and the Nepal China Boundary Treaty maps.

540. **Trekking map : Gasainkund, Helambu, Langtang** ; also showing the Kathmandu Valley and the Arniko Rajpath from Kathmandu to the Chinese border. Kathmandu : International Graphic Art, 1972.

A map of 69 by 78 cm., folding to 18 by 12 cm., on a scale of 1:126,720 or 2 miles to 1 inch. This is based on a map provided by I. R. Harvey. Facilities and the heights of the highest and lowest points are marked along the main routes. Includes a Nepali glossary.

541. **Trekking map: Jomosom to Jumla,** showing the Dhaulagiri Himal and Kanjiroba Himal. Kathmandu : International Graphic Art [1971].

A map of 68 by 82 cm., folding to 18 by 12 cm., on a scale of 1:250,000 or 4 miles to 1 inch. Facilities and the heights of the highest and lowest points are marked along the main routes. Includes a Nepali glossary.

542. **Trekking map : Kathmandu to Pokhara, showing the new road.** Kathmandu : International Graphic Art, 1971.

A map of 61 by 99 cm., folding to 17 by 11 cm., on a scale of 1:126,720 or half an inch to the mile. It is based on a map provided by I. R. Harvey. Facilities and the heights of the highest and lowest points are marked along the main routes. Includes a Nepali glossary.

543. **Trekking map : Pokhara to Jomosom, showing whole of the Annapurna Himal.** Kathmandu : International Graphic Art, 1971.

A map of 61 by 61 cm., folding to 16 by 10 cm., on a scale of 1:126,720 or half a inch to the mile. It is based on a map provided by I. R. Harvey. Facilities and the heights of the highest and lowest points are marked along the main routes. Includes a Nepali glossary.

544. **Village panchayats in Nepal.** *Regmi Research Project : Miscellaneous Reports*, no. 40 (22 April 1969), pp. 1-125; no. 47 (28 May 1969), pp. 1-74.

Names of village panchayats in different districts and their distance from their district headquarters are given. These were originally compiled by the Planning, Progress, and Statistics Division, Ministry of Home and Panchayats.

17

GEOLOGY

545. **Aryal, R.K.** Geological report on the salt occurrence of Chharka-Bhot Gaon area. Kathmandu : His Majesty's Government of Nepal. Ministry of Industry and Commerce, Nepal Geological Survey, 1973. 9 leaves. 2 maps. bibliog.

This report deals with the salt occurrence in the Chharka-Bhot Gaon area, Dolpa District, Dhaulagiri Zone. The purpose of the work was to investigate brine water resources and their potential for domestic and industrial use. The area under consideration falls into the Survey of India toposheet 62O/8. Mimeographed.

546. **Aryal, R.K.** and **Sharma, R.R.** Geology of Tarap and salt occurence [sic] of Namda and Thingi area. Kathmandu : His Majesty's Government of Nepal, Ministry of Industry and Commerce, Nepal Geological Survey, 1974. 10 leaves. map.

A preliminary geological investigation of salt encrustation in the Namda and Thingi area. A reconnaissance geological map showing the salt-encrustated area has been prepared from this field observation. The area is covered by the Survey of India toposheet 62. Mimeographed.

547. **Bashyal, R.P.** Geology of Dang-Sallyan area, Dang-Sallyan and Rolpa districts : report of the field season, 2027-2028. Kathmandu : His Majesty's Government of Nepal, Ministry of Industry and Commerce, Nepal Geological Survey, 1972. 38 leaves. 2 maps. bibliog.

Includes a regional geological map showing about 380 square miles in the Dang-Sallyan and Rolpa districts (western Nepal). The mapped area lies in the Survey of India toposheets 62 L/7 and 62 L/8. In the map area, Siwalik group, Mahabharat sedimentaries and metamorphic rocks were observed. The Siwaliks are exposed to the south of the main boundary fault. Mimeographed.

548. **Bashyal, R.P.** Geology of Taplejung area, Taplejung District : report of the field season, 2026-2027. Kathmandu : His Majesty's Government of Nepal, Ministry of Industry and Commerce, Nepal Geological Survey, 1970. 29 leaves. 3 maps. 4 charts.

Deals with the regional geological mapping carried out by the author in the field season 1969-70. The area lies in Taplejung District, Mechi Zone, in the eastern part of Nepal, and falls in the Survey of India toposheet number 72 M/15 and half of the eastern part of number 72 M/11. Mimeographed.

549. **Bashyal, R.P.** Report on the geology of phosphorite basin of Barahakshetra-Tangsar area (Sunsari, Udaypur, Sindhuli districts). Kathmandu : His Majesty's Government of Nepal, Ministry of Industry and Commerce, Nepal Geological Survey, 1973. 56 leaves. 4 maps. bibilog. 3 charts.

This report deals with the preliminary geological investigations of a phosphorite basin lying between Barahakshetra and Tangsar (Sundhuli). The study was undertaken to determine the extension of the Barahakshetra-Takure phosphorite basin to the west and to measure the thickness and P^2O^5 concentration of the basin. This area is covered by Survey of India toposheets 72 N/1, 72 J/13, 72 J/9, 72 J/5, and 72 I/8, 72 I/4. Mimeographed.

550. **Bashyal, R.P.** Report on the phosphorite rocks of the south-eastern Nepal. Kathmandu : Nepal Geological Survey, Ministry of Industry and Commerce, 1975. 29 leaves. bibliog.

An account of field work on the geology of the southern and far eastern parts of Nepal. The main purpose of the study was to search for phosphorite rock and to review previous work; this report represents the last phase in the investigations in the south-eastern part of the country. It falls into Survey of India toposheets 72 E/3, 72 E/7, 72 E/10, 72 E/11, 72 E/15, 72 I/3, 72 I/4, 72 I/8. 72 I/12, 72 J/9, 72 J/13, 72 N/1, 72 N/5, 72 N/9, 72 N/13, 78 B/1, and covers various districts in the Bagmati, Narayani, Janakpur, Sagarmatha, Koshi, and Mechi zones. Mimeographed.

551. **Bhandari, A.N.** The geology of Pyuthan, Rolpa, and Argha Khanchi districts. Kathmandu : His Majesty's Government of Nepal, Ministry of Industry and Commerce, Nepal Geological Survey, 1972. 15 leaves. map. bibliog.

This report deals with the geology of a portion of Pyuthan, Rolpa and Arghakhanchi districts in Rapti Zone, mapped by the author during 1971-72. The mapped area, measuring 250 square miles, is covered by Survey of India toposheet number 62 L/16 and consists entirely of metamorphic rock which has been divided into seven categories to its lithological and textual variations. The main metamorphics are phyllites, quartzites, shales, and schists. Mimeographed.

552. **Bhattarai, K.D.** The geology of a portion of Pyuthan and Argha Khanchi district[s]. Kathmandu : His Majesty's Government of Nepal, Ministry of Industry and Commerce, Nepal Geological Survey, 1977. 34 leaves. 2 maps.

A report on the geology of a part of the Pyuthan and Gulmi districts of the Rapti and Lumbini zones of western Nepal. The area mapped by the author covers about 250 square miles; half of the area is shown on the Survey of India toposheet number 62 M/1 and the other half on number 63 I/13. The mapped area consists of Siwalik group and Mahabharat sedimentaries. Mimeographed.

553. **Chaturvedi, G.P.** Study of beryl bearing pegmatites from Debighat to Sundarijal, Bagmati Anchal. Kathmandu : His Majesty's Government of Nepal, Ministry of Industry and Commerce, Nepal Geological Survey, 1969. 10 leaves. map. bibliog.

The report of a geological study of the Debighat-Sundarijal area of the Bagmati Zone, undertaken to investigate the mining potential of the beryl-bearing pegmatites in the area. Mimeographed.

554. **Jha, J.** and **Aryal, R.K.** Geology of Lalitpur area (Lalitpur, Makwanpur, and Kabre Palanchok districts) : report of field season, 2030-2031. Kathmandu : His Majesty's Government of Nepal, Ministry of Industry and Commerce, Nepal Geological Survey, 1974. 25 leaves.

A report on the geology of the Lalitpur, Makwnpur and Kabhre Palanchok districts in the central Nepal. The area covered lies mainly in Lalitpur District and appears in the Survey of India toposheets 72 E/6 and 72 E/7. The representative rocks are carbon-eceous phyllite, limestones, chlorite-sericite phyllite and granites which are exposed just the north of the main boundary fault. The Siwalik formations are exposed south of the main boundary fault. Mimeographed.

555. **Joshi, P.R.** The geology of a part of Baisekhani area around Dhorpatan, Baglung District, Dhaulagiri Anchal. Kathmandu : His Majesty's Government of Nepal, Ministry of Industry and Commerce, Nepal Geological Survey, Economic Geology Division, 1971. 25 leaves. map.

A geological study of a part of the Baisekhani area around Dhorpatan, appearing on the Survey of India toposheets 62 P/2 and 62 P/3. This area comprises metamorphic rocks, represented by limestone, slate, quartzite, carbonaceous schists, phyllites, garnetiferous schists, and other mica schists. Limestone, slate, quartzite, and carbonaceous shale are considered to be Mesozoic, whereas carbonaceous schist, phyllites, garnetiferous schist and other mica schists belong to the Palaeozoic period (Cambrian to Pre-Cambrian). Mimeographed.

556. **Joshi, P.R.** The preliminary investigation of salt occurrence at Jameri Khola, Phapherkhet Panchayat, Makawanpur District, Narayani Zone. Kathmandu : His Majesty's Government of Nepal. Ministry of Industry and Commerce, Nepal Geological Survey, Economic Mineral Division, 1975. 5 leaves. map.

The salt was observed on the right bank of Jameri Khola in the Siwalik sandstone about half a mile upstream from the mouth of the river. The area lies on toposheet no. 72 E/7 of the Survey of India. This paper deals with the investigations at Jameri Khola. Mimeographed.

557. **Kayastha, N.B.** The geology of Ilam District of south eastern Nepal. Kathmandu : His Majesty's Government of Nepal, Ministry of Industry and Commerce, Nepal Geological Survey, Division of Mapping, 1969. 25 leaves. map.

This report deals with the regional geological mapping carried out by the author on the pre-Tertiary geological formations in Ilam

District, Mechi Zone, southeastern Nepal during the field season 1968-69. The area corresponds to the Survey of India toposheet 72 N/13. The mapped area, biggest map in printing history about 225 square miles, is presented and the geological formations of the area are divided into three categories on the basis of lithological and textural variations. They possibly date from Pre-Cambrian to Lower Palaeozoic times. The metamorphics of the area include schists, phyllites, and quartzites, and are thrust upon the tertiary Siwalik sandstones and shales to the south (main boundary thrust). Other structural features include folds and faults. Mimeographed.

558. **Kayastha, N.B.** Geology of southeastern part of Dhankuta and western Ilam districts, southeastern Nepal. Kathmandu : His Majesty's Government of Nepal, Ministry of Industry and Commerce, Nepal Geological Survey, Division of Mapping, 1968. 15 leaves. map.

This report deals with geology of a portion of southeastern Dhankuta and western Ilam, in southeastern Nepal. The mapped area lies in toposheet number 72 N/9 of the Survey of India and consists entirely of pre-Tertiary metamorphics; the Tertiary Siwaliks to the south are separated from the metamorphics by the east-west trending main boundary thrust. The metamorphics are mainly made up of schists, phyllites, and quartzites, and have been divided into four subdivisions on the basis of lithological characteristics. Besides the main boundary thrust, the area is controlled by an eastward-plunging syncline and some faults. Mimeographed.

559. **Kayastha, N.B.** Report on phosphor bearing horizon of Takure, Barahakshetra area, Sunsari District, Kosi Anchal. Kathmandu : His Majesty's Government of Nepal, Ministry of Industry and Commerce, Nepal Geological Survey, 1971. 20 leaves. map. bibliog. 5 charts.

Deals with preliminary geological investigations of a phosphor-bearing horizon in the Takure-Barahakshetra. The investigators measured the extent, thickness and P^2O^5 concentration of the horizon by analysing material collected by trenching and channel sampling. Mimeographed.

560. **Oil and natural gas prospects in Nepal.** Dept. of Mines and Geology, Nepal. Kathmandu : His Majesty's Government of Nepal. Ministry of Industry and Commerce, Department of Mines and Geology, 1977. 11 leaves. map.

This publication contains five reports : Geology in brief; Sedimentary basins; Opinion of experts; The present status of geological works; Blocks of the promising areas for petroleum exploration. Mimeographed.

561. **Panta, M.R.** A note on the geochemical sampling of Baraghari deposit. Kathmandu : His Majesty's Government of Nepal. Ministry of Industry and Commerce, Nepal Geological Survey, 1972. 26 leaves. 5 maps.

This survey of geochemical sampling over an area of one-third of a square mile in the Baraghari region was carried out in April 1970. Chemical tests for lead, zinc, copper, and molybdenum were conducted on 522 samples. Higher values were observed in certain regions which are shown in the maps.

562. **Sharma, Chandra K.** Geology of Nepal. Kathmandu : Mani Ram Sharma, 1973. 189 p. maps. bibliog.

A geological account of various parts of Nepal, with details of physical features, the Himalayan geological setting, and mineral occurrences.

563. **Singh, Vinod.** Geological investigation of the Labdi iron deposit, District Bandipur, West no. 3, Gandaki Anchal. Kathmandu : Nepal Geological Survey, Ministry of Industry and Commerce, His Majesty's Government of Nepal, 1968. 22 leaves.

A geological investigation of the Labdi iron deposit undertaken while preparing a geological map of the area. Surveying was done by prismatic and bronton compass; channel samples were taken from six exposed portions of the ore. The extension of the ore-bearing formation was traced in the area, which is shown on toposheets 72 A/5 and 72 A/3 of the Survey of India and lies in Bandipur District of Gandaki Anchal. Mimeographed.

564. **Singh, Vinod.** A geological report of Amlekhgunj-Thankot : field trip with O.N.G.C. party of Government of India, field season, March-May 1960. Kathmandu : His Majesty's Government of Nepal, Ministry of Industry and Commerce, Mineral Resources Division [1960 ?]. 22 leaves. map.

The object of this field trip was to study the geology of a section between Amlekhgunj (Terai) and Kathmandu Valley and to analyse in detail the Siwalik formation between Amlekhgunj and

Hitaura. The group hoped to find evidence of oil in the Terai belt of Nepal. The area covered is about 62 square miles. Mimeographed.

565. **Singh, Vinod.** The geological report of Dang Deukhuri area, Rapti Anchal, western Nepal. Kathmandu : His Majesty's Government of Nepal, Ministry of Industry and Commerce, Nepal Geological Survey, 1971. 33 leaves. map.

During 1970-71, a field trip was organized to prospect for oil in the Terai region of Dang Deukhuri-Nepalgunj in western Nepal. The Survey mapped an area of about 340 square miles, covered by the Survey of India toposheet number 63 I/9 and the western part of number 63 I/13. The area embraces five districts: Dang Deukhuri, Gulmi, Puthan, Sallyan, and Suraj Khajani. Mimeographed.

566. **Singh, Vinod.** A summary of the coal occurrences in Nepal. Kathmandu : His Majesty's Government of Nepal, Ministry of Commerce and Industry, Nepal Geological Survey, 1971. 19 leaves. map. bibliog.

An assessment of all the occurrences of coal in Nepal,based on the information contained in records and reports available in Nepal Bureau of Mines and Nepal Geology Survey Library. This report fulfills one of important duties of the Economic Geology Division, by evaluating the country's economic mineral resources and by examining what will need to be done to explore such deposits. Mimeographed.

567. **Tater, J.M.** Ammonites from Muktinath area. Kathmandu : Nepal Geological Survey, 1968. 12 leaves. 2 maps.

This paper presents a study of ammonites collected by the author from the Muktinath area in northern Nepal during the field season 1965-66. The occurrence of ammonites in this particular area is confined to dark-grey to black shale which is referred here as saligram shale. In all, 7 species were identified and the fossil assemblage indicates that the shale dates from the Upper Jurassic period. Mimeographed.

568. **Tshering, L.D.** The geology of phosphate rock of Takure (Dharan), Barah[a]kshetra area. Kathmandu : His

Majesty's Government of Nepal, Nepal Geological Survey, Economic Division, 1971. 22 leaves. map. bibliog.

During 1970-71, detailed geological mapping, pitting, trenching and sampling were conducted in Dharan in order to search for phosphate rock. The area mapped by the author covers about thirty-nine square miles and corresponds to Survey of India toposheets 72 N/1 and 72 N/5 in the Kosi Administrative Zone of eastern Nepal. Mimeographed.

569. **Tshering, L.D.** Report on the regional map of Rolpa, Piuthan, and Baglung districts of Rapti and Dhaulagiri zones. Kathmandu : His Majesty's Government of Nepal, Ministry of Industry and Commerce, Nepal Geological Survey, 1972. 16 leaves. 3 maps.

A report on the regional geology of the Rolpa, Piuthan, and Baglung districts. The area mapped covers most of the Survey of India toposheets 62 L/11, 62 L/15, and 62 P/3. The area mainly consists of metamorphic rocks. Mimeographed.

570. **Vaidya, Y.L.** Preliminary geochemical investigation in the Myagdi Khola map area. Kathmandu : His Majesty's Government of Nepal, Ministry of Industry and Commerce, Nepal Geological Survey, 1972. 16 leaves. bibliog.

This report is a supplement to the report *Geology of Myagdi Khola area*. A preliminary geochemical soil survey and a drainage sediment survey were carried out over about 265 square miles in the Myagdi Khola map area. Geochemical maps and results are presented, an attempt is made to simplify the statistical treatment of the geochemical data, and the difficulties and problems in the interpretation of the data are discussed. Mimeographed.

571. **Yadav, R.N.** The geology of Gulmi map area, western Nepal. Kathmandu : His Majesty's Government of Nepal, Ministry of Industry and Commerce, Nepal Geological Survey, 1974. 22 leaves. map. bibliog.

Presents a regional geological map of the Gulmi area, covering 500 square miles. The area is shown on Survey of India toposheet number 62 P/4, the southern half of number 62 P/8 and the eastern half of number 62 P/12. The exposed rock is mainly comprised of shales, phyllites, quartzites, dolomitic limestones and schists, etc. Mimeographed.

572. **Yadav, R.N.** Preliminary geological report of Gorkha Durbar area. Kathmandu : His Majesty's Government of Nepal, Ministry of Industry and Commerce, Nepal Geological Survey, 1975. 6 leaves. map. chart.

This survey of the Gorkha Durbar area was undertaken to study the causes of landslides and how to prevent them. This area lies in the southern part of the Survey of India toposheet 71 D/12. Mimeographed.

18

HISTORY

ARCHIVES, SOURCES & INSCRIPTIONS

573. **Aitihasika patrasangraha.** Vol. 1 compiled by Dhanvajra Vajracharya; Gyanmani Nepal; vol. 2 compiled by Ramji Tewari; Bholanath Paudel; Deviprasad Bhandari; Shankarman Rajavanshi; Dhanvajra Vajracharya. Kathmandu : Nepal Sanskritika Parishad, 1957-64. 2 vols. map.

Collection of letters arranged chronologically covering the period 1744-1831. The letters date from the beginning of Gorkha rule, set up by Maharaja Prithvi Narayan Shaha Deva, and the collection includes some letters written by Maharaja Prithvi Narayan Shaha Deva before he became King of Nepal. Some important letters on the period of power struggle between the monarchy and nobility are included as well as some letters from and to the Nepalese envoys to different countries, which throw light on Nepal's foreign relations. Other letters give information about the British-Nepal war. All the letters are in Nepali and several are accompanied by the compilers commentary on their historical importance.

574. **Bendall, Cecil.** A journey of literary and archaeological research in Nepal and northern India during the winter 1884-85. Reprint. Kathmandu : Ratna Pustak Bhandar, 1974. 100 p. illus (Bibliotheca Himalayica, Series III, vol. 2)

A reprinted edition of a book published in 1886 by Cambridge University Press, England. Part one presents an archaeological and general report. Part two contains lists of manuscripts, with notes, subdivided into a classified list of manuscripts personally collected; a rough list of manuscripts from Bombay; notes on particular manuscript acquired; and notes on manuscripts in private possession. The work includes three appendices: inscriptions; a rough list of Jain manuscripts at Benares; and revised tables of the Kings of Nepal.

575. **Erhard, Franz-Karl.** Tibetan texts in the National Archives, Kathmandu.

For full entry refer to Bibliographies section.

576. **Gnoli, Raniero.** Nepalese inscriptions in Gupta character. Rome : Istituto Italiano per il Medio ed Estremo Oriente, 1956. (Serie Orientale Roma, 10. Materials for the Study of Nepalese History and Culture, 2)

A study of inscriptions in Gupta characters.

577. **Hofer, Andras.** On re-reading *Le-Nepal* : what we social scientists owe to Sylvain Levi.

For full entry refer to History—General section.

578. **Hunter, W.W.** Life of Brian Houghton Hodgson, British Resident at the court of Nepal.

For full entry refer to History—Biographical works.

579. **Macdonald, Alexander W.** A Nepalese copper plate from the time of Prithvinarayan Shaha's father. *Kailash : a Journal of Himalayan Studies*, vol. 1, no. 1 (Mar. 1973), pp. 6-7.

Presents details of a *tama-patra* (copperplate) which the author photographed in the bazar at Bodhnath in February 1962. The copy of the *tama-patra* is included, with a location map and the inscriptions have been transliterated into Roman script.

580. **Manandhar, Thakurlal.** A leaf from the Bendall 'Vamsavali'. *Contributions to Nepalese Studies*, vol. 1, no. 2 (June 1974), pp. 99-102.

This is an inquiry into the text. The author corrects some misgivings which appear in Bendall's article, "The history of Nepal and the surrounding kingdoms".

581. **Medieval Nepal (colophons and inscriptions)**. Collected by Hem Raj Shakya; edited by Hem Raj Shakya; T.R. Vaidya. Kathmandu : T.R. Vaidya, 1970. 243 p. bibliog.

After 1951, Nepali historians felt free to evaluate events in an unbiased historical context, and this ushered in a period during which scholars searched for new materials and sought to make the history of Nepal as factual as possible. This book, a collection of twenty-four colophons and seventy-two inscriptions, will aid the study of Nepalese history. Most of these colophons and inscriptions were previously unpublished, and the few which were already available have been restored to their original forms. The colophons which date from A.D. 1011 to 1768, are in the Newari, Bhujimol, Ranjana scripts and in the Newari and Sanskrit languages. The inscriptions, on political, religious, devotive, and commercial topics, are in Newari, Ranjana, Pancamol, Devanagari, and Maithili scripts and in Newari and Sanskrit languages. They date from A.D. 1242 to 1768.

582. **Narahari Nath, Yogi.** Itihāsaprakāśa. Kathmandu : The Author, 1965. 784, 73 p. illus. (Gorakshagranthamalā pushpa 85)

The first volume of a set which is to be completed in five volumes. This is a chronologically arranged collection of treaties between the rulers of different small states of Nepal prior to its unification. Most of the work is devoted to the treaties of Gorkha period, between Nepal and British India as well as Tibet, although the earlier period is also represented. The compiler has taken care to include treaties not only located in archives but also those on copper plates from earlier periods, found at several placcs throughout Nepal. Documents relating to relations and exchanges of view between Nepal and some European countries during the administration of Bhim Sen Thapa and Jung Bahadur are of great interest. The last part (73 p.) presents copies of some original documents and copper plates, and illustrations of some important historical places. In Nepali.

583. **Narahari Nath, Yogi**, ed. Itihāsaprakāśamā sandhipatrasaṅgraha. Dang, Nepal : Adhyatmika Sammelana, 1966. vol. 1- (Gorakshagranthamalā pushpa 85).

This is the first volume of a series presenting treaties of historical importance, arranged chronologically. This collection is concerned with economic aid. In Nepali.

584. **Narahari Nath, Yogi** and **Vasnyat, Narendra Man Singh.** Itihāsaprakāśama sandhipatrasaṅgraha. Itihas prakasama

sandhi patra sangraha. Kathmandu: The Authors, 1964. 48 p.

A collection of treaties of historical importance from the period 1790 to 1956, arranged chronologically. In Nepali.

585. **Pant, Nayaraj**. Śrī Pāñca Pṛthvīnārāyaṇa Śāhako upadeśa. Edited by Gautamvajra Vajracharya; compiled by Deviprasad Bhandari; with Dinesh Raj Pant. Lalitpur, Nepal: Jagdamba Prakashan [n.d.] 1200, 146 p.

Despite its title, this is a collection of material about Prithvi Narayan Shaha, who ruled from 1743-75, and his ancestors. The text is in Nepali and Sanskrit. The compilers consulted literary sources and archival material, and have presented in chronological order contemporary documents, proclamations, correspondence, inscriptions, and portions of creative writings which are in any way related to the life and achievements of Prithvi Narayan Shaha. The book includes some texts in old Nepali, and the compilers have given modern Nepali versions for these so that the scholars can understand the material easily. The last group of pagination (146 p.) includes subject index and notes. This is source material for research scholars.

586. **Poudyal, Nayanath**. Bhāshā vaṃśāvalī. Kathmandu: Archaeological Department, Royal Nepal Archives, 1963. 86 p. (Purātatva Prakāśana Mālā, 21)

This old Nepali manuscripts, preserved in Royal Archives, is a traditional history of Nepal up to the end of the Malla period. This is an anonymous work and was probably compiled gradually as records. As a traditional account, this intermingles both history and myth, but it nevertheless records valuable information and presents details about the kings of Nepal. This also gives histories of the establishment of some old temples in Nepal. A portion of the work is based upon the Puranic text of *Hemavat khanda*.

587. **Rajvanshi, Shankarman**, ed. Bhaktapura Śilalekha sucī.

For full entry refer to Bibliographies section.

588. **Regmi, D.R.** The mediaeval calendar of Nepal. *Nepal Digest*, vol. 2, no. 11-12 (Oct. 1973-Jan. 1974), pp. 71-73.

Describes the characteristics of the Newari calendar, which originated in the Nepali era corresponding to A.D. 879.

589. **Regmi, Jagadish Chandra,** comp. and ed. Dictionary of Nepalese cultural geography. Assistant editor : Sheshraj Shivakoti. Kathmandu : Office of Nepal-Antiquary, 1980. 137, 96, 31 leaves. illus.

Extracts from Kirkpatrick's *An account of the Kingdom of Nepaul* published in 1811 and from Hamilton's *An account of the Kingdom of Nepal* published in 1819. The author, one of Nepal's top scholars, has arranged the accounts under suitable headings. This work will be useful to historians as a source on the beginning of the modern period of Nepal and on the earlier period. Mimeographed.

590. **Regmi, Jagadish Chandra,** comp. and ed. The great King Prithivi Narayan Shah special. Kathmandu : Office of the Nepal-Antiquary, 1979. 30 leaves.

This is a special issue of *Nepal-Antiquary*; *Journal of Socio-Historical Research and Digest* (no. 10, Jan. 1979), produced as a Nepal's unity-day special to commemorate the anniversary of the king's 256th birthday. (*27 Paush 2035, 10 Jan. 1979*). This contains a collection of excerpts on historical events and geographical features from documents and official records.

591. **Riccardi Theodore, Jr.** An account of Nepal from the Vir Vinod of Shyamaldas. *Kailash : a Journal of Himalayan Studies*, vol. 3, no. 3 (1975), pp. 199-286.

The *Vir Vinod* was written towards the end of the last century by Kaviraj Shyamaldas, court poet of Maharana Sajjan Singh of Mewar. It is one of the great works of Hindi historiography and is of major importance for the history of Rajasthan. An account of Nepal is included because of the traditional importance of relations between Nepal and Rajasthan. This portion, known as '*Nayapalaka itihasa*' (History of Nepal), describes the geography, history, and castes of Nepal. In this article, the author gives a short introduction in English followed by the original text *Vir Vinod* in Hindi.

592. **Sahakalina, etihasika ciththipatra sangraha**. Compiled by Buddhisagar Parajuli; edited by Shankarman Rajvanshi; vol. 2 revised by Babukrishan Dhakala. Kathmandu : Bir Pustakalaya, Archaeology Department, Ministry of Education, Nepal [1966 ?] 2 vols. (Purātattva Prakāśanamālā, 35-36).

A collection of historical correspondence from the Shaha dynasty. The letters are arranged chronologically from 1813 to 1864 and are addressed to prime ministers and other officers. These volumes cover the reigns of Girvana Juddha Bikram Shaha Deva, Rajendra Bikram Shaha Deva, and Surendra Bikram Shaha Deva, and include letters bearing on Anglo-Nepalese relations. Some of the letters have yet to be studied in the context of the history of modern Nepal. This is a useful source material for historical research. The letters are preserved in the Royal Archives of Nepal.

593. **Shakya, Hem Raj**, ed. Abhilekha prakash=Abhilekha prakāśa ; Licchavi period. Translated by : Asha Ram Shakya. Lalitpore, Nepal : Karuna Prakashan, 1969. 23 p.

Presents eleven inscriptions from the Licchavi period. There is a catalogue giving the text of the inscriptions in English.

594. **Shakya, Hem Raj.** Śrī Hiraṇyavarṇa Mahāvihārasthita piṇḍipātra-abhilekha. Kathmandu : Mukt Bahadur Dhakhva, 1980. 36 p.

A collection of Newari inscriptions on the begging bowls of monks preserved in the Hiraṇyavarṇa Mahāvihāra, at Buddhist monastry in Lalitpur, Napal. The book includes an introduction explaining the religious importance of the offering bowls. The book is in Newari or Sanskrit, with an introduction in Newari.

595. **Sharma, Aishvarya Dhar.** Three unpublished inscriptions concerning the Devabhājus of Patan. *Journal of the Nepal Research Centre*, vol. 1 (Humanities) (1977), pp. 130-138.

This paper presents three hitherto-unpublished inscriptions of the Malla period which provide with some information about the Devabhāju Brahmins of Patan. The location, size, and script of the inscriptions is given, along with a translation of the Newari portion into English.

596. **Srivastava, K.P.** Source material in U.P. State Archives on Nepal and Afghanistan. Lucknow, India : Uttar Pradesh State Archives [1978 ?]. 9 p.

The author is the Director of U.P. State Archives, Lucknow, India. The records of Gorakhpur, Kumaun and Varanasi (Benares) Divisions now preserved in the U.P. State Archives afford ample material for a detailed study of the history of trade with Nepal and of the Anglo-Nepalese War. These records furnish important raw material for understanding the economic and political histories of Nepal and Afghanistan. Includes a glossary of terms.

597. **Stiller, Ludwig F.** ed. Letters from Kathmandu : the Kot Massacre. Kathmandu : Research Centre for Nepal and Asian Studies, Tribhuvan University, 1981. 388 p. 2 maps. illus.

This is a documentary history dealing with one of the great turning points in the history of Nepal, the 1846 massacre in Kathmandu which marked the beginning of Rana rule. The documents, presented here is an edited form, describe the events as they were observed and interpreted by the British Residents of Nepal. Without trying to eliminate the bias, the editor has indicated in his notes and introductory explanations the special areas in which the reader and student of history should be especially alert for distortions or questionable interpretation. The result is a gripping story that develops step-by-step with each document.

598. **Thapa, Ramesh Jung.** The archives movement and Nepal. Kathmandu : Department of Archaeology, His Majesty's Government of Nepal, 1967. 23 p. illus.

The archives movement in Nepal can easily be traced to the days of Prithvi Narayan Shaha, who ruled between 1743-75. This booklet traces the impact of the archives movement both in Nepal and abroad. The author decribes the kinds of archives in Nepal: *sandhi-patras* (treaties, with local and foreign powers), *chitthi-patra* (correspondence), *khadga nishanas, dui-chappes, ek-chappes,* and *lal mohars* (seals).

599. **Vajracharya, Dhan Vajra** and **Shreshtha, Tek Bahadur.** Śāhakālaka abhilekha. Kathmandu : Institute of Nepal and Asian Studies, Tribhuvan University, 1980. 598 p.

A collection of inscriptions belonging to the period of the Gorkha kings (the present ruling house) of Nepal, edited with good introduction by two well-known scholars. This very important source material for research in Nepalese history provides 164 inscriptions covering the period 1609-1815, with explanations. In Nepali or Sanskrit.

600. **Vajracharya, Gautamavajra.** Recently discovered inscriptions of Licchavi Nepal. *Kailash : a Journal of Himalayan Studies*, vol. 1, no. 2 (1973), pp. 117-133. illus.

Stone inscriptions are a most important source for the study of the Licchavi period. Most of the inscriptions come from the

Kathmandu Valley, the dynastic seat of the Licchavis from A.D. 300 to 850, and are written in Sanskrit and inscribed in Gupta characters. The author describes ten recently discovered inscriptions, with illustrations, and presents their texts with translations.

BIOGRAPHICAL WORKS

601. **Acharya, Baburam.** Śrī Pāñca Baḍamahārājādhirāja Pṛthvīnārāyaṇa Śāha; saṅkshipta jīvanī, 1723-75. Kathmandu : His Majesty's Government, Press Secretariat, 1967-68. 3 vols.

Maharaja Prithvi Narayan Shah was the Gorkha king who founded the Gorkha dynasty in Nepal. He introduced Nepali as the national language and is called the father of Nepali nationalism. This biography deals with the beginning of the Gorkha Kingdom; the main events in the life of Prithvi Narayan Shah; the idea of the unification of Nepal; victories over the other Nepalese states; social, religious, and economic reforms; local revolts; relations with the East India Company; and the establishment of Union of Nepal. Each volume includes a genealogical table of Gorkha Kings. Nevertheless this is not a very authentic biography of Prithvi Narayana Shah.

602. **Bajracharya, Manik Lal.** Birendra—the King with a difference. Kathmandu : Eastern Trading and Investment, 1974. 151 p. illus.

A short biography of the King of Nepal, Birendra Bir Bikram Shah Deva, who was born in 1945.

603. **Genealogical chart of the Chandra Shumshere family.** Place and publishers not known, 1975. 15 leaves.

Descendants of Chandra Shumshere Jung Bahadur Rana, 1862-1929, former prime minister of Nepal. Mimeographed.

604. **Genealogical chart of the Juddha Shumshere family.** Place and publisher not known, 1975. 23 leaves.

Descendants of Juddha Shumshere Jung Bahadur Rana: 1875-1952, former prime minister of Nepal. Mimeographed.

605. **Hunter, W.W.** Life of Brian Houghton Hodgson, British Resident at the court of Nepal. London : John Murray, 1896. 390 p.

Brian Houghton Hodgson was Assistant Resident of Nepal, 1825-33, and Resident of Nepal, 1833-43. This book describes his life in detail and also gives historical information on Nepal and its policies in the 19th century. Includes an index to the manuscripts Hodgson presented to the India Office Library.

606. **Limbu, Keshar Kumar**, comp. and ed. Imānasiṅa Cemajoṅa ko jīvanī. Darjeeling, India : Brhat Sahitya Sansthan, 1978. 33 p.

This Nepali publication is a biography of Iman Singh Chemjong, 1904-76, Limbu linguist and historian. This includes a brief history of the Kiratis and their religion.

607. **Masters, John**. Bugles and a tiger : a volume of autobiography. New York : Viking ; London : Michael Joseph, 1956. 312 p. illus.

A lively portrait of Gurkha troops in British India which tells how a gifted officer learned his profession prior to the Second World War.

608. **Masters, John**. The road past Mandalay : a personal narrative. London : Michael Joseph, 1961. 343 p. maps. (Book Society Choice)

A continuation of the preceding item. This includes an account of Gurkha troops in action during the Burma campaign.

609. **Pant, Naya Raj**. Paṇḍita Gopāla Pāṅḍe ra unako ghanamūla lyāune rīti. Kathmandu : Royal Nepal Academy [1980?]. 87 p.

A biography of Gopal Pande, 1848-1921, the Nepalese mathematician and astronomer. This includes an exposition of his method of extracting cubic roots according to the Hindu mathematical system.

610. **Prasad, Ishwari**. The life and times of Maharaja Juddha Shumsher Jung Bahadur Rana of Nepal. New Delhi : Ashish Publishing House, 1975. 384 p.

Maharaja Joodha Shumshere Jung Bahadur Rana, 1875-1950, was the Prime Minister of Nepal. This book is an account of his life and career as Prime Minister, and provides great insight into the history of Nepal during his tenure of the office.

611. **Rana, Pudma Jung Bahadur.** Life of Maharaja Sir Jung Bahadur of Nepal. Editor: Abhay Charan Mukerji. Reprint. Kathmandu: Ratna Pustak Bhandar, 1974. 314 p. (Bibliotheca Himalayica, Series II, vol. 8).

A reprint of the 1909 edition printed at the Pioneer Press, Allahabad. This is a biographical account of Maharaja Sir Jung Bahadur, 1817-77. He was Prime Minister of Nepal during 1846-56 and 1857-77. Includes 10 leaves of illustrations.

612. **Sesya, Ch.** and **Paul, Dh.** Rare gems of Nepal. Kathmandu: Ratna Pustak Bhandar, 1966. 94 p. illus.

Short biographical sketches of eminent people from Nepal.

613. **Shah, Rishikesh.** Jung Bahadur, the strongman of Nepal. Place not given; Durga Pokhrel [1978?]. 37 p.

A biographical account of Maharaja Sir Jung Bahadur; 1817-77. He was Prime Minister of Nepal, 1846-56 and 1857-77, and this work throws light on his role in the politics of the period.

614. **Stiller, Ludwig F.** Prithwinarayan Shah in the light of Dibya upadesh.

For full entry refer to History—General section.

GENERAL

615. **Acharya, Baburam.** Nepālako saṅkshipta vṛttānta. Kathmandu: Pramod Shamsher and Nirabikram 'Pyasi', 1965. 169 p. map.

The author, great historian and patriot, always wrote to glorify the history and culture of Nepal. This brief history examines the ruling periods of Prithvi Narayan Shah, Pratap Singh Shah, Rana Bahadur Shah, 1743 to 1799.

616. **Adhikari, Krishna Kant.** A brief survey of Nepali historiography. Kathmandu: Buku, 1980. 72 p. bibliog.

This work is divided into four chapters. The first chapter describes the development of historiography in Europe along with the development of Nepali historiography in the 19th century. The second chapter deals with Nepali historiography in the 20th century. An introduction to source materials for the study of

Nepali history is given in chapter three. The final chapter points out some of the shortcomings in Nepali historiography, together with some remedial suggestions.

617. **Aryal, I R.** and **Dhungyal, T.P.** A new history of Nepal. Kathmandu : Voice of Nepal, 1970. 274 p. bibliog.

A brief outline of historical facts, intended for students of history. This would be a suitable textbook for high schools and colleges where history is taught in the English language. Includes two appendixes: 'Nepal's relation with India' and 'Significance of the word Nepal'.

618. **Bhandari, Dundi Raj.** Nepālako itihāsika vivecanā. Varanasi, India : Krishna Kumari, 1968. 367 p. 2 maps. illus. Distributed by Madhav Prasad Sharma.

A reliable history of Nepal, from ancient times through to around 1960. The chapters are arranged chronologically, and the book is divided into three broad sections covering the ancient, mediaeval, and modern periods. The work includes objective appraisals of prominent people, particularly of modern Nepal.

619. **Datta, C.L.** Ladakh and western Himalayan politics : 1819-1848. New Delhi : Munshiram Manoharlal, 1973. 239 p. maps.

Chapter six contains an account of British policy during the period and Nepal's responses to it. The study presents important information on this era in Nepal's history.

620. **Edwards, Daniel W.** Nepal on the eve of the Rana ascendancy. *Contributions to Nepalese Studies*, vol. 2, no. 1 (Feb. 1975), pp. 99-118.

The administrative institutions in Nepal in 1843 are described in the light of relevant historical documents and texts, and the names and functions of personnel, the central government officers, are given.

621. **Hamilton, Francis Buchanan.** An account of the Kingdom of Nepal and of the territories annexed to this dominion by the house of Gorkha. Reprint. New Delhi : Manjusri Publishing House, 1971. 364 p. illus. (Bibliotheca Himalayica, Series I, vol. 10).

The author visited Nepal for fourteen months in 1802-03 with the mission of Captain Knox. The author himself travelled extensively in order to collect information from the people. As a result, this book is the most comprehensive, yet concise, history of Nepal from Prithvi Narayan Shah to 1814. It was first published in 1819. The book is illustrated with engravings. Includes a register of the weather from February 1802 to March 1803; a map of the dominions of the house of Gorkha; and calculations of the altitudes of a number of mountains.

622. **History of Nepal.** Translated from the Parbatiya by Shew Shunker Singh; Pandit Gunanand; edited with an introduction by Daniel Wright. Reprint. Kathmandu : Nepal Antiquated Book Publishers, 1972. 320 p. illus.

Originally published in 1877 by Cambridge University Press, this is a history of Nepal, with particular reference to Kathmandu Valley, covering the period up to 1829. It includes Newari songs; a list of the rājās (kings) of Nepal from the time of *Ne Muni*, extracted from the history; and a catalogue of the editor's collection of Sanskrit manuscripts obtained in Nepal for the University of Cambridge.

623. **Hofer, Andras.** On re-reading *Le-Nepal* : what we social scientists owe to Sylvain Levi. *Kailash : a Journal of Himalayan Studies*, vol. 7, no. 3-4 (1979), pp. 176-190. bibliog.

Sylvain Levi, generally considered an Indologist, undertook his first journey to Nepal and India in 1897 and his *Le Nepal* released in 1905-08. In this article the author summarizes of Levi's conclusions, without criticizing Levi's research results, some of which are now outdated. Levi's style remains vivid and his diary of two months in Nepal bears evidence of his humanistic commitment, a characteristic rarely found in other accounts of 'Old Nepal', such as Hodgson's or Oldfield's.

624. **Jain, M.S.** Emergence of a new aristocracy in Nepal (1837-58). Agra, India : Sri Ram Mehra, 1972. 220 p. bibliog.

An account of the two decades which led to the emergence of Rana rule in Nepal. Jung Bahadur's plans to usurp power, his administration, and his relations with British India during the period have been highlighted.

625. **Khatry, Prem Kumar.** The samantas in ancient Nepalese polity. *Nepalese Culture*, vol. 1 (1979), pp. 14-20.

Depicts the role of the *samantas* in the polity of ancient Nepal. In its historical context, the term *samanta* bears different meanings. Generally it means a chief—regional or state—who had limited autonomy over his feudal holdings but owed allegiance to a higher sovereign. It can also mean a neighbouring or an adjoining ruler. In some cases, *samanta* was given as a title by a ruler to aides or advisers who served in ministerial positions. From the early historical documents it appears that the *samanta*, either as a court official or as a regional or provincial ruler, exerted considerable influence on the administration of Nepal.

626. **Kirkpatrick, William**. An account of the Kingdom of Nepaul, the substance of observations made during a mission to that country in the year 1793. Reprint. New Delhi : Manjusri Publishing House, 1969. 386 p. map. illus.

Originally published by William Miller, London, 1811. Colonel Kirkpatrick's mission to Nepal was undertaken from 13 February to 3 April 1793, and he was perhaps the first foreigner to describe the scenery of the Himalayas. By writing this book the author hoped to increase the prospects of trade and commerce with Nepal; he felt that Nepal, particularly because of its proximity to Tibet, would be a highly interesting commercial partner. In addition, he describes the land, flora, fauna, agriculture, history, government, people, folklore, crafts, festivals, architecture, and historical places, etc. A twenty-eight-page word list in Nepali and Newari and four pages in Magar and Limbu is furnished to illustrate the comparative vocabulary of these languages. The accompanying illustrations are not very accurate, but the author's most serious mistake was misrecording the death dates of Prithvi Narayan Shah and Pratap Singh Shah.

627. **Kumar, Satish**. Rana polity in Nepal : origin and growth. Bombay : Asia Publishing House, 1967. 195 p. map. bibliog.

A revised version of the author's dissertation, *Political system of Nepal under the Ranas: 1846-1909*, submitted to Delhi University in 1962. The present study offers a perspective on the Rana period as a whole, based on Nepali-language documents, archival records of British India, and interviews with many eminent persons in Nepal, It includes appendixes listing: kings, regents, and prime ministers after 1769; genealogical tables of the royal and Rana families; Rana administration; the judicial structure under the Ranas; some important *lal-mohars*; rolls of succession; and a glossary of Nepali words.

628. **Landon, Perceval**. Nepal. Reprint. Kathmandu : Ratna Pustak Bhandar, 1976. 2 vols. in 1. 4 maps. bibliog. illus. (Bibliotheca Himalayica, Series I, vol. 16)

Originally published in 1928, this is one of the most comprehensive books on Nepal, written at the request and with the help of Prime Minister Chandra Shamshere Rana. This includes material on Nepal's history, political situation, people, land, towns, tracks, flora and fauna, coins, etc. The coverage is from earlist times to 1926. It also contains more than 200 contemporary photographs of considerable historical interest and three genealogical tables.

629. **Manandhar, Thakurlal**. Nepal in the early medieval period : gleanings from the Bengali Vaṁśāvali. *Journal of the Nepal Research Centre*, vol. 1 (Humanities) (1977), pp. 83-88.

The *Bendall Vaṃśāvalī*, later named as the *Gopālarāja Vaṃśavalī*, is now preserved in the National Archives, ms. no. 1-1593 (Jtihasa 6). In this article, the author supplements information derived from the *Bendall Vaṃśāvalī* with the testimony of contemporary inscriptions and colophons from Nepalese manuscripts.

630. **Manandhar, Thakurlal**. Two letters from Ranga Nath Pandit to B.H. Hodgson. *Kailash: a Journal of Himalayan Studies*, vol. 3, no. 1 (1975), pp. 77-83.

Ranga Nath Pandit accepted the office of Prime Minister during 1837-38 on two occasions, but rapidly realized that the drawbacks of the post were greater than the dignity and emoluments it conferred. He was received little support and after the Kot massacre, he was forced to flee the country along with other nobles. This article contains two letters from Ranga Nath Pandit, Prime Minister during 1837-38 to Mr. B.H. Hodgson, in Nepali with English translations. They reveal that since the time of Bhim Sen Thapa, who was Prime Minister during 1806-37, Ranga Nath Pandit was in favour of establishing friendly relations with the British to save the country from ruin.

631. **Oldfield, H. Ambrose**. Sketches from Nepal, historical and descriptive; with an essay on Nepalese Buddhism and illustrations of religious monuments and architecture. Reprint. Delhi : Cosmo, 1974. 2 vols.

Vol. 2 includes a reproduction of the title-page of the 1880 edition, published by W.H. Allen, London, giving the full title: *Sketches from Nepal, historical and descriptive, with anecdotes of the court life and wild sports of the country in the time of Maharaja Jung Bahadur, G.C.B., to which is added an essay on Nepalese Buddhism, and illustrations of religious monuments, architecture, and scenery from the author's own drawings.*

632. **Pandey, Madhav Raj**. How Jang Bahadur established Rana rule in Nepal. *Contributions to Nepalese Studies*, vol. 1, no. 1 (Dec. 1973), pp. 50-53.

Describes Jung Bahadur's (1817-76) role during the Kot massacre and the Bhandarkhal incident, his rise to power, his offer of help to the British during the Indian Mutiny and other events connected with life and times.

633. **Pemble, John**. The invasion of Nepal : John Company at war. London : Oxford University Press, 1971. 389 p. maps. bibliog. illus.

A study of the Anglo-Nepalese war of 1814-16 and its consequences. The author discusses the part played by John Company, a regiment developed by East Indian Company of Bengal army.

634. **Petech, Luciano**. Mediaeval history of Nepal, c. 750-1480. Roma : Istituto Italiano per il Medio ed Estremo Oriente, 1958. 238 p. (Serie Orientale Roma, 10. Materials for the Study of Nepalese History and Culture, 3).

This book is the result of author's two-month stay in Nepal in 1956 and his research in Calcutta, Cambridge, London, and Paris. The history of Nepal can be divided into four periods: 1. Licchavi and their successors (c. 400-750); 2. Thākurī and early Malla (c. 750-1480); 3. The three Malla kingdoms (1480-1768); 4. The Gorkha dynasty (after 1768). This book deals with the Thākurī and early Malla period. Includes two genealogical tables.

635. **Rana, Pramode Shamshere J.B**. Rana Nepal : an insider's view. Kathmandu : R. Rana, 1978. 175 p. illus.

An account of the period of Rana rule, 1846-1951. Includes genealogical tables.

636. **Regmi, D.R**. Ancient Nepal. 3rd ed. Calcutta : Firma K.L. Mukhopadhyay, 1969. 364 p. maps. bibliog. (Political and Economic History of Nepal from the Ancient Times to 1846 A.D.)

This is an authentic history of Nepal by a well-known historian.

This work is the result of strenous research during the past several years. The source materials for the study were mostly inscriptions, numismatics, chronicles, and old correspondence. A great many of them are still unpublished, and some were personally traced by the author and are brought to light for the first time in this work. The author presents new interpretations of old material and all the source material has been objectively evaluated. The work includes general observations on some aspects of Nepalese life and culture and describe the early Lichhavi rulers, Amsuvarman and his Gupta successors, the Lichhavi restoration, and political and economic conditions in ancient Nepal.

637. **Regmi, D.R.** A century of family autocracy in Nepal. 2nd ed. Kathmandu : Nepal National Congress, 1958. 267 p.

The account of the last century of Rana autocracy, 1846-1949. Appendixes contain the Treaty of Sugowlie, 1875, the treaty of 1923 between Nepal and Great Britain, and the treaty of peace between Nepal and Tibet, 1856.

638. **Regmi, D.R.** Medieval Nepal. Calcutta : Firma K.L. Mukhopadhyay, 1965-66. 3 vols. maps. bibliog. illus.

A well-authenticated study of the mediaeval history of Nepal. The contents are volume 1: *Early medieval period*; *750-1530 A.D.*; volume 2: *A history of the three kingdoms, 1520-1768 A.D.*; volume 3: *Source materials for the history and culture of Nepal, 740-1768 A.D.* contains inscriptions, chronicles, diaries, etc. in Sanskrit, Newari, and Nepali. These volumes are supplemented by the fourth volume published by the author in 1966 from Patna which covers selected inscriptions, 1524-1728; giving verification and corresponding dates according to Gregorian calendar. The text of vol. 4 are covered in vol. 3.

639. **Regmi, D.R.** Modern Nepal. Calcutta : Firma K. L. Mukhopadhyay, 1975. 2 vols. maps. bibliog. illus.

Volume 1: *Rise and growth in the eighteenth centnry*; volume 2: *Expansion, climax, and fall*. This work by a well-known historian describes modern history of Nepal.

640. **Regmi, Jagadish Chandra.** Licchavi-saṃskṛti. Kathmandu : Ratna Pustak Bhandar, 1969. 463 p. bibliog. illus.

The period of the Licchavi rulers is the most ancient age known in Nepal's history. Though no systematic chronological history has been published so far, a cultural history can be reconstructed from the abundant material still extant in the country. In this Nepali work, the author has attempted such a history, using both numismatic and epigraphic records to reconstruct the cultural history from the 4th century B.C. to 9th century A.D. Many interesting areas such as religion, literature, art, architecture, and development of popular languages are fully covered by this work.

641. **Regmi, Mahesh C.** Some questions on Nepali history. *Contributions to Nepalese Studies*, vol. 3, no. 2 (Sept. 1976), pp. 1-5.

The author is well-known scholar and has written several books and articles on the history of Nepal. In this paper he discusses certain questions of the Kiratas, the Licchavis, and on defining historical periods as ancient, mediaeval, and modern. He presents the views of other scholars along with his own.

642. **Regmi Research Series.**

For full entry refer to Professional periodicals section.

643. **Riccardi, Theodore, Jr.**, ed. and tr. Sylvain Levi : the history of Nepal. Pt. I. *Kailash : a Journal of Himalayan Studies*, vol. 3, no. 1 (1975), pp. 5-60.

The first part of this article describes the life and work of the historian Sylvain Levi, 1863-1935. This is followed by the general description of Levi's *Le Nepal : Etude Historique d'Un Royaume Hindou* which is in three volumes published between 1905-08. This article presents the portion of *Le Nepal* dealing with the history of Nepal, which appears in the second volume of the original work.

644. **Sen, Jahar.** Slave trade on the Indo-Nepal border in the nineteenth century. *Kailash : a Journal of Himalayan Studies*, vol. 1, no. 2 (1973), pp. 159-166.

Slavery was an ancient institution both in India and Nepal and an important element of trade in Asia. In this article, the author discusses the history of slavery on the Indo-Nepal border throwing light on the role of the East India Company and various officials of the border states. The author also describes the social and legal measures taken by Jung Bahadur, Prime Minister, 1846-77, to stop slavery business, as well as the action taken by the government of India.

645. **Shrestha, Ava.** Regency of Bahadur Shah. Kirtipur, Nepal : History Instruction Committee, 1976. 113 p. bibliog.

Discusses the political achievements of Bahadur Shah, Prince of Nepal, who was born around 1737. This is the author's M.A. dissertation. Mimeographed.

646. **Shrestha, D.B. and Singh, C.B.** The history of ancient and medieval Nepal in a nutshell, with some comparative traces of foreign history. Kathmandu : The Authors, 1972-74. 2 vols. maps.

Volume one of this title covers the ancient and medieval period and volume two covers the modern period.

647. **Shrestha, Devi Chandra.** Mallakara in its economic and historical perspective. *Contributions to Nepalese Studies*, vol. 5, no. 2 (June 1978), pp. 1-6.

Various types of taxes played a role in the public finance of ancient Nepal. Taxes were levied on produce at the point of origin and there are numerous references to production taxes on a wide variety of commodities. Among these, the most frequent reference has been to the *mallakara*. However, historians, whether Nepalese or foreign, have been far from unanimous with regard to the meaning of *mallakara*. Some of their hypotheses are fascinating, and a brief review of these is presented as an introduction to the explanation of *mallakara* in this article.

648. **Singh, Harischandra Lal.** Principal records of Nepal. Kathmandu : Satish Singh, 1980. 88 p.

A chronological list of important events in the fields of administration; arts, culture, and religion; communications; education; economy; foreign policy; history; health services; humanitarian and social services; industry and commerce; literature; politics; sports; transport; and tourism.

649. **Stiller, Ludwig F.** Prithwinarayan Shah in the light of Dibya upadesh. Kathmandu?: publisher not known, 1968. 74 p.

On the personality of Prithvi Narayan Shah, King of Nepal, 1723-75, as a nation builder and a ruler as revealed in his Divya Upadesh, a work on the basic tenets of polity.

650. **Stiller, Ludwig F.** The rise of the house of Gorkha : a study in the unification of Nepal, 1768-1816. New Delhi : Manjusri Publishing House, 1973. 390 p. 6 maps. bibliog. illus. (Bibliotheca Himalayaica, Series XIV, vol. 15).

Discusses the rise of the Shaha dynasty in Nepal, with special emphasis on the King Prithvi Narayan Shah's historic campaign for the unification of Nepal. The author also analyses the causes of the Anglo-Nepalese war and Nepal's relations with the British in India, Tibet, and China during the period. This very useful book will be for those interested in the political and military history of Nepal.

651. **Stiller, Ludwig F.** The role of fear in the unification of Nepal. *Contributions to Nepalese Studies*, vol. 1, no. 2 (June 1974), pp. 42-89.

A review of the role the British played in the unification of Nepal. The author credits the unification to Prithvi Narayan Shah.

652. **Stiller, Ludwig F.** The silent cry : the people of Nepal, 1816-1839. Kathmandu : Sahayogi Prakashan, 1976. 344 p. 2 maps. bibliog.

War with the East India Company and the Treaty of Sagauli severely challenged Nepal. This account begins with the Treaty of Sagauli in 1816 and continues through to the death of Bhim Sen Thapa in 1839. The author calls these transition years the 'silent years' because historians have generally neglected this period. However, this book testifies eloquently to the impact of the 'silent years' on today's Nepal. Includes genealogical tables.

653. **Thapa, Netra Bahadur.** A short history of Nepal. Revised by M.D. Moran. 4th ed. Kathmandu : Ratna Pustak Bhandar, 1973. 296 p.

A simply written history of Nepal. Following a chapter on geographical features the author divides the history of Nepal into three chapters: Ancient Nepal; Medieval period; and Modern Nepal. The topics are arranged almost in chronologicol order. The book includes genealogical charts of the Shah rulers.

654. **Tucci, Giuseppe.** Nepal : the discovery of the Malla. English translation from the Italian by Lovett Edwards. New York : Dutton ; London : Allen & Unwin, 1962. 96 p. illus.

Originally entitled *Alla Scoperta Dei Malla*, this is an account of the author's journey to western provinces of Nepal and the area around Jumla. In Dullu, the author discovered some inscriptions which throw light on the western kingdom of the Malla known as the Khasa Kingdom during the early Middle Ages.

655. **Tucci, Giuseppe.** Preliminary report on two scientific expeditions in Nepal. Roma : Instituto Italiano per il Medio e Estremo Oriente, 1956. 153 p. illus. (Serie Orientale Roma, 10. Materials for the Study of Nepalese History and Culture, 1)

A report of the author's visit to west Nepal, where he studied the inscriptions and temples of Jumla and its surroundings in order to find information about the Khasa rulers of western Nepal.

656. **Tuladhar, Daman R.** Contemporary Nepal, 1945-1955. Kathmandu : Laxmi Publications, 1980. 340 p.

An exhaustive account of political change in Nepal, from the rule of the Ranas to the short-lived democracy.

657. **Voice of History.**

For full entry refer to Professional periodicals section.

REGIONAL

658. **Burleigh, Peter.** A chronology of the later kings of Patan. *Kailash : a Journal of Himalayan Studies*, vol. 4, no. 1 (1976), pp. 21-71.

A chronology of the later Malla kings of Patan which also deals with the history of Patan during its last period of artistic, and especially architectural glory. It covers the period 1598-1768.

659. **Clarke, Graham E.** A Helambu history. *Journal of the Nepal Research Centre*, vol. 4 (Humanities) (1980), pp. 1-38. map. bibliog. illus.

Helambu is situated in the middle of a triangle formed between Kathmandu in the south and the border towns of Kyirong and Nilam (or Nyennam, formerly known as Kuti) in Tibet to the north. Administratively it is located within the Sindhupalchok District of the Bagmati Zone of Nepal, but the area is not a clear geographical unit. The author stayed in Helambu for fourteen months during 1974-77. After giving a brief introduction of the area, he describes the social organization and development, and early history of the area. The appendixes contain lineage charts, Helambu documents, and a summary list of Helambu Ghyangs and associated temples.

660. **Edwards, Dan.** The relationship between Kathmandu and Palpa in the Rana period. *Kailash : a Journal of Himalayan Studies*, vol. 4, no. 1 (1976), pp. 72-84.

Because Palpa is a long way from Kathmandu, it was very difficult for the central government to exercise control over Palpa. The government therefore gave more power to the *Bada Hakim*, or chief administrator (also called *Tainathwalla*) to govern the district. This article discusses the relations between the central government and the officials of Palpa District between 1933-50.

661. **Gutschow, Niels and Shakya, Hemraj.** The monasteries (Bāhā and Bahī) of Patan : a contribution towards the cultural topography of a Newar town. *Journal of the Nepal Research Centre*, vol. 4 (Humanities) (1980), pp. 161-174. 3 maps. illus.

This paper is a part of an extensive survey of the Newar towns of the Kathmandu Valley and was made possible by a grant from the German Research Council. The former monasteries of Patan were traced in March 1974. This paper aims at nothing more than providing dates. The authors examine the pattern of distribution of monasteries (*mahāvihāra*) and branch monasteries (*vihāra*) which so well determine the cultural, social, as well as spatial structures of Patan.

662. **Jackson, David P.** Notes on the history of Se-rib, and nearby places in the upper Kali Gandaki Valley. *Kailash : a Journal of Himalayan Studies*, vol. 6, no. 3 (1978), pp. 195-227. map. bibliog.

In Nepal's upper Kali Gandaki Valley, one of the main regions is Thak Khola which contains many temples, caves, and ruins. A distinct land and people called Se-rib once existed in upper Thak Khola. This article presents the author's findings on the history of Se-rib in particular, and of upper Thak Khola in general.

663. **Joshi, Satya Mohan.** Karṇālī loka saṃskṛti, vol. 1: itihāsa. Kathmandu : Royal Nepal Academy, 1971. 156 p. 4 maps. bibliog. illus.

Little is known about the natural resources and the people of the hilly Karnali Zone. This book is volume 1 of a series presenting the comprehensive history of Karnali Zone since medieval times. A complete chronology of the rulers of the different dynasties has been reconstructed on the basis of available material, e.g. epigraphy and tradition. The periods preceding and following the unification of Nepal are treated separately. There is a table of the historical remains and inscriptions found in this area, and the book also includes several illustrations of inscriptions.

664. **Peissel, Michael.** Mustang, the forbidden kingdom : exploring a lost Himalayan land. New York : Dutton, 1967. 318 p. maps. illus.

Mustang District, a part of Dhaulagiri Zone, had a population of 26,944 in 1971. The district is isolated and not well known to other parts of the world. This book describes the history and customs of Mustang.

665. **Pradhan, Bhuwan Lal.** Lumbini, Kapilwastu, Dewadaha. Kirtipur, Nepal : Research Centre for Nepal and Asian Studies, Tribhuvan University, 1979. 100 p. map. illus.

Lumbini, Kapilvastu, and Dewadaha are associated with Gautama Buddha and these places have great importance to Buddhists. The Research Centre for Nepal and Asian Studies decided to publish this work as its contribution to Lubini Year in 1979. The book contains articles on the history and antiquities of the three ancient cities of Nepal.

666. **Stiller, Ludwig F.** An introduction to Hanuman Dhoka. Kirtipur, Nepal : Institute of Nepal and Asian Studies, Tribhuvan University, 1975. 57 p. map.

A historical study of the old royal palace complex in Kathmandu. The text is based on the Nepali work entitled *Hanuman Dhoka—ek adhyayan* by Gautam Vajra Vajracharya.

667. **Vajracharya, Dhanvajra** and **Shreshtha, Tekbahadur.** Dolakhāko etihasika ruparekhā. Kathmandu : Institute of Nepal and Asian Studies, Tribhuvan University, 1974. 200 p. (Tribhuvan University. Institute of Nepal and Asian Studies, Etihasika sāmagrī mālā, 8)

Under the early Malla kings, Dolakha was an independent state and later it became part of the empire of Prithvi Narayan Shah. This work presents Dolakha's chronological and dynastic history from the 11th century until the Gorkha period and studies its social, economic, and cultural conditions through the ages. It includes information on the Hindu and Buddhist religious places which once played an important role in the formation of the local culture. The result of an original research project, this study is based on the extensive use of source materials. It also contains the text of important inscriptions found in the area, historical happenings, and Dolakhali folk-tales.

668. **Yatri, Purna Prakash Nepal.** Setīañcala digdarśana: vividha anusandhānātmaka vishayasamanvīta.

For full entry refer to Geography—General section.

19

INDUSTRY

669. **Acetic acid plant.** Prepared for Nepal Industrial Development Corporation by Industrial Services Centre Kathmandu : Industrial Services Centre, 1979. 36 leaves.

This report deals with the feasibility of an acetic acid plant in Nepal. The study concentrated on area of market, availability fo raw materials, and the technicality of production. Various possible alternatives for raw material have also been discussed. The study revealed that the proposed unit of acetic acid plant is found to be unfeasible. To make this project feasible, measures are also suggested in the report. This mimeographed study has cover title: Study report on acetic acid plant.

670. **Audyogika ganana 2022 ko parinama, Kathamadaum Upatyaka** = Results of the census of manufacturing establishments, 1965, Kathmandu Valley. Trade and Industries Statistics Division, Central Bureau of Statistics, Nepal. Kathmandu : His Majesty's Government, National Planning Commission Secretariat, Central Bureau of Statistics, 1970. 149 p.

This is the first attempt of the Trade and Industries Statistics Division in this field and this publication relates to Kathmandu, Lalitpur, and Bhaktapur districts of Kathmandu Valley, Nepal. In Nepali.

671. **Audyogika ganana 2022 ko parinama, madhya Tarai**= Results of the census of manufacturing establishments, 1965, middle Terai. Trade and Industries Statistics

Division, Central Bureau of Statistics, Nepal. Kathmandu : His Majesty's Government, National Planning Commission Secretariat, Central Bureau of Statistics, 1972. 78 p.

This publication covers Rautahat, Bara, Parsa, Makawanpur, Chitwan of middle Terai. In Nepali.

672. **Audyogika ganana 2022 ko parinama, pasicama Tarai**= Results of the census of manufacturing establishments 1965, western Terai. Trade and Industries Statistics Division, Central Bureau of Statistics, Nepal. Kathmandu : His Majesty's Government, National Planning Commission Secretariat, Central Bureau of Statistics, 1970. 74 p.

This publication gives information regarding districts of Nawal Parasi, Rupandehi, Kapilvastu of western Tarai, Nepal. In Nepali.

673. **Audyogika ganana 2022 ko parinama, purvi Tarai** = Results of the census of manufacturing establishments, 1965, eastern Terai. Trade and Industries Statistics Division, Central Bureau of Statistics, Nepal. Kathmandu : His Majesty's Government, National Planning Commission Secretariat, Central Bureau of Statistics, 1970. 63 p.

This publication relates to districts of Saptari, Siraha, Dhanusha, Mahottari, Sarlahi of eastern Terai, Nepal. In Nepali.

674. **Audyogika ganana 2022 ko parinama, sudura pascima Tarai** = Results of the census of manufacturing establishments, 1965, far western Tarai. Trade and Industries Statistics Division, Central Bureau of Statistics, Nepal. Kathmandu : His Majesty's Government, National Planning Commission Secretariat, Central Bureau of Statistics, 1970. 82 p.

Covers districts of Banke, Bardia, Kailali, Kanchanpur of far western Tarai, Nepal. In Nepali.

675. **Audyogika ganana 2022 ko parinama, sudura purva Tarai** = Results of the census of manufacturing establishments, 1965, far eastern Terai. Trade and Industries Statistics Division, Central Bureau of Statistics, Nepal.

Kathmandu : His Majesty's Government, National Planning Commission Secretariat, Cenrtal Bureau of Statistics, 1970. 85 p.

Information regarding districts of Jhapa, Sunsari, and Morang of far eastern Terai, Nepal. In Nepali.

676. **Audyogika ganana, 2030** = Census of the manufacturing establishments, 1972-73. Trade & Industries Statistics Division, Central Bureau of Statistics, Nepal. Kathmandu : His Majesty's Government, National Planning Commission Secretariat, Central Bureau of Statistics, 1975. 151 leaves.

This publication is in English and Nepali and covers census of all manufacturing units in Nepal by economic activity, legal status and size, number of persons engaged and year of the commencement, total amount of wages and salaries paid, gross out put during the year, source of finance, fuels consumed, raw material consumed, and principal commodities produced during the year. Mimeographed.

677. **Audyogika ganana ko prarambhika natija** = Preliminary results of the census of manufacturing establishments, 1965. Trade and Industries Statistics Division, Central Bureau of Statistics, Nepal. Kathmandu : His Majesty's Government, Ministry of Economic Planning, Central Bureau of Statistics, 1966. 55 leaves.

The preliminary results, of the country's first census of manufacturing establishments. In Nepali.

678. **Bakery industry at Chitwan**. Prepared for Nepal Industrial Development Corporation by Industrial Services Centre. Kathmandu : Industrial Services Centre, 1977. 32 p.

This study relates to assessment of the existing bakery industries at Chitwan, and raw material, market, technical, and financial aspects of establishing a new bakery industry. The study revealed that it is feasible to have additional bakery plant at Chitwan and also suggested its location. This mimeographed study has cover title: Study report on bakery industry at Chitwan.

679. **Brick and tile making plant in Surkhet/Nepalgunj**. Prepared for Nepal Industrial Development Corporation

by Industrial Services Centre. Kathmandu : Industrial Services Centre, 1978. 47 leaves.

The objective of this study was to examine viability of a brick and tile making plant in Surkhet and Nepalgunj. The study revealed that additional brick making plant is not desirable in Surkhet. Therefore, the study team concentrated more in Nepalgunj. This report deals with the desirability of a brick making plant from techno economic point of view and indicated the feasibility of a brick making plant in Nepalgunj. This mimeographed study has cover title: Study report on brick & tile plant in Surkhet/ Nepalgunj.

680. **A dry-cell battery manufacturing plant at Kathmandu.** Prepared for Nepal Industrial Development Corporation by Industrial Services Centre. Kathmandu : Industrial Services Centre, 1979. 158 p.

This study deals with the marketing, technical know-how, materials to be used, plant location, manpower and organization, engineering, management, financial and economic aspects of dry-cell battery manufacturing plant and indicates the feasibility of such a plant at Kathmandu. Includes 41 pages annexes having statistical data. This mimeographed study has cover title: Study report on a dry-cell battery manufacturing plant at Kathmandu.

681. **The feasibility of a cotton spinning mill at Butwal.** Prepared for Nepal Industrial Development Corporation by Industrial Services Centre. Kathmandu : Industrial Services Centre, 1979. 194 leaves.

The study reveals that the project is relatively very large and the sums of money involved are high where as the rate of return is very low. Without tariff protection the project would not be profitable to equity investors. This study has not examined the economics of a large integrated textile project but it is understood that cost advantages can be obtained by integrating weaving, dyeing, and finishing with spinning. This mimeographed study has cover title: Study report on the feasibility of a cotton spinning mill at Butwal.

682. **The feasibility of establishing timber seasoning plants at Dharan and Dhangadi**. Prepared for Nepal Industrial Development Corporation by Industrial Services Centre. Kathmandu : Industrial Services Centre, 1979. 77 leaves.

This study was designed to cover the demand, supply, scale of plant, financial analysis, etc., of the feasibility of establishing timber seasoning plants at Dharan and Dhangadi. The study indicates that a timber seasoning plant would be feasible at Dharan but the export-oriented plant proposal to be located at Dhangadi would not be feasible. This mimeographed study has cover title : Study report on the feasibility of establishing timber seasoning plants at Dharan and Dhangadi.

683. **Feasibility study of housing industry in Kathmandu.** Centre for Economic Development and Administration. Kathmandu : Centre for Economic Development and Administration, 1972. 41 p.

This study was undertaken by the centre on behalf of the Nepal Bank, Kathmandu. The main aim was to find out the investment potential of the housing industry in Kathmandu.

684. **Feasibility study on plywood and chipboard industry :** report for the Nepal Industrial Development Corporation. Battelle Institut. Kathmandu : Nepal Industrial Development Corporation, 1965. 96 p.

The study was designed to cover the demand, supply, scale of plant, financial analysis, etc., in order to ascertain the feasibility of establishing a plywood and chipboard industry in Nepal. Includes folded illustrations.

685. **Fruit and vegetable preservation plant in Nepal.** Prepared for Nepal Industrial Development Corporation by Industrial Services Centre, Feasibility Branch. Kathmandu : Industrial Services Centre, 1979. 41 p.

This report reveals there is no scope to set-up the additional unit in this industry for domestic market. If export potentialities increase, additional unit may be added. However, this is not possible due to the shortage of fresh fruits and vegetables. At the proposed Eastern Region plant, the study was done only to process pea, tomato, and chilli and didnot cover the preservation of mushroom, asparagus, and bamboo shoots products. Therefore a separate and specific study on these products is needed in future if Nepal has to develop this industry. This mimeographed study has cover title: Study report on fruit and vegetable preservation plant in Nepal.

686. **Gharelu tatha sana udyoga sarvekshana, 2030** = Sample survey of the cottage and small scale industries, 1972/73.

Central Bureau of Statistics, Nepal. Kathmandu : His Majesty's Government, National Planning Commission Secretariat, 1973. 64 p.

This publication contains eleven tables in both English and Nepali. These are concerning number of industries by region, size, investment; number of employees; production; consumption; sales; and raw material, etc.

687. **A ginger oil distillation plant at Nepalgunj**. Prepared for Nepal Industrial Development Corporation by Industrial Services Centre. Kathmandu : Industrial Services Centre, 1979. 37 p.

From the report it is clear that in the present state of affairs there is not much scope for ginger drying in the Far Western Region. At present the only possibility is a ginger oil distillation plant. The report is in mimeograph form, includes 20 pages of annexes, and has cover title: Study report on a ginger oil distillation plant at Nepalgunj.

688. **Isdoc Bulletin**. Kathmandu : Industrial Services Centre, 1974- quarterly.

Industrial services documentation bulletin.

689. **Jute carpet industry**. Prepared for Nepal Industrial Development Corporation by Industrial Services Centre. Kathmandu : Industrial Services Centre, 1979. 50 leaves.

This study deals with feasibility of jute carpet industry in Nepal. Jute carpets are imported from India, despite the existence of two jute industries in Nepal alongwith the abundance availability of jute indigeneously. The study surveyed the market situation, technical and economical aspects of the production and recommended that establishment of a jute carpet industry in Nepal is not feasible. This mimeographed study has cover title: Study report on jute carpet industry.

690. **Kathamadaum upatyakako udyoga karyalayako namasuci** = Kathmandu Valley manufacturing establishments directory. Trade and Industries Statistics Division, Central Bureau of Statistics, Nepal. Kathmandu : His Majesty's Government, Ministry of Economic Planning, Central Bureau of Statistics, Trade and Industries Statistics Division, 1967. 49 p.

A directory of manufacturing establishments in three districts, Kathmandu, Lalitpur, and Bhaktapur, of Kathmandu Valley. In Nepali.

691. **Khadka, Krishna Ram**. Study of effective protection in Nepal with reference to some selected industries. Kathmandu : Centre for Economic Development and Administration, Tribhuvan University, 1980. 98 p. bibliog.

This study is an attempt to analyse the interdependence of the trade and industrial policies of Nepal. An analysis has been made of the effective protection enjoyed by selected import substituting industries of Nepal. An analytical presentation of effective tariff protection granted in Nepalese industries is also discussed. The study will be useful to Nepalese policymakers, planners, and others association with Nepal's foreign trade and industrial development. Mimeographed.

692. **Nepal Journal of Management**. Kathmandu : Management Consultants 1972- quarterly.

This is a publication of Management Consultants. Discusses the management problems relating to business, industry, etc. A useful publication for scholars and students. This is published irregularly.

693. **Occupational tools : carpentry & masonary**. Prepared for Nepal Industrial Development Corporation by Industrial Services Centre. Kathmandu : Industrial Services Centre, 1979. 74 leaves.

This study deals with the feasibility of establishing carpentry and masonry tools (occupational tools) production unit in Nepal. The study was initiated with a view to promote the industry of this type so as to bring about the import substitution of the products which is now being met through imports largely from India and China. This mimeographed study has cover title: Study report on occupational tools (carpentry & masonry).

694. **Performance of public enterprises in Nepal : a managerial analysis**. Industrial Services Centre. Kathmandu : His Majesty's Government of Nepal, Corporation Coordination Council and Industrial Services Centre, 1980. 124 p.

This is believed to be the first comprehensive research work in public enterprises in Nepal. This will be useful to policy makers and planners to have a better perspective of public enterprises and to formulate appropriate policy measure to help them to improve their performance.

695. **Preliminary results of the census of manufacturing establishments, 1965**. Prepared under the supervision of : Trade & Industry Statistics Division, Central Bureau of Statistics, Nepal. Kathmandu : His Majesty's Government of Nepal, Ministry of Economic Planning, Central Bureau of Statistics, 1966. 55 p.

This census, which is the first of its kind, relates to the fiscal year 1964/65. Its aim was to provide statistics on the running condition of existing establishments and the total production of the industrial sector, in order to aid future plans for industrial development.

696. **Prospects of industrial investment in Nepal.** Nepal Industrial Development Corporation. Kathmandu : Nepal Industrial Development Corporation, 1973. 255 p. maps.

Provides comprehensive information on Nepal's industries, investment prospects, industrial policies, and development programmes. The information is supported by tables.

697. **Report of animal feed**. Prepared for Nepal Industrial Development Corporation by Industrial Services Centre, Feasibility Branch. Kathmandu : Industrial Services Centre, 1979. 55 leaves.

This study was undertaken in Eastern Development Region to examine whether an animal feed industry in Eastern Region is feasible or not. The scope of the study was designed to cover various aspects such as demand and consumption pattern, existing animal feed industry, requirement of raw materials and their supply, suggestion for the scale of the plant, financial analysis, etc. This report is in mimeograph form and has cover title: Study report on report of animal feed.

698. **Result of the pilot survey of manufacturing establishments, 2020 [1963 A.D.]**. Trade and Industries Statistics Division, Central Bureau of Statistics, Nepal Kathmandu : His Majesty's Government, Ministry of Economic Planning, Central Bureau of Statistics, Trade & Industries Division, 1965. 12 leaves.

The results of a pilot survey of manufacturing establishment in the three industrial towns of Birgunj, Biratnagar, and Nepalgunj leading to a country-wide census of manufactures which was due to begin soon. The major objective of the census was to obtain the fundamental statistical data, regarded as the first step to acquiring facts under the various aspects of the manufacturing establishments, and to make use of it. Mimeographed.

599. **Seminar-cum-Workshop on Management of Industries, Jan. 15, 1973-Jan. 24, 1973**; seminar report. Prepared by Ramesh Singh and Rajendra Suwal. Kirtipur, Nepal : Centre for Economic Development & Administration, 1973. 79 p.

The seminar was organized by the Centre for Economic Development and Administration. The cover title is *Report of the Seminar on Management of Industries.*

700. **Sharma, Suresh P.** Estimation of the production function of Nepalese manufacturing industry. Kirtipur, Nepal : Centre for Economic Development and Administration, Tribhuvan University, 1980. 45 p.

This study is an attempt to add to the existing knowledge about the manufacturing sector of Nepal. The "production function" approach has been used as a theoretical guide to provide answers to the resource as well as efficiency aspects to this sector. This study will prove useful to the policymakers and others association with the development of this sector. Includes statistics. Mimeographed.

701. **Sharma, Suresh P.** Import substitution in hotel industry in Nepal : a research report. Kirtipur, Nepal : Centre for Economic Development and Administration, Tribhuvan University, 1979. 49 p.

This study is conducted for the Ministry of Tourism, His Majesty's Government, Nepal. The basic aim of this study is to find out the import content of hotel industry in Nepal and to look at the possibility of establishing import-substituting industries within the country. The study revealed that while the hotel industry is seen to use the products of other sector of the economy, there is ample opportunities to increase such linkages even more. This can be done by improving the standard of food and dairy products and also by giving Nepalese touch to the hotels. Mimeographed.

702. **Soyabean processing industry in Nepal.** Prepared by Industrial Service Centre for National Industrial Development Corporation. Kathmandu : Industrial Services Centre, 1979. 39 p.

The purpose of this study is to examine the feasibility of setting up a soybean processing industry in Nepal. The study is segmented to the different aspects like the introduction on soybean, soybean and soybean products, soybean as raw material, market, technical, and financial aspects. Includes statistics. Mimeographed. Cover title : Study report on soyabean processing industry in Nepal.

703. **Trier, Jesper.** Ancient paper of Nepal; results of ethno-technological field work on its manufacture, uses, and history—with technical analyses of bast, paper, and manuscripts. Copenhagen : Jutland Archaeological Society, 1972. 271 p. 4 maps. bibliog. (Jutland Archaeological Society, publications, vol. x, 1972).

This publication deals with the production, use, and history of paper in Nepal. During the studies it emerged that the development of paper in Nepal as well as in the rest of Himalaya can only be satisfactorily explained if the broad outline of the use of paper in India and Tibet is known. The results of the investigations which is relevant to Nepal are included in the work. The work is based on three journeys of the author to Nepal. The study is supported by 239 plates, tables, and diagrams. The plates deal with the people of Nepal; species of Thymelaeaceae for making-paper; paper-making; manuscripts, letters, wood-cuts, ritual cards, horoscope rolls, etc.; and fibre photographs. The tables and diagrams deal with macroscopical analysis. Includes an index.

20

LANGUAGES AND DIALECTS

SOURCE BOOKS

704. **Chemjong, Iman Singh.** Tūm Yākthūṅ nīnvāphū sāplā. Prathama Kirāta pāṭhya pustaka = Kirat primary book. Darjeeling, India : Akhil Bharatiya Kirat Chumlun Sabha, 1970. 39 p.

The Limbu community settled in eastern Nepal and Sikkim are known as Kirata because of their descent from the ancient Kirati tribe. Their language is called Limbu. This is a primary book for Kirats, written in Limbu, Nepali, and English, with reading selections in Limbu.

705. **Clark, T.W.** Introduction to Nepali : a first-year language course. Cambridge, England : W. Heffer & Sons, 1963. 421 p.

This book is designed to guide different types of students who wish to learn Nepali. It is divided into three sections. Section one is concerned with spoken Nepali. In section two, the material is selected to provide experience of both spoken and written Nepali. At the end of each chapter is a set of twenty sentences to be used as exercises. Section three presents the characters of the Devanāgarī syllabary as used in Nepali, a large number of conjunct characters are analysed to show their components separately.

706. **Das Gupta, Bidhu Bhushan** and **Karmacharya, Madhav Lal.** Nepali self-taught. Calcutta : Das Gupta Prakashan, 1964. 216 p.

A useful grammer of Nepali, the official language of Nepal. As well as Nepali, this publication gives the grammar of neighbouring tribal languages of the Himalayan regions. The authors present conversational lessons, letters, and useful vocabulary material, and this work will be useful to beginners as well as to teachers. Nepali alphabets and words with their English equivalents and Nepali pronunciation in the Romanized form are given. The authors also include some specimens of translations, passages for translation, idioms and proverbs, and notes on letter writting and correspondence. An appendix gives a list of words used commonly in Nepali.

707. **Hari, Anna Maria**, ed. Conversational Nepali. Kathmandu : Summer Institute of Linguistics, Institute of Nepal Studies, Tribhuvan University, 1971. 1 v.

The Summer Institute of Linguistics, Institute of Nepal Studies, Tribhuvan University, issued this publication so that scholars visiting Nepal converse in Nepali with local people. This publication is a revised and expanded version of two mimeographed lessons produced by the Summer Institute of Linguistics.

708. **Joshi, Achut B.** Nepali thru English. Kathmandu : Himalayan Pioneer, 1963. 169 p.

A guide to the Nepali language. English words and sentences are provided with Nepali translations (in Roman script), together with rules of the grammar. A useful publication for those who wish to get along in Nepal and do not have the time to undertake a serious study of the language.

709. **Lock, John K.** Godāvarī śabda suddhi. Godavari, Nepal : St. Xaviers School, 1968. 22 p.

At Godavari, in Nepal, is the famous St. Xaviers School. The principal of this school compiled this list to help students to overcome a problem that Nepali has in common with other Eastern dialects. In writing, the Sanskrit orthography and alphabet are used, but phonetics have greatly deviated from Sanskrit. As a result, the average person will commit mistakes in writting his own language. This book is a guide to writing Nepali words correctly, especially for those who do not know Sanskrit. There is a general trend towards simplifying spelling, and one result of this has been the introduction of unscientific words. This book intends to put a check to the introduction of such unscientific words.

710. **Magar, Keshar Jung Baral**. Magara kurā kūṭa jāṭma ṅākke? = Magara bhāshā kasarī bolne? Kathmandu : Suresh Ale, 1980. 91 p.

A beginner's text book of conversational Magar, a Tibeto-Burman language spoken in some parts of Nepal This book will also help visiting scholars who want to do research on people in Magar-speaking areas, but who have no knowledge of Magar language.

711. **Pradhan, Indramani**. An introduction to the Nepali vowel and consonant sounds. Darjeeling, India : The Author, 1969. 31 p.

A brief introduction for those who want to learn Nepali.

712. **Robers, G.G.** Colloquial Nepali. Calcutta, Thacker Spink, 1950. 124 p.

This book was compiled from notes prepared by the author when he was employed as a Nepali instructor with the Gurkha Brigade during the Second World War. The book aims to present the student with a simple form of the language as spoken in eastern and western Nepal, that is, a pure form of the language as used by the young soldier or recruit in any Gurkha regiment. Includes a Nepali to English vocabulary.

713. **Shafer, Robert**, ed. Bibliography of Sino-Tibetan languages.

For full entry refer to Bibliographies section.

714. **Shastri, Shukraraj**. Nepālabhāshā-vyākaraṇa. Calcutta : The Author, 1928. 256 p. bibliog. (Śrīcandragranthamālā, 1)

The origins of the Newari language (Nepalabhasha) are uncertain, but it hasbeen strongly influenced by the Tibeto-Burman languages, particularly in its phonology. This work is divided into chapters corresponding to the topics in a full-fledged Sanskrit grammar, but it is arranged according to a Western system. The author examines the phonology in terms of the Sanskrit alphabet, but is not concerned with Newari as it is actually spoken. Although this book is not very thorough from a research point of view, it is very useful for anyone who wants to learn the language.

715. **Shrestha, Chij K.** and **Karki, Tika B**. Basic course in spoken Nepali. Rev. and enl ed. Kathmandu : The Authors [1980 ?]. 279 p. bibliog.

A book written for foreigners who want to learn Nepali. The material is based on spoken Nepali. There are regional variations in spoken Nepali as well as in its grammar, and so the authors have chosen the usages which in their experience and knowledge, appear to be most common.

716. **Sresthacharya, Iswaranand** [et al]. Conversational Newari. Kathmandu : Summer Institute of Linguistics, Institute for Nepal Studies, Tribhuvan University, 1971. 245 leaves.

This book, intended mainly for foreign scholars who want to learn Newari, is the first part of a language course in Newari. The emphasis is on the rudiments of grammar, especially the morphology of nouns and verbs. The dialect presented is that of Kathmandu, it differs considerably, both phonologically and lexically, from that of Bhaktapur. This mimeographed publication has two appendixes: 'Conversation in Devanagari' and 'Glossary'.

717. **Subba, B.B.** and **Subba, P.S.** Yākthuṅ huhāsi = Limbu self-taught. Gangtok, India : Text Book Unit, Directorate of Education, Government of Sikkim, 1978. 88 p.

An introduction to the Limbu language for the beginners, using Limbu, English, and Nepali texts to aid interpretation and comprehension. This textbook can also be used as general reading material. The presentation of phonetical expressions, linguistic and grammatical forms and a vocabulary list has amplified to the usefulness of this book.

718. **Thapar, Udhir Samsher.** Know Nepal and Nepali.

For full entry refer to Tourism & Travellers' Accounts—Guidebooks section.

719. **Verma, M.K.** and **Sharma, T.N.** Intermediate Nepali reader. New Delhi : Manohar, 1979. 186 p.

This is volume two of a set and is intended to be used in conjunction with its companion volume, *Intermediate Nepali structure* (see the following item). This reader contains lessons which present reading passages, graded in terms of language complexity and selected in terms of style. The purpose is to expose students to writings on various subjects in different styles and to introduce the language, people, and culture of Nepal. At the end of the book is a consolidated dictionary of all the words used in the lessons. Tape lessons are included both the reader and the structure guide.

720. **Verma, M.K.** and **Sharma, T.N.** Intermediate Nepali structure. New Delhi : Manohar, 1979. 227 p.

This is volume one of a two-volume set that provides a comprehensive packet of instructional materials for students who have completed a first-year course in basic Nepali. It is intended to be used in conjunction with its companion volume, *Intermediate Nepali reader* (see the preceding item) and is designed to enable students to attain fluency in the grammatical structure of Nepali. It presents the crucial aspects of the structure of Nepali. To strengthen the usefulness of these volumes further, two sets of tapes are provided: one for the volume on structure and one for the reader.

DICTIONARIES

721. **Bajracharya, Adi Bajra**. Nigūgu paryāyavācī kosha. Kathmandu : Basant Raj Tuladhar, 1980. 78 p.

A very useful dictionary of Newari synonyms.

722. **Chemjong, Iman Singh**. Rōṅ-Lūṃ-Mikdum-riṅkō = LāpacāNepālī-Angrejī śabdakośa = Lepcha-Nepali-English dictionary. Kathmandu : Cultural Department, Royal Nepal Academy, 1969. 340 p.

Lepcha belongs to Tibeto-Burman family of languages and is spoken by Lepcha tribe in the Ilam District of east Nepal, Darjeeling, Kalimpong, Sikkim, and Bhutan. This dictionary of Lepcha gives meanings in Nepali and English.

723. **Chemjong, Iman Singh**. Yākthuṅ-Pene Mikphulāpan-chekā = Limbū-Nepālī-Aṅgarejī-śabda-kośa = Limbu-Nepali-English-dictionary. Kathmandu : Nepal Academy, 1962. 58, 376 p.

The Limbu community settled in eastern Nepal and Sikkim are known as the Kirata because of their descent from the ancient Kirati tribe. They have their own language called Limbu. This dictionary of Limbu language gives meanings in Nepali and English. It also includes some information on their social life.

724. **Dixit, Narendra Mani Acharya,** ed. Aṅgrejī Nepālī Sājhā saṅkshipta śabdakośa. Kathmandu : Sajha Prakashan, 1976. 644 p. bibliog.

An English-Nepali dictionary.

725. **Glover, Warren W.** [et al]. Gurung-Nepali-English dictionary, with English-Gurung and Nepali-Gurung indexes. Canberra : Department of Linguistics, Researeh School of Pacific Studies, Australia National University, 1977. 316 p. bibliog. (Pacific Linguistics, Series C, no. 51)

Gurung belongs to the Tibeto Burman group of languages. This dictionary of Gurung gives Nepali and English meanings.

726. **Gorkhali, Chandra Prasad.** Vijñāna-śabdāvalī, Aṅgrejī-Nepālī = A glossary of scientific terms, English-Nepali. Kathmandu : Royal Nepal Academy, 1979. 50 p.

This glossary, the first of its kind in Nepal, is intended to further the use of Nepali in education at all levels.

727. **Gurung, Chitra Kumar** and **Nyaupane, Kedar.** Prāvidhika śabdārthāvalī. = Technical vocabulary. Kathmandu : Tribhuvan University, Institute of Medicine, Research Division, 1979- vol. 1.

A Nepali-English, English-Nepali technical vocabulary. This volume, the first in a series, covers medicine and basic sciences.

728. **Jorgensen, Hans.** A dictionary of the classical Newārī. Copenhagen : Levin & Munksgaard, 1936. 178 p.

Newari (Nepalabhasa) is the language spoken by the Newars, who are the original inhabitants of the Kathmandu Valley. This dictionary is a considerably enlarged and improved edition of the author's *Versuch eines Worterbuches der Nevārī-Sprache*. It will be very helpful to anyone wishing to translate works in Newari or to study Tibeto-Burmese comparative philology. Classical Newari is the language used in ancient manuscripts as opposed to modern spoken Newari, which is somewhat different.

729. **Joshi, Panna Prasad.** Saṅkshipta Nepāla Bhāshā śabda-kośa. Kathmandu : Ratna Prasad Joshi, 1956. 283 p.

This compact Newari-Nepali dictionary is based on the modern Newari language spoken in the Kathmandu Valley. It does not cover words from mediaeval Newari literature even though modern Newari authors use ancient and mediaeval Newari terms, and so in a real sense this book is only partially useful. This book has an appendix having additional words and meanings. In the same year, the author also issued a separate thirty-nine-pages supplement to update this work.

730. **Joshi, Satya Mohan.** Satya-kośa : Aṅgreja bhāy-Nevā bhāy. Kathmandu : Hemant Raj Joshi, 1979. 88 p.

A concise dictionary of English-Newari.

731. **Kotapish, Carl** and **Kotapish, Sharon.** A Darai-English, English-Darai glossary. Assisted by Antaman Darai and Tul Bahadur Darai. Kathmandu : Summer Institute of Linguistics, Institute of Nepal and Asian Studies, Tribhuvan University, 1975. 152 p. bibliog.

Darai belongs to the Indo-Aryan languages and is the least-known language of Nepal. It is spoken only in the western hills area of the Tanhun and Palpa districts and the flat plains of Chitwan, by approximately 1600 people. The dialect studied in this book is spoken by the people of the village of Pipaltar, located along the Kali Gandaki River in Ramjakot Panchayat, Tanhu District. Includes seven appendixes on kinship, religious ceremonies, pronominal cross-reference markings in nouns and verbs, weights and measures, days of the week, months of the year, and numbers.

732. **Mainwaring, George Byres,** comp. Dictionary of the Lepcha language. Revised and completed by Albert Grunwedel. Kathmandu : Ratna Pustak Bhandar, 1979. 522 p. (Bibliotheca Himalayica, Series II, vol. 6)

A reprint of the only existing comprehensive dictionary of the Lepcha language, which is spoken in the border towns of Nepal, Darjeeling, and the Sikkim hills. It is based on material collected by the compiler during the 1870s and 1880s, but the final editing was done under the supervision of Dr. Albert Grunwedel. The book was first published by Unger Bros., Berlin, in 1898 by the order of H.M.'s Secretary of State for India.

733. **Nanda, Ishwara.** Dhukū pikū, Nepāla Bhāsāy mukka kriyāyā dhukū = The Nepal bhasha-verbs. Kathmandu : Sudha Devi [1963?]. 209 p.

Nepalabhasha is the name for Newari, the language of Newars. This is a dictionary of Newari verbs.

734. **Paryavaci sabda-kosa.** Kathmandu: Royal Nepal Academy, 1973. 186 p. 30 maps.

Fourteen languages are spoken by different ethnic groups in Nepal, and the individual languages are not spoken exclusively in particular localities. So there is much bilingualism or multilingualism in Nepal. Though the government of Nepal has only recognized Nepali, an Indo-Aryan language, as the official language of the state, they have accorded due place to other languages. This multilingual vocabulary attempts to make these languages understandable to one another. It is not a full-fledged dictionary, but rather a vocabulary of words, taking the Nepali as the base. Apart from Nepali the languages covered are Chepang, Gurung, Lepcha, Limbu, Magar, Newari, Bantawa Rai, Sunwar, and Tamang of the Tibeto-Burman group, and Bhojpuri, Danuwar, Maithili, and Tharu of the Indo-Aryan group.

735. **Pradhan, Babulal**. English-Nepali dictionary. Calcutta, A.C. Chakravarti, 1967. 696 p.

Nepali belongs to the Indo-Aryan group of languages and is the official language of Nepal. This dictionary gives English words with their Nepali meanings.

736. **Pradhan, Paras Mani**. Nepālī muhāvarā. 2nd ed. Kalimpong, India : The Author, 1960. 128 p.

Gives idiomatic expressions and phrases and their meanings, in Nepali only.

737. **Rana, Pushkar Shamsher J.B.** Nepālī ukhāna ra tukkāko, varṇakarmānusārī sūcī ra vākyaṃśa, vākpaddhati, ityadiko kosha. Kathmandu : The Author, 1941. 2 vols.

Nepali to Nepali dictionary, volume 1 includes proverbs and volume 2 includes idiomatic phrases.

738. **Sharma, Bal Chandra**. Nepālī śabda-kośa. Kathmandu : Royal Nepal Academy, 1963. 1146 p.

Includes approximately 55,000 Nepali words with their meaning in Nepali, their pronunciation and their grammatical form.

739. **Sharma, Harsha Nath**, ed. Bṛhat Nepālī śabdakosha. Biratnagar, Nepal : Nepali Sahitya Bhandar, 1966. 893 p.

A Nepali to Nepali dictionary.

740. **Shreshtha, Krishna Prakash**, ed. Saṅkshipta Aṅgreji-Nepālī pāribhāshika śabdāvalī. Moscow : Vishva Sahitya Anuvada Sansthan, 1981. 120 p.

This English-Nepali technical glossary was published in the USSR and printed in Kathmandu.

741. **Shrestha, Durga Bahadur**, comp. A guide to common terms on various subjects : English-Roman-Nepali, more than 10,000 terms. Kathmandu : The Author, 1975. 554 p. illus.

An English-Nepali dictionary.

742. **Subba, B.B.** Limbu, Nepali, English dictionary. Gangtok: Text Book Unit, Directorate of Education, Government of Sikkim, 1979. 199 p.

This dictionary is the first ever written in the Limbu script. It contains about 6,000 words of Limbu, with Nepali and English meanings. The dictionary is useful not only to teachers and students, but also to anyone interested in learning the Limbu language.

743. **Toba, Sueyoshi** and **Toba, Ingrid**. A Khaling-English, English-Khaling glossary. Editor: Austin Hale. Kathmandu : Summer Institute of Linguistics, Institute of Nepal and Asian Studies, Tribhuvan University, 1975. 86 p. bibliog.

Khaling is a Tibeto-Burman language belonging to the Rai group; it is spoken in the Solukhumbu and Khotang districts of Sagarmatha Zone, Nepal. This glossary includes Khaling words which are used in everyday speech. Not included are the majority of geographical names, onomatopoetic words, and many Nepali loan-words. There are two appendixes: Khaling kinship terms; Numbers.

744. **Tuladhar, Sugat Dass.** Nepālabhasha śabda-saṅgraha, vākya, vākyamśaya chagū pāṭhasahita = A collection of colloquial Newari words, phrases, and sentences with their equivalents in English, Nepali, and Hindi. 6th ed. Kathmandu : Himalayan Pioneer Publications, 1965. 85 p.

The *Nepalabhasa* (Newari) words, phrases, and sentences contained in this collection are mainly colloquial. The book is intended for those who know Newari and want to learn English, Nepali, and Hindi. The pronunciation of English words is also given in Devanagari script.

745. **Turner, Ralph Lilley**. A comparative and etymological dictionary of the Nepali language. 2nd ed. London : Routledge & Kegan Paul, 1965. 932 p.

The author was Professor of Sanskrit, University of London; Fellow of Christ's College, Cambridge and sometime Adjutant of the 2nd Battalion 3rd QAO (Queen Alexandra's own) Gurkha Rifles. This Nepali dictionary, which contains 26,000 entries, was first published in 1931, after the author had spent sixteen years compiling it. As well as Nepali itself, this dictionary includes indexes of words quoted from other Indo-Aryan languages (Asokan inscriptions, Assamese, Bengali, Bihari, Dardic dialects, Gujarati, Hindi, Kashmiri, Kumaoni, Lahnda, Oriya, Pali, Panjabi, Prakrit, Sanskrit, Sindhi, Sinhalese, West Pahari dialects). These indexes, comprising 48,000 entries, were compiled by the author's wife, Dorothy Rivers Turner, to enable those interested in Indo-Aryan languages other than Nepali to use the etymological material collected here.

746. **Vajra, Adi**. Chuṃ paryāyavācī kosha. Kathmandu : The Author, 1954. 58 p.

A classified dictionary of Newari synonyms with Sanskrit synonyms included in some instances. The book includes approximately 1200 words and will be useful for the general reader.

747. **Watters, David** and **Watters, Nancy**. An English-Kham, Kham-English glossary. Kirtipur, Nepal : Summer Institute of Linguistics, Institute of Nepal and Asian Studies, 1973. 126 p.

Kham is a Tibeto-Burman language spoken by about 40,000 people living in the Dhaulagiri and Rapti Zones of Western Nepal. This glossary is based on the dialect spoken at Taka, Baglung District, by about 1500 people. The glossary is introduced by a very short summary of Kham phonology and of the orthography used in spelling of the Kham entries, and a note on major phonetic variants and pronunciation. Includes three appendixes: A special class of quantities which are immeasurable in terms of specific weights and measures; locations and directionals; weight and measures.

LINGUISTIC STUDIES

748. **Acharya, Jayaraj**. Traditional grammars, English and Nepali : a study ; the influence of J. C. Nesfield's *idiom, grammar, and synthesis* on Somnath Sharma's *Madhya-*

chandrika, a middle Nepali grammar. Kathmandu : The Author, 1980. 248 p. bibliog.

An excellent empirical enquiry into the structure and content of an established textbook of Nepali grammar. The author analyses not only the influence of Nesfield as such, but also diagnose its causes. The infilteration of the Nesfield tradition into a piece of work believed to have been a popular adaptation of the Royal Preceptor's codification is revealing.

749. **Acharya, Shivaraja.** An elucidatory note on the nature of the Sanskrit long vowels. *Journal of the Tribhuvan University*, vol. 7, no. 1 (Nov. 1972), pp. 74-83.

Discusses the use of vowels in Nepali language, with Sanskrit examples.

750. **Allen, N. J.** Sewala puja Bintila puja : notes on Thulung ritual language. *Kailash : a Journal of Himalayan Studies*, vol. 6, no. 4 (1978), pp. 237-256. bibliog.

The Thulung Rai of East Nepal possess their own language and have a tendency towards endogamy. They also have their own *diumla*, which means religion, lore or custom, and this makes them a distinct social group. In this article the author discusses Thulung ritual language, its collective linguistic competence, its structure, invocations, melodic phrases, elucidation, phonology, typology, etc.

751. **Allen, N. J.** Sketch of Thulung grammar with three texts and a glossary. Ithaca, New York : China-Japan Program, Cornell University, 1975. 254 p. (Cornell University East Asia papers, no. 6/1975)

The Thulung language belongs to the Tibeto-Burman group, and is spoken around the Dudh Kosi and the Solu River in the southern part of Solukhumbu District in Nepal. There may be only 8000 speakers and they also speak Nepali. The book covers phonology, personal pronouns and verbs and gives brief comments on other parts of speech and diachronic topics. It includes texts and a Thulung-English glossary of 1600 words. The book gives detailed information about the language and is a valuable contribution to its study.

752. **Bandhu, Chuda Mani.** Karṇālī loka saṃskṛti. Vol. 4 : Bhāshā. Kathmandu : Royal Nepal Academy, 1971. 114 p. 2 maps.

This is one of several books in a series intended to portray the civilization, economic and social conditions, history, geography, etc., of Karnali. This volume deals with the language. The Sinjali dialect of Nepali is very influential in the area, particularly in the phonetics of the surrounding Tibeto-Burman languages and dialects. This dialect is scientifically studied in this book. The vocabulary is arranged by subject and classified in a more comprehensive way than Grierson's languages survey. A few mediaeval inscriptions found in the Karnali Zone and written in this dialect have been used for the historical study of the dialect.

753. **Bieri, Dora** and **Schulze, Marlene**. A guide to Sunwar tone. Kathmandu : Tribhuvan University and Summer Institute of Linguistics, 1971. 38 leaves. (Guide to tone in Nepal, pt. 4)

Sunwar belongs to the Tibeto-Burman group of languages.

754. **Bieri, Dora** and **Schulze, Marlene.** A vocabulary of the Sunwar language. Kirtipur, Nepal : Summer Institute of Linguistics and Institute of Nepal Studies, Tribhuvan University, 1971. 40 leaves. (Comparative vocabularies of languages of Nepal)

Sunwar belongs to the Tibeto-Burman group of languages. English terms are given in Sunwar (Romanized) in this vocabulary of words for everyday use. For the categories of the words, see *Comparative vocabularies of languages of Nepal : English*.

755. **A Brief introduction to Nepali language and literature.** Nepali Bhasa Samiti. Darjeeling, India : Nepali Bhasa Samiti, 1972. 19 p

Though not very comprehensive, this small book has its own importance. It has been compiled and published as a part of the movement for the official recognition of the Nepali language in India, and it presents some bibliographical information about Indian Nepali writing.

756. **Caughley, Ross** C. A vocabulary of the Chepang language. Assisted by Bhobikan Chepang. Kirtipur, Nepal : Summer Institute of Linguistics and Institute of Nepal Studies, Tribhuvan University, 1972. 40 leaves. (Comparative vocabularies of languages of Nepal)

Chepang belongs to the Tibeto-Burman group of languages. This vocabulary gives the Chepang equivalents (Romanized) of English terms and it contains words for day-to-day use. For a list of the categories of the words, see *Comparative vocabularies of languages of Nepal : English.*

757. **Chand, Geeta** [et al.]. Studies in bilingualism in Nepal. Kathmandu : Institute of Nepal and Asian Studies, Tribhuvan University, 1975. 67 p. maps. bibliog.

A survey of bilingualism and primary education in the Bara and Chitwan districts of Narayani Zone, Nepal. This is a report on pilot project no. 2 relating to a 1975 survey.

758. **Chemjong, Iman Singh.** Tūm Yākthūṅ hūppān sāplā = Kirāta byakaraṇa (Limbu) = The Kirat grammar (Limbu). Darjeeling, India : Jasahanga Maden, 1970. 66 p.

The Limbu community settled in eastern Nepal and Sikkim are known as the Kirata. They are descendants of the ancient Kirati tribe, and have their own language called Limbu. This work is a basic Kirat grammar in the Limbu language, and it also includes a chapter on invention of Kirat script. Words are given in the Limbu language, with their Romanized form in English and Nepali and with English equivalents.

759. **Clause, sentence, and discourse patterns in selected languages of Nepal.** Kathmandu : University Press, Tribhuvan University, 1970. 4 vols. (Summer Institute of Linguistics publications in linguistics and related fields, no. 40)

The publications in this series were sponsored by the Summer Institute of Linguistics of the University of Oklahoma, Norman; the editor of the series is Irvine Davis. The volumes are: 1. *General approach*, edited by Austin Hale; 2. *Clause*, edited by Austin Hale and David Watters; 3. *Texts*, edited by Austin Hale; 4. *Word lists*, edited by Austin Hale.

760. **Collected papers on Khaling, Kulunge, Darai, Newari, Chitwan Tharu.** Kirtipur, Nepal : Summer Institute of Linguistics, 1973. 87 p. (Nepal studies in linguistics, 1)

A collection of papers on some of the Tibeto-Burman languages spoken in Nepal. The contents are: The Khaling verb, by I. Toba; Kulunge Rai clause types, by A. Holzhausen; Darai cases, by S. Kotapish; Case and role in Newari, by A. Hale and T. Manandhar; Chitwan Tharu narrative introduction, by W.M. Leal; A bibliography of SIL in South Asia, by D. Hargrave and M. Hale.

761. **Collected papers on Sherpa, Jirel.** Kirtipur, Nepal : Summer Institute of Linguistics, Institute of Nepal and Asian Studies, 1973. 176 p. (Nepal studies in linguistics, 2)

A collection of four papers on Sherpa and Jirel, two of the Tibeto-Burman languages spoken in Nepal: Clause patterns in Sherpa. Vowels and tone in the Sherpa verb, by B. Schottelndreyer; Clause patterns in Jirel by E. Strahm; Report on the 1974 linguistic institute by T.R. Kansakar; A bibliography of SIL in South Asia by D. Hargrave.

762. **Comparative vocabularies of languages of Nepal : English.** Summer Institute of Linguistics. Kirtipur, Nepal : Summer Institute of Linguistics, Institute of Nepal and Asian Studies, Tribhuvan University [1971?]. 40 leaves.

Scholars from all over the world visit Nepal for research purposes and they find it difficult to communicate with the local people. With this in mind the Summer Institute of Linguistics, Institute of Nepal Studies, Tribhuvan University, decided to issue vocabularies in the different languages of Nepal. This first publication is in English and serves as a key to the series of comparative vocabularies of the languages of Nepal. Each book in the series contains a list of words under the following categories: Swadesh 100 words; Human body parts; Animals; Plants; Time, weather, geography; House and home; Food and clothing; Tools, instruments, metals; Numbers and quantifiers; Emotions, diseases, supernatural; Role and social structure; Attributes: human; matters; space, dimension, form, and motion; abstract relations; miscellaneous function words; Activities and states of human body; Activities concerning animals; Activities concerning plants and cultivation; Verbs concerning time, weather, and geography; Activities concerning house and home; Activities concerning food; Activities concerning clothing; Activities with tools and metals; Activities of the human mind and soul; Activities concerning role and social structure. Mimeographed.

763. **Comparative vocabularies of languages of Nepal : Jirel.** Summer Institute of Linguistics. Kirtipur, Nepal : Summer Institute of Linguistics, Institute of Nepal and Asian Studies, Tribhuvan University [1971?]. 18-40 leaves.

Jirel belongs to the Tibeto-Burman group of languages. English terms are given in Jirel (Romanized) in this vocabulary of words for day-to-day work. For the categories of the words, see *Comparative vocabularies of languages of Nepal : English.*

764. **Fisher, James F.** A vocabulary of the Kaike language. Assisted by Tagla Tsering Budha. Kirtipur, Nepal : Summer Institute of Linguistics and Institute of Nepal Studies, Tribhuvan University, 1971. 25 leaves (Comparative vocabularies of languages of Nepal)

The Kaike language (dialect), or Terali Kham as it is called in Nepali, is a Tibeto-Burman dialect spoken (but never written) in only three villages and it is not mutually intelligible with any of the Tibetan or Magar dialects spoken elsewhere in Nepal. Tagla Tsering Budha, whose mother-tongue is Kaike, supplied all the words for this work. Equivalents of English terms are given in Kaike (Romanized) and this vocabulary contains approximately 1000 Kaike terms for day-to-day conversation. For the categories of the words, see *Comparative vocabularies of languages of Nepal : English.*

765. **Glover, Warren William.** Sememic and grammatical structures in Gurung (Nepal). Kirtipur, Nepal : Summer Institute of Linguistics, 1974. 232 p. maps. (Publications in linguistics and related fields - Summer Institute of Linguistics, no. 49)

Gurung is a Tibeto-Burman language spoken in central Nepal. This publication was originally the author's thesis, submitted to the Australian National University in 1973. The book was sponsored by the University of Oklahoma, Norman.

766. **Glover, Warren William.** A vocabulary of the Gurung language. Assisted by Deu Bahadur Gurung. Kirtipur, Nepal : Summer Institute of Linguistics and Institute of Nepal Studies, Tribhuvan University, 1972. 40 leaves. (Comparative vocabularies of languages of Nepal)

The Gurung language belongs to the Tibeto-Burman group of languages. The Gurung forms presented here were supplied chiefly by Deu Bahadur Gurung of Ghachok Village, Kaski District, Nepal. English terms are given in Gurung (Romanized), and this vocabulary contains words for day-to-day work. For the categories of the words, see *Comparative vocabularies of Languages of Nepal : English.*

767. **Glover, Warren William** and **Glover, Jessie.** A guide to Gurung tone. Kathmandu : Tribhuvan University and

Summer Institute of Linguistics, 1972. 34 leaves. (Guide to tone in Nepal, pt. 6)

A tone guide to one of the Tibeto-Burman languages of Nepal.

768. **Gupta, Sagar Mal** and **Tuladhar, Jyoti.** Dative subject constructions in Hindi, Nepali, and Marathi and relational grammar. *Contributions to Nepalese Studies*, vol. 7, no. 1-2 (Dec. 1978-June 1980), pp. 119-153. bibliog.

Attempts to present a systematic description of Dative Subject Construction (DSC) in Hindi, Nepali, and Marathi. In the first section the authors discuss verbs of sense-perception, verbs of mental and emotional experiences, verbs denoting health conditions, and verbs obligatorily taking Dative Subject Construction. In the second section, they investigate some of the semantic and pragmatic properties of DSC. In the third section, they discuss some syntactic processes of DSC in all the three languages, and in the last section, they comment on Relational Grammar, suggesting a solution of DSC within the framework of Relational Grammar.

769. **Hale, Austin** and **Shresthacharya, Iswaranand.** Is Newari a classifier language? *Contributions to Nepalese Studies*, vol. 1, no. 1 (Dec. 1973), pp. 1-21.

This paper looks at Newari in the light of Joseph Greensberg's study, with a view to determine whether Newari can be considered as a classifier language, and if so, upon what basis. In section one, the authors review various evidence that might be misused to lead to an affirmative answer to the question. In section two, the authors present evidence that supports an affirmative answer using Greensberg's criteria. In section three, the authors try to give a representative sample of the true classifier of Newari.

770. **Hale, Margrit** and **Hale, Austin.** A vocabulary of the Newari language. Kirtipur, Nepal : Summer Institute of Linguistics and Institute of Nepal Studies, Tribhuvan University, 1971. 40 leaves. (Comparative vocabularies of languages of Nepal)

The Newari language is also known as *Nepalabhasha*. Most people accept that it belongs to the Tibeto-Burman group of languages, although this is still a debated question. This vocabulary contains Newari words (Romanized), that are useful in day-to-day life. For the categories of the words, see *Comparative vocabularies of languages of Nepal : English.*

771. **Hari, Anna Maria.** A guide to Tamang tone. Kathmandu : Tribhuvan University and Summer Institute of Linguistics, 1970. 36 leaves. (Guide to tone in Nepal, pt. 1)

Tamang belongs to Tibeto-Burman group of languages. This book is one of a series of tone guides published by the Summer Institute of Linguistics and Tribhuvan University, to help visitors deal with Nepalese languages.

772. **Hari, Anna Maria.** A guide to Thakali tone. Kathmandu : Tribhuvan University and Summer Institute of Linguistics, 1971. 48 leaves. (Guide to tone in Nepal, pt. 2)

Thakali is a Tibeto-Burman language spoken in the Dhaulagiri Zone of western Nepal. This book is one of a series of tone guides published by the Summer Institute of Linguistics and Tribhuvan University, to help visitors deal with Nepalese languages.

773. **Hari, Anna Maria.** Tentative systemic organization of Nepali sentences. Kirtipur, Nepal : Summer Institute of Linguistics, Institute of Nepal Studies, Tribhuvan University, 1972. 62 p.

A rather specialized study of sentences in Nepali.

774. **Hari, Anna Maria,** ed. A vocabulary of the Nepali language. Kirtipur, Nepal : Summer Institute of Linguistics, Institute of Nepal Studies, Tribhuvan University, 1971. 34 leaves. (Comparative vocabularies of languages of Nepal)

In order to help foreign visitors, the Summer Institute of Linguistics, Institute of Nepal Studies, Tribhuvan University, decided to issue vocabularies in the different languages of Nepal. They first of all issued *Comparative vocabularies of languages of Nepal : English*, to serve as a key to the series. This vocabulary contains the same words in Nepali, in the same sequence as those listed in *Comparative vocabularies of languages of Nepal : English.* It presents the Nepali equivalents (in Devanagari script) of English words.

775. **Hari, Anna Maria.** A vocabulary of the Thakali language. Kirtipur, Nepal : Summer Institute of Linguistics and Institute of Nepal Studies, Tribhuvan University, 1971. 40 leaves. (Comparative vocabularies of languages of Nepal)

Thakali belongs to Tibeto-Burman group of languages. This book contains Romanized Thakali equivalents of English terms. The vocabulary presents words useful for day-to-day work. For the categories of the words, see *Comparative vocabularies of languages of Nepal : English.*

776. **Himalangue.** Kathmandu : Basudev Sharma, 1973- three number a year.

An English periodical on linguistics.

777. **Hoehlig, Monika** and **Hari, Anna Maria.** Kagate phonemic summary. Kathmandu : Summer Institute of Linguistics, Institute of Nepal and Asian Studies, Tribhuvan University, 1976. 78 p.

Kagate belongs to the Tibeto-Burman group of languages, and it is spoken by the Syuuba, a group of people from Likhu and Khimti Khola, Ramechhap District, Janakpur Zone. This study is a phonemic analysis of Kagate language.

778. **Holzhausen, Andreas.** Phonological survey report of the Kulunge language. Kirtipur, Nepal : Summer Institute of Linguistics, Tribhuvan University, 1973. 12 leaves.

Kulunge belongs to the Tibeto-Burman group of languages, and it is spoken in Solukhumbu and Sankhuwasabha districts of Nepal.

779. **Hugoniot, Richard D.,** ed. A bibliographical index of the lesser known languages and dialects of India and Nepal.

For full entry refer to Bibliographies section.

780. **Journal of the Tribhuvan University** : special linguistic number. Kirtipur, Nepal : Tribhuvan University, [1968?]. 160 p.

Contains five articles: Three Gurung equivalents of English be by W. W. Glover; Structure and function in the Gurung interrogative by J. R. Glover; Tamang weaving by D. Taylor; Some dimensions of contrast in Sherpa phonology by A. Hele; and An introduction to transformational studies of the English comparative by A. Hale.

781. **Kansakar, Tej R.** Linguistic survey of Nepal : a proposal. *Journal of the Tribhuvan University*, vol. 7, no. 1 (Nov. 1972), pp. 35-48.

Discusses the needs for linguistic survey and research in Nepal.

782. **Kansakar, Tej R.** Linguistics and the study of Newari language. *Journal of the Tribhuvan University*, vol. 7, no. 1 (Nov. 1972), pp. 49-58.

A brief linguistic description of Newari phonology and grammar.

783. **Kansakar, Tej R.** Rhythm and intonation in colloquial Newari. *Contributions to Nepalese Studies*, vol. 5, no. 1 (Dec. 1977), pp. 1-14.

Since rhythm is an important factor in the intelligibility of speech, in the first part of this paper the author briefly examines the nature and function of rhythm in Newari, based on his own speech as a native speaker of the language. Intonation consists of the non-segmental or suprasegmental features of speech. In the second section, the author has briefly discussed the nature of intonation patterns in Newari and how they relate to syntactic units such as clauses and sentences.

784. **Kotapish, Carl** and **Kotapish, Sharon.** A vocabulary of the Darai language. Kirtipur, Nepal : Summer Institute of Linguistics, Institute of Nepal and Asian Studies, Tribhuvan University, 1973. 40 leaves. (Comparative vocabularies of languages of Nepal)

The Darai language belongs to the Indo-Aryan group of languages, and is spoken in the Tanhun and Chitwan districts of Nepal. This is a vocabulary of Darai in Roman script. The vocabulary presents words useful for day-to-day work. For the categories of the words, see *Comparative vocabularies of languages of Nepal : English*.

785. **Kuegler, Klaus P.** and **Kuegler, Doris.** Danuwar Rai phonemic summary. Kathmandu : Summer Institute of Linguistics, Institute of Nepal and Asian Studies, Tribhuvan University, 1974. 91p.

The Danuwar Rai language belongs to the Indo-Aryan languages group. It is spoken in the Makwanpur and Sindhuli districts of Nepal.

786. **Leal, Dorothy.** Chitwan Tharu phonemic summary. Kirtipur, Nepal : Summer Institute of Linguistics and Institute of Nepal Studies, Tribhuvan University, 1972. 40 leaves. (Nepal Indo-Aryan series, 1)

An examination of the dialect spoken in and around Devauli Village, near Bharatpur, Chitwan District. The dialect belongs to the Indo-Aryan group.

787. **Leal, Dorothy.** A vocabulary of the Tharu language. Kirtipur, Nepal : Summer Institute of Linguistics, Tribhuvan University, 1973. 40 leaves.

A vocabulary of Tharu, an Indo-Aryan language spoken in the Chitwan District of the Narayani Zone of Nepal. The vocabulary presents words useful for day-to-day work. For the categories of the words, see *Comparative vocabularies of languages of Nepal : English*.

788. **Linguistics of the Tibeto-Burman Area.** Berkeley, California : Department of Linguistics, University of California. 1974- semiannual.

A journal devoted to linguistic studies of languages either in the Tibeto-Burman family or in the Tibeto-Burman linguistic area.

789. **Malla, Kamal Prakash.** Linguistic archaeology of the Nepal Valley : a preliminary report. *Kailash : a Journal of Himalayan Studies*, vol. 8, no. 1-2 (1981), pp. 5-23. bibliog.

The author attempts to assign non-Sanskritic nominals to the Tibeto-Burman sub-family of the Sino–Tibetan family of languages, mainly by tracing some of the roots to the Bodic division. He also tries to show the relationship between these nominals and the modern Newari language. The other major aim of the paper is to explore the possibilities of using linguistics as an instrument for the study of the prehistory of the Nepal Valley. The non-Sanskrit nominals are documented here as evidence of the 'Kirata Period' in ancient Nepalese history, for which there is as yet no archaeological evidence other than mediaeval chronicles.

790. **Malla, Kamal Prakash.** Linguistic studies in Nepal. *Vasudha*, vol. 15, no. 5 (Dec. 1974-Jan. 1975), pp. 17-24.

A summary of linguistic studies since 1912 in Nepal.

791. **Malla, Kamal Prakash** and **Kanaskar, Tej R.**, ed. Occasional papers in the humanities and social sciences. Kathmandu : Institute of Humanities and Social Sciences, Tribhuvan University, 1978. 157 p. illus.

A collection of highquality research papers written specially for this publication. The contents are: The British approach to the teaching of phonetics by Tej R. Kanaskar; Literary heritage of Nepal by Ram Niwas Pandey; Nepal : the politics of nomination by Lok Raj Baral; Systems derivative : input output analysis by Dharma Bahadur Shakya; Nature of society in John Dewey and Josiah Royce by Premlata Ghimire; The part Gandhi played in provoking communal tensions by Prem Uprety ; The spatial diffusion of public policy innovations in the United States : modelling the diffusion process and its empirical validation by Bal Kumar K.C.; Taxation and development finance in Nepal by S.K. Singh; Katherine Mansfield the feminist by Indira Shrestha; Diaglossomania in Nepali English, by Ramesh Shrestha.

792. **Mazaudon, Martine.** Consonantal mutation and tonal split in the Tamang sub-family of Tibeto-Burman. *Kailash : a Journal of Himalayan Studies*, vol. 6, no. 3 (1978), pp. 157-179. map.

It is assumed that a language is either entirely tonal or is not, and that tonal languages have always been and will always be tonal. These are fallacies. The Tibeto-Burman languages of Nepal described in this article are semi-tonal or marginally tonal. They also exemplify how languages can become tonal from being non-tonal, or, can become more tonal from being slightly tonal. The eight languages or dialects are Risiangku, Sahu, Taglung, Tukche, Marpha, Syang, Ghachok, and Manang. These belong to the Tibeto-Burman family of Sino-Tibetan languages, according to the classification of Robert Shafer.

793. **Meerendonk, M.** Basic Gurkhali grammar. 3rd rev. ed. [London] : The Author, 1964. 277 p. (Distributed by Bailey Bros. & Swinfen, London).

Gurkhali is an earlier name for Nepali, the official language of Nepal. The Gurkhali language belongs to the Indo-Aryan, or Sanskrit, family of languages, and it has much in common with Hindi. This book, in Roman script, deals with Gurkhali grammar. The orthography in this book is the standard form of Roman Gurkhali; it was devised by the author, a major in the Royal

Army Educational Corps, for the British army in 1948 and adopted for practical purposes after consultation with the School of Oriental and African Studies of the University of London. The book was first published in 1949.

794. **Michailousky, Boyd** and **Mazaudon, Martine.** Notes on the Hayu language. *Kailash : a Journal of Himalayan Studies*, vol. 1, no. 2 (1973), pp. 135-152.

The authors discuss the Hayu language as spoken in the village of Murajor, Sukajor Village panchayat. The Hayu language belongs to the Tibeto-Burman family of languages and appears to be closely related to the 'Rai' language of Nepal. This study covers word and syllable structure, vowels, initial consonants, final consonants, word, medial consonant-combinations, and residue.

795. **Nepalarajakiya-Virapustakalayasthahastalikhitapustakanam brhatsucipatram.**

For full entry refer to Libraries and Museums section.

796. **Proceedings of the First Symposium of Nepali and German Sanskritists, 1978.** Dang, Nepal : Institute of Sanskrit Studies, Tribhuvan University ; Kathmandu : Nepal Research Centre, 1980. 172 p.

This symposium was held between 17-22 October 1978, as a joint venture between the Institute of Sanskrit Studies, Tribhuvan University, and the Nepal Research Centre in Kathmandu. Its chief aim was to create a platform by means of which Nepali and West German Sanskritists could exchange information and ideas on certain problem areas in the field. The papers are chiefly on Sanskrit language, literature and history, and on the antiquity of Nepal. They are written in English and Sanskrit. The work includes five leaves of plates showing Hindu gods in various temples of Nepal.

797. **Reinhard, Johan** and **Toba, Tim.** A preliminary linguistic analysis and vocabulary of the Kusunda language. Kirtipur, Nepal : Summer Institute of Linguistics and Tribhuvan University, 1970. 31 leaves.

A study of a little-known language spoken in scattered places in central and western Nepal.

798. **Schmidt, Ruth L.** The Nepali system of honorific registers. *Kailash : a Journal of Himalayan Studies*, vol. 4, no. 3 (1976), pp. 213-226.

Like Bengali language there are three grades of address forms in Nepali, corresponding to the three second person pronouns : *tā̃*, *timī, and tapāī*. *Tā* is a low grade honorific, *timī*, a middle grade honorific, *tapāī*, a high grade honorific. A survey was conducted in Kathmandu about the use of these address forms and this article presents the results of the survey.

799. **Schottelndreyer, B.** and **Schottelndreyer, H.** A vocabulary of the Sherpa language. Kirtipur, Nepal : Summer Institute of Linguistics and Institute of Nepal Studies, Tribhuvan University, 1971. 18 leaves.

Sherpa belongs to the Tibeto-Burman group of languages. English terms are given in Sherpa (Romanized) in this vocabulary of words for day-to-day use. For the categories of the words, see *Comparative Vocabularies af Languages of Nepal : English*.

800. **Schoettelndreyer, Heiderose.** A guide to Sherpa tone. Kathmandu : Tribhuvan University and Summer Institute of Linguistics, 1971. 46 leaves. (Guide to tone in Nepal; pt. 5)

The Sherpa language belongs to Tibeto-Burman group of languages. This book is one of a series of tone guides published by the Summer Institute of Linguistics and Tribhuvan University, to help visitors deal with Nepalese languages.

801. **Schulze, Marlene** and **Bieri, Dora**. Chaining and spotlighting : two types of paragraph boundaries in Sunwar. Kirtipur, Nepal : Summer Institute of Linguistics and Tribhuvan University, 1971. 26 leaves.

A rather specialized study of Sunwar, a language of the Tibeto-Burman group.

802. **Seaward, Larry L.** and **Hale, Austin**. Index to word lists and comparative vocabularies. Kirtipur, Nepal : Summer Institute of Linguistics, Institute of Nepal and Asian Studies, Tribhuvan University, 1974. 25 p. bibliog. (Comparative vocabularies of languages of Nepal)

Scholars from all over the world visit Nepal for research purposes and they find it difficult to communicate with the local people. With this in mind, the Summer Institute of Linguistics and Institute of Nepal and Asian Studies, Tribhuvan University, decided to issue the series *Camporative Vocabularies of Nepal.* These vocabularies contain words from the different languages of Nepal, to enable the visitor to deal with everyday affairs. This publication is an English index, alphabetically arranged, to the word-lists and vocabularies published by the Summer Institute of Linguistics.

803. **Senior, H. W. R.,** comp. A vocabulary of the Limbu language of eastern Nepal. Reprint. Kathmandu : Ratna Pustak Bhandar, 1977. 86 p. (Bibliotheca Himalayica, series II, vol. 13)

This book was first printed in 1908. Limbus are among the oldest recorded populations of Nepal and their features indicate that they are descendants of early Tibetan settlers of Nepal. They speak the Limbu language, which belongs to the Tibeto-Burman family. This book is a vocabulary of the Limbu language, and it includes numerals and some useful sentences at the end.

804. **Shakyavansha, Hemaraj**. Nepāla lipi saṅgraha, or, a collection of Nepalese alphabets. 2nd ed. Kathmandu, Mandas & Sugatdas, 1957. 40 p.

The author is an authority on the subject. The first edition of this book contained Devanagari equivalents only, but this edition has both Devanagari and Roman equivalents. The alphabets presented in this book are almost all the alphabets discovered so far in ancient and modern Nepali books, inscriptions, and other sources. These are: Ranjana, Bhujinmol, Kunmol, Kwanmol, Golmol, Pachumol, Himol, and Litumol. Also included are: the alphabet currently used in Nepal; miscellaneous alphabets in Nepalese book and inscriptions; and Kutakshar, a monogram type of Ranjana alphabet. This book will be of great help to those undertaking research on Nepal.

805. **Sharma, Mohan Raj**. Śabda-racanā ra varṇa vinyāsa : bhāshā-vaijñānika paddhati. Kathmandu : Syllabus Development Centre, Tribhuvan University, 1979. 394 p. bibliog.

An excellent Nepali-language work on morphology and orthography : linguistic approach by a very competent scholar.

806. **Shepherd, Gary** and **Shepherd, Barbara**. A vocabulary of the Magar language. With assistance from Krishna Bahadur Thapa Magar. Kirtipur, Nepal : Summer Institute of Linguistics and Institute of Nepal Studies, Tribhuvan University, 1972. 40 leaves. (Comparative vocabularies of languages of Nepal)

Magar belongs to the Tibeto-Burman group of languages. This word-list represents the Magar language as spoken in Yanchok Village, Tanhun District, Gandaki Zone. Short visits by the authors in the Palpa District, specifically the village of Arakhala, resulted in the discovery of many Magar words to replace the Nepali loan-words of the Yanchok dialect. English terms are given in Magar (Romanized). For the categories of the words, see *Comparative vocabularies of languages of Nepal : English*.

807. **Sresthacharya, Iswaranand**. Jyāpu vocabulary (preliminary report). Consultation for the English translation : Nirmal Man Tuladhar. Kathmandu : Institute of Nepal and Asian Studies, Tribhuvan University, 1976. 136 p.

The project was originally conceived as a study of certain taxonomic relations within the vocabulary of the Newari farming communities of Pāngā and NagĀĀ. The term Jyāpu was not intended as a dialect designation but rather as an occupational designation. The Jyāpus in Bhaktapur, Kathmandu. and Patan speak different dialects of Newari and this study deals only with the Jyāpus of Patan. The author list variant pronunciations of the Newari words, using a phonetic transcription. Although the pronunciation of various individual words in NagĀĀ differs from the commonly accepted Kathmandu pronunciation, the contrastive system of phonemes appears to be the same.

808. **Sresthacharya, Iswaranand**. Some types of reduplication in the Newari verb phrase. *Contributions to Nepalese Studies*, vol. 3, no. 1 (Jan. 1976), pp. 117-127. bibliog.

Reduplication is a syntactic process which is quite common in both spoken and written Newari. The author here provides a brief survey of the use of reduplication in certain constructions closely associated with the Newari verb. He distinguishes the following varieties of reduplication : reduplication of the finite forms of the verb; reduplication of non-finite form of the verb; reduplication of proverbal elements.

809. **Srivastava, Dayanand.** Nepali language, its history and development. Calcutta, Calcutta University, 1962. 145 p.

This work presents the history and development of Nepali language according to historical principles. The linguistic analysis is entirely based on author's observations from examining Nepali-language documents. After a brief introduction, the work is divided in two parts: part one deals with phonology, and part two with morphology.

810. **Strahm, Esther** and **Maibaum, Anita.** A vocabulary of the Jirel language. Kirtipur, Nepal : Summer Institute of Linguistics, Institute of Nepal Studies, Tribhuvan University, 1971. 17 leaves. (Comparative vocabularies of languages of Nepal).

The Jirel language belongs to the Tibeto-Burman group of languages. This vocabulary presents English terms in Jirel in a Romanized form. It contains words for day-to-day work. For the categories of the words, see *Comparative vocabularies of languages of Nepal : English.*

811. **Subba, Subhadra.** Bilingualism in Nepal Terai : report on a pilot project. Kathmandu : Institute of Nepal and Asian Studies, Tribhuvan University, 1975. 93 leaves. bibliog. (Studies in bilingualism in Nepal, 1)

This report is the result of field study on the bilingual situation in the eastern Terai of Nepal, carried out by the Institute. As well as studying the special characteristics of the two major languages spoken in the area—Maithili and Nepali—the attitude of the people of each language community towards the other and towards the language of the other community is also examined. Another purpose of this study is to discover what difficulties are faced by minority language speakers who have Nepali as their national language. The study should be very useful for planning and extending literary programmes in the Nepali language.

812. **Subba, Subhadra.** The medium question in Nepalese higher education.

For full entry refer to Education section.

813. **Tamsang, K. P.** Rōṅ rīṅ hrīm=A grammar of the Lepcha language. Kalimpong, India : Lyangsong Tamsang, 1978. 92 p.

The Lepcha people live around the border between India and Nepal and speak the Lepcha language, which belongs to the

Tibeto-Burman group. This is a Lepcha grammar written in a traditional fashion. This book will meet a need long felt by the Lepchas.

814. **Taylor, D.** [et al.]. A vocabulary of the Tamang language. Kirtipur, Nepal : Summer Institute of Linguistics and Institute of Nepal Studies, Tribhuvan University, 1972. 40 leaves. (Comparative vocabularies of languages of Nepal)

Tamang belongs to the Tibeto-Burman group of languages. This word-list represents the dialect of Tamang spoken in the village of Sahugaon in the Nuwakot District. English terms are given in Tamang (Romanized) form, and the vocabulary contains words for day-to-day work. For the categories of the words, see *Comparative vocabularies of languages of Nepal : English.*

815. **Tibeto-Burman phonemic summaries.** Summer Institute of Linguistics. Kirtipur, Nepal : Summer Institute of Linguistics and Tribhuvan University, 1969. vols. 1-12.

Twelve volumes of this publication have been released so far : 1. *Gurung phonemic summary* by W. W. Glover; 2. *Sherpa phonemic summary* by K. Gordon; 3. *Thakali phonemic summary* by M. Hari; 4. *Chepang phonemic summary* by R. C. Caughley; 5. *Newari phonemic summary* by Margrit Hale and Austin Hale; 6. *Sunwar phonemic summary* by D. Bieri and M. Schulze; 7. *Tamang phonemic summary* by D. Taylor; 8. *Magar phonemic summary* by Gary Shepherd and Barbara Shepherd; 9. *Sunwar phonemic summary; revised version* by D. Bieri and M. Schulze; 10. *Kham phonemic summary* by David E. Watters; 11. *Jirel phonemic summary* by Esther Strahm and Anita Maibaum; 12. *Khaling phonemic summary* by Sueyoshi and Ingrid Toba.

816. **Toba, Sueyoshi** and **Toba, Ingrid**. A vocabulary of the Khaling language. Kirtipur, Nepal : Summer Institute of Linguistics, Tribhuvan University, 1972. 40 leaves. (Comparative vocabularies of languages of Nepal)

The Khaling belongs to the Tibeto-Burman group of languages and is spoken in the Solukhumbu and Khotang districts of Sagarmatha Zone. Equivalents of English terms are given in Khaling (Romanized) in this vocabulary containing words for everyday use. For the categories of the words, see *Comparative vocabularies of languages of Nepal* : *English.*

817. **Trail, Ronald L.** [et al.]. Patterns in clause, sentence, and discourse in selected languages of India and Nepal.

Kathmandu : University Press, Tribhuvan University, 1973. 4 vols. (Summer Institute of Linguistics publications in linguistics and related fields, no. 41)

Vol. 1. Sentences, discourse, vol. 2. Clauses; vol. 3. Texts; and vol. 4. Word lists. This is a publication of Summer Institute of Linguistics of the University of Oklahoma, Norman.

818. **Troyer, Les**. Linguistics and development in Nepal. *Contributions to Nepalese Studies*, vol. 1, no. 2 (June 1974), pp. 107-118.

Believing that linguistics has an important contribution to make national progress, the former Vice-Chancellor of Tribhuvan University, Dr. Trailokya Nath Upraity, initiated a joint project with the Summer Institute of Linguistics (an international voluntary agency) to begin a serious research programme and to assist in developing linguistic facilities in Nepal. In this article the author discusses: The linguistic configuration of Nepal; some benefits gained from linguistic research; linguistic projects and programmes accomplished and in process; and linguistic projects planned for the future.

819. **Tuladhar, Nirmal M.** and **Tuladhar, Suman K.** Testing Nepali as a second language.

For full entry refer to Education section.

820. **Watters, David E.** A guide to Kham tone. Kathmandu : Tribhuvan University and Summer Institute of Linguistics, 1971. 43 leaves. (Guide to tone in Nepal, pt. 3)

A tone guide to Kham, one of the Tibeto-Burman languages of Nepal. It is spoken in the Dhaulagiri and Rapti zones of western Nepal.

821. **Watters, David E.** and **Watters, Nancy**. A vocabulary of the Kham language. Kirtipur, Nepal : Summer Institute of Linguistics and Institute of Nepal Studies, Tribhuvan University, 1972. 40 leaves. (Comparative vocabularies of languages of Nepal)

The Kham language belongs to the Tibeto-Burman group of languages. For the compilation of this vocabulary, Hasta Ram Budha of Taka Village, Dhaulagiri Zone, contributed a number of words. The vocabulary contains equivalents of English terms in Kham (Romanized) and presents words for day-to-day use. For the complete categories of the words, see *Comparative vocabularies of languages of Nepal : English*.

822. **Yadav, Ramawatar.** Generative phonology and the aspirated consonants of colloquial Maithili. *Contributions to Nepalese Studies*, vol. 4, no. 1 (Dec. 1976), pp. 77-91. bibliog.

The Maithili language belongs to the Indo-Aryan group, and is spoken by about 21 million people of Bihar, India, and the Terai of Nepal. This paper describes the aspirated consonants of Maithili in the framework of generative phonology, with examples from colloquial Maithili. The author covers the phonological inventory, aspiration, frequency, pregenerative approach, and the framework of generative phonology.

823. **Yadav, Ramawatar.** The influence of aspiration on vowel duration in Maithili. *Contributions to Nepalese Studies*, vol. 7, no. 1-2 (Dec. 1979-June 1980), pp. 1-8. bibliog.

The Maithili language belongs to the Indo-Aryan group of languages and is the second major language spoken in Nepal. This study examines the influence of post-vocalic consonants on vowel duration.

824. **Yadav, Ramawatar.** Maithili language and linguistics : some background notes. *Kailash : a Journal of Himalayan Studies*, vol. 8, no. 1-2 (1981), pp. 71-87. bibliog.

Maithili is spoken by a total of about 21 million people in the eastern and northern regions of the Bihar State of north India and the Terai of Nepal. In the past, Maithili was regarded either as a dialect of Bengali or Eastern Hindi, or as one of the three dialects of a spurious language called Bihari but now it is written in Devanagari script. Demographically, Maithili is the second most widely spoken language of Nepal and the sixteenth largest language of India. It is recognized as a distinct language and taught as such in several universities in India and Nepal. This article covers the following points: the language and the area; important works on the Maithili; the term 'Bihari'; and genetic classification. The study also includes the earliest written Maithili text.

21

LIBRARIES AND MUSEUMS

825. **Bendall, Cecil.** Catalogue of the Buddhist Sanskrit manuscripts in the University Library, Cambridge, with introductory notices and illustrations of the palaeography and chronology of Nepal and Bengal. Cambridge: University Press, 1883. 225 p.

Presents historical introduction, palaeographical introduction, excursus on two manuscripts of the 9th century A.D.

826. **Dwivedi, Pashupati Kumar.** Museum in Nepal. Kathmandu : Sushila Dwivedi, 1976. 172 p. 1 map. bibliog.

On the National Museum of Nepal, issued on the occasion of Mahendra Memorial and Constitution Day.

827. **A Glimpse of the Natural History Section of the National Museum of Nepal.** Compiled by National Museum of Nepal. Kathmandu : National Museum of Nepal, 1975. 29 p.

Describes about the collection of Natural History Section of the Museum. Includes illustrations.

828. **Journal of Natural History Museum.** Kathmandu : Natural History Museum, Tribhuvan University, 1977.

Publishes scholarly articles on plants and herbs of Nepal.

829. **Nepalarajakiya-Virapustakalayasthahastalikhitapustakanam brhatsucipatram.** Kathmandu : Bir Pustakalaya, 1960-65. 7 vols. (Purātattvaprakāśanamālā; 5-6, 9, 25, 29-30, 44)

This catalogue is in Sanskrit language. Contents: vol. 1: Astrology; vol. 2: Literature; vol. 3: Drama; vol. 4: Tantras; vol. 5: Ayurveda; vol. 6: Grammar; vol. 7: Buddhism.

830. **Sen, Siva Narayan.** The Nepal Museum. Kathmandu : Nepal Museum, 1939. 9 p.

The leaflet contains information about Nepal Museum and its collection. Includes illustrations.

831. **Talwar, Kay** and **Krishna, Kalyan.** Indian pigment paintings on cloth.

For full entry refer to Arts section.

832. **Thierry, Solange.** Le Népal dans les collections du Musée de l' Homme. *Objects et mondes,* tome 9, fasc. 1 (1969), pp. 125-142.

The purpose of this article is to offer a general survey of the Nepalese collections of the Musee de l'Homme (Ethnographical Museum in France). The first part deals with the representative quality of the ethnographic object. Second part deals with the history of the collections and a brief enumeration of their contents. Few interesting pieces are described in the light of their ethnological and sociological context. Includes illustrations.

22

LITERATURE

HISTORY & CRITICISM

833. **Baral, Ishwar.** Balkrishna Sama. *Kailash : a Journal of Himalayan Studies*, vol. 2, no. 3 (1974), pp. 189-197.

Balkrishna Sama was a typical prodigy of Nepali renaissance. He started writing verse at the age of eight and later tried his hand at painting, photography, drama and also at music. This article describes the life and works of this major force in Nepali literature giving who gave an impetus to new trends.

834. **Bendall, Cecil.** A journey of literary and archaeological research in Nepal and northern India during the winter 1884-85.

For full entry refer to History—Archives, sources, and inscriptions section.

835. **Bennett-Campbell, Lynn.** Locally produced plays as a medium of communication between village and government in Nepal. Kathmandu : Remote Areas and Local Development Department, His Majesty's Government of Nepal/UNICEF, 1974. 15 leaves. (Research-cum-Action project paper—Remote Areas and Local Development Department, His Majesty's Government of Nepal/ UNICEF, no. 8)

The main aim of locally produced plays is the rural uplift. This publication includes comments by Ferdinand E. Okada.

836. **A Brief introduction to the Nepali literature**; presented by Nepali Sahitya Sansthan on the occasion of the literary seminar held in Kathmandu from 11th June to 13th June 1963. Kathmandu : Nepali Sahitya Sansthan, 1963. 37 p.

A brief introduction to Nepali literature presented by the Nepali Literary Organization.

837. **Chhetri, Sarad.** Kehī rekhāṅkana, kehī samālocanā. Darjeeling, India : Shyam Brothers Prakashan, 1980. 103 p.

A study of some contemporary Indian Nepali authors, by an eminent poet and critic. The work outlines the latest trends in Indian Nepali literature.

838. **Goma.** Sāhityika phūlabārīka phūlaharū. Kathmandu : Bhagirath Kaphale, 1980. 133 p.

The author presents a critical estimate of some eminent Nepali poets and analyses their views on society.

839. **Hahn, Michael.** Gopadatta's Kapīśvarajātaka. *Journal of the Nepal Research Centre*, vol. 4 (Humanities) (1980), pp. 133-159.

The *Kapisvarajataka* deals with a former existence of the Bodhisattva, in which he was reborn as a king of monkeys or kapisvara. One of the main purposes of this paper is to give a short report on the studies which are being undertaken in connection with editions of the known parts of Gopadatta's work.

840. **Hridaya, Chittadhar.** comp. Jhīgu sāhitya ; Nepāla Bhāshā sāhityayā itihāsa sambandhī lekhayā saṅgraha. Kantipur, Nepal : Nepal Bhasha Parishad, 1967. 186 p. (Nepāla bhāshā saphū, no. 13).

The compiler, a well known poet who writes in the Newari language, has revived the literary traditions of Newari. This work outlines the general history of Newari literature since the late mediaeval period. In particular, it emphasises the revival movement. The book comprises eleven essays on different writers in Newari, who made an important contribution to the revival movement.

841. **Hridaya, Chittadhar.** Nepāla Bhāshā sahityayā jātaḥ. Kantipur, Nepal : Nepal Bhasha Parishad, 1971. 266 p.

The author, a respected poet and scholar of mediaeval Newari literature, was sent to prison for six years during the 1940s for propagating the Newari language. Even in the prison he prepared manuscripts for several works and completed his greatest epic *Sugata Saurabha*. The major part of the ancient and mediaeval Newari literature is forgotten. In this book, the author attempts to write the history of Newari literature from the beginning. All the aspects of Newari literature, Buddhism, Tantras, music, songs, etc., are described in this book, which is more an inventory than a criticism. This very useful source of Newari literature also provides extracts from mediaeval Newari works.

842. **Journal of the Nepal Research Centre.** Wiesbaden/BRD : Kommissionsverlag Franz Steiner GmbH, 1977-

This journal is the first one to be published by foreign scientists working in or on Nepal whose mother-tongue is not the English language. It is intended to communicate quickly the research results of the scholars working at/from the Nepal Research Centre to the Nepalese scholars and to interested general public. It also aims at republishing in the English language some of the more significant articles on Nepal, originally written in the German language which otherwise would escape the attention of Nepalese scholars. The journal also contains the English translation of outstanding articles written in the Nepali language, which because of similar reasons would escape the attention of Western scholars interested in Nepal or in Hindu and Buddhist studies.

843. **Malla, Kamal P.** Classical Newari literature : a sketch. Kathmandu : Nepal Study Centre, 1981. 81 p. bibliog.

A preliminary essay on the literature written in the older dialects of the Newari language available mostly in the manuscripts dated between ca. 1360 and 1900. Being a programmatic rather than a final statement on the nature of the literature, part of the purpose of this study is to erect a firm chronology without which no history can be attempted.

844. **Malla, Kamal Prakash.** Nepāla bhāshāya dhvānā saphūyā dhalaḥ, Ne. sam. 1020-97 = Bibliography of Nepal Bhasha, 1900-77.

For full entry refer to Bibliographies section.

845. **Mitra, Rajendra Lal.** The Sanskrit Buddhist literature of Nepal.

For full entry refer to Bibliographies section.

846. **Nepalarajakiya-Virapustakalayasthahastalikhitapustakanam brhatsucipatram.**

For full entry refer to Libraries and Museums section.

847. **Pradhan, Krishan Chandra Singh.** Nepālī upanyāsa ra upanyāsakāra. Lalitpur, Nepal : Sajha Prakashan, 1980. 375 p. bibliog.

A comprehensive, up-to-date, and scholarly study of the novelists of Nepal. The author studies various trends in modern Nepali novel writing, and provides useful bibliographical information.

848. **Pradhan, Paras Mani.** Adikavi Bhanubhakta Acharya. Kalimpong, India : Bhagya Laxmi Prakashan, 1979. 96 p. bibliog. (Makers of Nepali literature series, no. 3)

This study by an eminent Indian Nepali writer, describes the life and works of Bhanubhakta (1812-1868), called the first Nepali poet. Includes selections from Bhanubhakta's works with English translation.

849. **Pradhan, Paras Mani.** Balakrishna Sama. Kalimpong, India : Bhagya Laxmi Prakashan, 1980. 80 p. bibliog. (Makers of Nepali literature series)

Balakrishna Sama, born in 1903, is a former Vice-Chancellor of the Royal Nepal Academy, and is a well known poet and playwright. This book describes his life and works and includes a selection of Sama's poetry with an English translation.

850. **Pradhan, Paras Mani.** Kavishironmani Lekhanath Paudyal. Kalimpong, India : Bhagya Laxmi Prakashan, 1979. 80 p. bibliog. (Makers of Nepali literature series)

Describes the life and works of the Nepali poet Lekh Nath Sharma Paudyal, born in 1884. Includes a selection of Paudyal's poetry with English translation and a portrait of him.

851. **Pradhan, Paras Mani.** Mahakavi Laxmi Prasad Deokota. Kalimpong, India : Bhagya Laxmi Prakashan, 1978. 82 p. (Makers of Nepali literature series)

On the life and works of the poet, Laxmi Prasad Deokota, 1908-1959. Includes passages in Hindi and Nepali.

852. **Riccardi, Theodore, Jr.** A Nepali version of the Vetālapañcaviṃśati. New Haven, Connecticut : American Oriental Society, 1971. 206 p. bibliog. (American oriental series; v. 54)

This work was originally submitted, in a somewhat different form, as a doctoral dissertation to the Department of Oriental Studies of University of Pennsylvania in 1968. This work contains the romanized text of a Nepali translation of Kṣemendra's Sanskrit Vetālapañcaviṃśati, a book of twenty-five stories narrated by ghosts. An oral indigenous version of these stories may yet turn up in the Nepalese hills. The author also provides an annotated English translation of his version of the stories with a short but useful introduction and a grammatical sketch of the language of the manuscript. The stories are clearly, if not always elegantly, told and are not lacking in drama and humour.

853. **Risal, Ram Mani.** Nepālī kavya ra kavi. Kathmandu : Sajha Prakashan, 1974. 459 p. bibliog.

In the introductory chapter, the author outlines the whole history of Nepali poetry. He goes on to study in separate sections, epic poems, short poems, lyrics, and modern poetry, including an analysis of the latest trends. In each section, biographical accounts of all the major poets are included with bibliographical information about their works.

854. **Sharma, Nara Dev.** Kavivara Motīrāma Bhaṭṭako jīvanī. 2nd ed. Kathmandu : Sajha Prakashan, 1980. 88 p.

A biography of the Nepali poet Motiram Bhatt, 1866-1896, which was originally published in 1938. Though there are other more comprehensive writings on Bhatt, this, the first biography by one of the poet's associates has its historical value. Includes a list of the poet's works.

855. **Shreshtha, Bhagavati Prasad.** Nepāla bhāsha patra-patrikāyā jātah.

For full entry refer to Bibliographies section.

856. **Shreshtha, Dayaram** and **Sharma, Mohanraj.** Nepālī sāhityako saṃskshipta itihāsa. Kathmandu : Royal Nepal Academy, 1977. 151 p. bibliog.

Nepali literature has progressed with great strides since the last quarter of the 19th century. In the present century, modern literature of all types has developed, including fiction, plays, and poetry. This work gives a brief but thorough survey of the whole of Nepali literature, with emphasis on the modern period. The present trends, which can be divided into traditional and progressive, have been accorded a balanced treatment. An appendix includes a bibliography of important Nepali publications on the Nepali language.

857. **Subedi, Abhi.** Nepali literature : background history. Kathmandu : Sajha Prakashan, 1978. 228 p. bibliog.

Presents the background and history of Nepali literature, and will be helpful even for the Nepali readers both at the university and outside.

858. **Thapa, Himanshu.** Sāhitya-paricaya. Kathmandu : Sajha Prakashan, 1980. 308 p. bibliog.

An exhaustive introduction to Nepali literature, in the Nepali language.

TEXTS

859. **Alsop, Ian** and **Kansakar, Prem Bahadur.** A traslation of a Newari version of the Cāṇakya Sār Saṁgraha. *Kailash : a Journal of Himalayan Studies*, vol. 7, no. 3/4 (1979), pp. 247-317. bibliog.

Cāṇakya, alias Kauṭilya, was the celebrated minister of Candragupta Maurya (4th-3rd century BC). His name has become practically synonymous with diplomacy and statecraft in Indian culture. The Cāṇakya Sār Saṁgraha belongs to the class of Indian literature known to early scholars as 'collections of gnomic verses'. Cāṇakya Sār Saṁgraha is one of the richest available sources for a study of the development of mediaeval written Newari. This translation is based on the edition by Prem Bahadur Kansakar, published by Cwasā Pāsā in 1971. This edition presents, essentially unedited, the Sanskrit and Newari of an edition of 1754, along with Prem Bahadur Kansakar's rendering of the maxims inmodern Newari. They have also referred to 1693 and 1960 editions. This work is in fact a translation-cum-commentary.

860. **Asa, S. P.** Mahāsāmanta. Kathmandu : Sajha Prakashan, 1979 or 1980. 190 p. bibliog.

A novel in Nepali, based on the history of Licchavis, people of ancient India and Nepal.

861. **Deep, Dhurba Krishna.** Lines of dreams : a collection of poems. Kathmandu : Iswar Man Shrestha, 1970. 32 p.

Most of these poems were originally written in Nepali, some in Newari and a few in English. Many have been published in literary magazines and newspapers prior to this English language edition.

862. **Dharmacharyya, Dharma Aditya** and **Barua, B.M.**, editors. Recent literary researches in Nepal : two original Sanskrit manuscripts discovered. *Buddhist India*, vol. 2, no. 2 (June 1928), pp. 124-125.

This article deals with (1) Suvanta Ratnakar : an original palm leaf manuscript written in the year 1190 A.D.; (2) Chhando-Manikya-Sastra, 1421 A.D.; (3) Dharani-Sangraha-Purana; (4) Vasundhara Dharani, 1364 A.D.; (5) Karanda vyuha, etc.

863. **Diwas, Tulsi**, ed. Seven poets. Kathmandu : Royal Nepal Academy, 1975. 163 p.

A collection of poems translated from Nepali with biographical accounts of the poets and illustrations.

864. **Dixit, Mani.** Come tomorrow. Kathmandu : Sajha Prakashan, 1980. 153 p.

Based on the lives of Gurkhas in the British army, this work of fiction provides an interesting look at Nepalese history.

865. **Hridaya, Chittadhar**. Chittadhar Hridaya's Nepal bhasa short stories. Translated by Tej R. Kansakar. Kathmandu : Nepal Bhasa Parishad, 1977. 90 p. (Nepal bhasa series; 34).

Newari short stories by Chittadhar Hridaya, translated into English. The author holds a very high position in the field of Newari literature, is a well known impartial critic and story writer. He writes with a patriotic spirit and cultural pride.

866. **Hridaya, Chittadhar**. Cittadhara 'Hṛdaya'ya degaḥ. Chittadhar Hridaya's pagoda. Translated by Vaikunth Prasad Lacoul. Kathmandu : Harsha Ratna Tuladhar, 1958. 68 p.

This is a collection of seventeen poems by Chittadhar Hridaya. born in 1906, in Newari and in English translation. Poet Keshari Chittadhar 'Hridaya' holds a very high position in the field of Nepal Bhasa (Newari) literature. His work emphasises current tastes, creeds, hopes, and sympathies. These poems show Chittadhar's patriotic feelings and his immense love for his country's literature and culture. His excellent power of minute observation is clearly demonstrated by his vital and complete descriptions of nature. The translator feels that there are many words for which an exact equivalent is hard to find.

867. **Jha, Pashu Pati.** Nepālasāmrājyodayam : mahākāvyam. Hoshiarpur, India : Sita Devi, 1980. 152 p.

A Sanskrit poem, written in the court epic style, describing the history of Nepal, from the unification of the country by Prithvi Narayan Shaha Deva to the coronation of the present monarch Birendra Bir Bikram Shaha Deva. The work is a superb piece of poetry, written in elegant but easy language which embodies all the poetic embellishments according to Sanskrit poetic norms.

868. **Lall, Kesar.** Nepalese fairy tales. Illustrated by Amar Chitrakar. Kathmandu : Sahayogi Prakashan, 1978. 60 p.

869. **Malla, Kamal Prakash.** The road to nowhere : a selection of writings, 1966-1977. Kathmandu : Sajha Publications, 1979. 255 p.

These essays display the author's impatience with the modern institutions of Nepal. These cover a wide range of topics, including educational planning, the university, teaching, linguistics, personalities, journalism, autobiography, culture, the intelligentsia, literature, and book reviews. The author attacks all the post-1950 institutions: the Royal Nepal Academy, Tribhuvan University, the *Rising Nepal*, the National Education System Plan, etc.

870. **Meserth, Andrew.** Riverfork. Kathmandu : The Author, 1978. 22 p.

A collection of poems about the mountains and people of Nepal.

871. **Modern Nepali poems.** Kathmandu ; Royal Nepal Academy, 1972. 327 p.

A collection of poems by different poets, with biograpoical data.

872. **Pandey, J. Raj.** The occult seeker. Kathmandu : Sharda Prakashan Griha, 1977. 200 p.

A novel.

873. **Parijat.** Blue mimosa. Translated from Nepali by Tanka Vilas Varya, assisted by Sondra Zeidenstein. Kathmandu : Sondra Zeidenstein, 1972. 100 p.

The translation of a novel : *Śirīshako phūla* originally written in Nepali.

874. **Paul, D.** The living lion : General Amar Simha Thapa. Kathmandu : Ratna Pustak Bhandar, 1968. 1 v.

A play about the Gurkha chief of Nepal, Amar Singh Thapa. 1748?-1816.

875. **Rana, Greta.** Distant hills. Kathmandu : Sharda Prakashan, 1977. 184 p.

A novel.

876. **Rana, Greta.** Nothing greener. Kathmandu : Sharda Prakashan Griha, 1977. 68 p.

This novel traces the personal growth and development of a young Nepalese woman.

877. **Sama, Balakrishna.** Amarasiṃha : ētihāsika nāṭaka. 2nd ed. Kathmandu : Ratna Pustaka Bhandar, 1964 or 1965. 128 p.

This is a historical play based on the life of Amarsingh Thapa, 1748?-1816, who lost his life during the 1814-16 war between the Nepalese and the British.

878. **Sama, Balakrishna.** Expression after death. Kathmandu : Sajha Prakashan, 1972 or 1973. 75 p.

A collection of poems, some of which are translated from Nepali.

879. **Sama, Balakrishna.** Prahlad. Translated by Madhusudan Devcota. Kathmandu : Royal Nepal Academy, 1969? 127 p.

A play, translated from Nepali.

880. **Saymi, Dhooswan.** The eclipse. Translated from the Newari by Tejratna Kansakar. Kathmandu : Vasudha Saymi, 1967. 203 p.

The translation of a novel, *Gaṅkī*, written in Newari.

881. **Shah, M.B.B.** A harvest of poems. Translated from Nepalese by Tirtha Raj Tuladhar. 2nd ed. Kathmandu : His Majesty's Government Press, 1964. 58 p.

An English translation of *Usaiko lāgi*, poems by Mahendra Bir Bikram Shaha Deva, Maharajadhiraja of Nepal. 1920-72. The first edition was issued in 1960 under the title : A choice of songs.

882. **Shah, M.B.B.** A harvest of poems. Translated from Nepalese by Tirtha Raj Tuladhar. Kathmandu : His Majesty's Government Press, 1964. 107 p.

English translation of *Pheri usaiko lāgi*, poems by Mahendra Bir Bikram Shaha Deva, Maharajadhiraja.

883. **Shrestha, Ramesh** [et. al]. Manas : a collection of poems. Kathmandu : The Authors, 1977. 66 p.

A collection of poems.

884. **Suyin, Han**. The mountain is young. London : Jonathan Cape ; New York : Putnam, 1958. 578 p.

The opening chapters of this novel present the western community's gossipy account of the Kathmandu political scene of the time.

885. **Vaidya, Karuna Kar**, comp. and tr. Nepalese short stories. Kathmandu : Purna Book Stall, 1971. 152 p.

English translation of eleven short stories, originally written in Nepali.

886. **Yogi, Nara Hari Nath**. Aitihāsika yatrā=Śikhariṇī yatrā. Kathmandu : Sangrah Prakashan, 1980. 36 p.

A long poem in Nepali describing the cultural history of Nepal and contextually of India also, by Yogi Naraharinath, a very learned monk of the Nātha sect of Nepal.

FOLKLORE

887. **Baidya, Karuna Kar**. Nepāyāgu pulām bākham. Kantipur, Nepal : V. R. Tuladhar, 1980. 101 p.

Newari folktales collected from oral traditions of various parts of Nepal, by a scholar engaged in research on folklore.

888. **Jangira, N.K.**, ed. Roṅ dūngit vam=Lepchā loka-gīta. Gangtok, India : Text Book Unit, Directorate of Education, Government of Sikkim, 1977. 91 p.

Lepchas stay in the bordering area of India and Nepal. They speak Lepcha language of Tibeto-Burman group of languages. This is a collection of Lepcha folk songs, collected from Darjeeling and Sikkim areas of India for the first time and published with Hindi translation and Devanagari transliteration.

889. **Kirpatrick, William**. An account of the Kingdom of Nepaul, the substance of observations made during a mission to that country in the year 1793.

For full entry refer to History—General section.

890. **Lall, Kesar.** Lore and legend of Nepal. 2nd ed. Kathmandu : Ratna Pustak Bhandar, 1965. 46 p.

Lore and legends tell about the civilization of a particular country or clan. This publication deals with the lore and legends of the Newars of Nepal.

891. **Lall, Kesar.** The seven sisters and other Nepalese tales. Kathmandu : I.M. Bajracharya, 1967. 58 p.

A collection of folk-tales of Nepal.

892. **Levine, Nancy.** The origins of *sTod-pa* : a nyinba clan legend. *Contributions to Nepalese Studies*, vol. 4, no. 1 (Dec. 1976), pp. 57-75. bibliog.

sTod-pa is one of the four villages located in the valley above the junction of the Humla Karnali and Dozam Khola and is not far from Simikot, the capital of Humla District in the Karnali Zone of northwestern Nepal. The four villages are collectively known as *Bod Yul-tsho bZhi* or *Nyin Yul-tsho bZhi*, that is the four Tibetan village districts or the four *Nyin* village districts. In 1975, lama *Drag-pa Chhos-ldan* who is from *sTod-pa's 'Khor dGon-pa* related the story regarding the origins of *sTod-pa* in Tibetan and this is translation of the legend in English.

893. **Lienhard, Siegfried.** Nevārīgītīmañjarī ; religious and secular poetry of the Nevars of the Kathmandu Valley. Stockholm : Almquist & Wiksell International, 1974. 332 p. bibliog. (Stockholm oriental series, no. 10) (Acta Universitatis Stockholmiensis)

A good collection of 100 old Newari religious poems, songs about love and marriage, epic poems, and didactic and enigmatic verses, with musical notation. The main purpose is to offer material on the thoughts of the Newars, their way of life, religious beliefs, and folklore. Most of the songs, the religious hymns as well as the folk-songs and ballads, are still very popular among Newars.

894. **Oakley, E.S.** and **Gairola, Tara Dutt.** Himalayan folklore : Kumaon and West Nepal. Kathmandu : Ratna Pustak Bhandar, 1977. 315 p. bibliog. (Bibliotheca Himalayica : series II, volume 10)

This book, first published in 1935. is the most comprehensive collection of Himalayan folklore and the first in a western language. The first section contains thirty-two legends of heroes, by Tara Dutt Gairola. These legends present a very vivid picture of the social, political, and religious life of the country during the middle ages and are useful source material for the history of that period. The second section contains folk-tales from E.S. Oakley and Pandit Ganga Dutt Upreti's collections, with a introduction and notes by Oakley. There is a introduction by Marc Gaborieau. The introduction discusses in detail certain lacunae in the first section of the book, and it serves as a guide to to the recent literature and research on the subject.

895. **Rimal, Pradip**. Karṇālī loka saṃskṛti. Vol. 5 : Sāhitya, saṅgīta, kalā. Kathmandu : Royal Nepal Academy, 1971. 118 p.

Karnali is a hilly area not much known about its natural resources as well as about its people to the outside world. This series is an attempt to bring to the light the civilization, economic, and social conditions, history, geography, etc., of that zone. This book is vol. 5 in the series and deals with the literature, music, and fine arts. The literature of this area is not a written literature of high society, it is a literature of the people. The work has representation of the main varieties of folk literature, folk songs from oral sources. Other cultural aspects of life namely folk dance of different types with a long traditional background has been described. There are important folk tales in this area and some are described in this work, though this field yet to be fully explored. Includes 17 illus.

896. **Sakya, Karna** and **Griffith, Linda**. Tales of Kathmandu : folktales from the Himalayan Kingdom of Nepal. Brisbane; Australia : House of Kathmandu, 1980. 255 p. bibliog.

A comprehensive analysis of folklore in general, as well as a thematic and structural study of Nepalese folk-tales. It draws comparisons between the genres of myth, legend, and folklore, pointing out some little known or forgotten characteristics of the latter. This work should help the reader to understand the most interesting customs and tradition of the Nepalese life-style. Each tale is illustrated with a line sketch.

897. **Some folk tales of Nepal**. Department of Culture, Nepal. Kathmandu : Department of Culture, Ministry of Information and Broadcasting, His Majesty's Government of Nepal, for the Nepal National Commission for UNESCO, Ministry of Education, HMG, 1968. 79 p.

Selected folk-tales of Nepal, published as part of UNESCO's programme of participation in the activities of its member states.

898. **Vinding, Michael.** The local oral tradition about the Kingdom of Thin Garab Dzong. *Kailash : a Journal of Himalayan Studies*, vol. 6, no, 3 (1978), pp. 181-193.

David Jackson in his article *Notes on the history of se-rib and nearby places in the upper Kali Gandaki* throws light on the importance of Thin Garab Dzong, which is now a ruin on a hill-top half a mile southeast of Thini, but was once important in the ancient Kingdom of Se-rib in the present Mustang District of Nepal. Jackson's study is based primarily on textual material from outside the area, due to the unavailability of local texts. During the author's stays in Thak Khola, he collected a few notes on the local oral tradition about the Kingdom of Thin Garab Dzong and published his findings as a supplement to Jackson's article. The local oral tradition is, for the local people, more than their history in a restricted sense, it can also serve to legtimate a past change and the world created by that change, and directly or indirectly gives people good advice about life.

23

MASS MEDIA

899. **Baral, Lok Raj**. The press in Nepal, 1951-74. *Contributions to Nepalese Studies*, vol. 2, no. 1 (Feb. 1975), pp. 169-186.

The history of the Press in Nepal actually begins with the revolution of 1950. This article describes the present conditions of the press in Nepal and also analysis the history of the press.

900. **Commoner**. Kathmandu : Commoner Alliance Press, 1957-

A daily newspaper.

901. **Devakota, Grishmabahadur**. Nepālako chāpākhānā ra patra-patrikāko itihāsa. Revised by Kashibahadur Shrestha. Kathmandu : Keshavprasad Lamsala, 1967. 651 p. bibliog.

Nepali journalism started in the real sense from India much earlier and in Nepal it started from 1950 only. This book is a comprehensive history of Nepali press and journalism starting from the beginning of the printing presses in Nepal and shows how journalism is developed in Nepal. The book also includes the complete history of struggle of freedom of the press during Rana Regime. Includes a list of periodicals issued from Nepal and on Nepal from other countries, particularly from India and Burma, arranged by subjects, giving information about title, language, frequency, place of publication, and name of the publishers. This publication, is a political mirror and very useful for research scholars as well as general reader having interest in the field of politics.

902. **Everest.** Kathmandu : Gorkha Printers, 1968- weekly.

A Pro-Chinese weekly.

903. **Foreign Affairs Journal.** Kathmandu : Bhola Bikrum Rana, 1976- three numbers a year.

A independent publication started with January/April 1976 issue.

904. **Himali, Bela.** Kathmandu : Himali Publishing House, 1970-

An independent newspaper.

905. **Jana Jagrti = Jan Jagriti.** Kathmandu : Gyanendra Man Shreshtha. weekly.

A general periodical in English and Nepali.

906. **Malla, Kamal Prakash.** The road to nowhere : a selection of writings, 1966-1977.

For full entry refer to Literature—Texts section.

907. **Motherland.** Kathmandu : Monika Press, 1958-

An independent newspaper.

908. **National Star.** Kathmandu : Star Printing Press, 1973-

A weekly on news and current affairs.

909. **Nepal Digest.** Kathmandu : Shakya Research Institute, 1971- monthly.

An independent English monthly started in March/April 1971.

910. **Nepal news.** Delhi : Royal Nepalese Embassy of India, 1961- weekly.

News about Nepal for the Indian public.

911. **Nepal Press Digest.** Kathmandu : Nepal Press Digest. weekly.

This presents the digest of articles from the Nepal press.

912. **Nepal Press Report.** Kathmandu : Regmi Research (Private) Ltd. irregular.

Translation of selected articles from the Nepal press. This was earlier published by Nepal Press Digest, Kathmandu. For sometime, this was issued with *Nepal gazette* and *Regmi Research Project, Miscellaneous reports.* Leter on this has absorbed *Regmi Research Project, Miscellaneous reports.*

913. **Nepal Review.** New Delhi : D. K. Jain, 1981- monthly.

A magazine on and about Nepal.

914. **Nepalese Perspective.** Kathmandu : Gorkhapatra Corporation, 1964- monthly.

From October 1964 to October 1971, this was a weekly publication. From November 1971, it is a monthly publication.

915. **Pen Times.** Kathmandu : Global Advertising Company.

A general periodical. Some volumes were published by Global Pen Pals, Kathmandu. A monthly publication but always issued irregularly.

916. **Regmi Research Series.**

For full entry refer to Professional periodicals section.

917. **Rising Nepal.** Kathmandu : Gorkhapatra Corporation, 1965-

A newspaper
Has maximum circulation among the English newspapers of Nepal.

918. **Vasudha.** Kathmandu : Tanka Lal Shrestha, 1959- monthly.

Publishes scholarly articles on general topics. This is a English monthly publication but not issued every month.

919. **Weekly Mirror.** Kathmandu : Mirror Printing Press, 1971-

Publishes news and current affairs. An independent weekly.

920. **Workshop/Seminar on Mass-communication.** Compiler: Nepal National Commission for UNESCO. *UNESCO Bulletin*, no. 6 (Apr. 1974), pp. 2-46.

The paper includes the following articles: 1. Role of mass-communications in a developing society, with reference to Nepal, by T.B. Khatri; 2. The communications plan, by M.R. Josse; 3. Co-ordination between mass media and development plans, by G.P. Pokharel; 4. Regional planning and mass-communication strategy, by M. Parajuli.

24

POLITICS

921. **Agrawal, H.N.** Monarchical Hindu state in Nepal. *Patna University Journal*, vol. 21, no. 1 (Jan. 1966), pp. 94-104.

The author attempts to prove that Nepal is the only Hindu kingdom in the world.

922. **Bhattarai, Muralidhar.** Culture and monarchy. Kathmandu : Pustak Bhandar [1960?]. 70 p. map. illus.

A treatise on the monarchy, with special reference to Nepal.

923. **Birendra Bir Bikram Shah Deva.** Speeches, proclamations, and messages, upto 1976. 2nd ed. Kathmandu : Department of Information, Ministry of Communications, 1977. 179 p.

Contains the speeches, proclamations, and messages of the ruling king, Birendra Bir Bikram Shah Deva, Maharajadhiraja of Nepal, born 1945.

924. **Chatterji, Bhola.** Palace, people, and politics : Nepal in perspective. New Delhi : Ankur Publishing House, 1980. 203 p.

This study is the product of a series of taped interviews the author had with Bishweswar Prasad Koirala, former Prime Minister of Nepal, over a nearly six-year period between October 1973 and July 1979. The interviews on which this book is based were conducted in Varanasi, New Delhi, Calcutta, and Patna; these are wide-ranging and reveal not only the man himself but also many facets of the complex history of Nepal since the late 1940s. The questions are candid and the answers are more so. The answers also have an autobiographical flavour is unlikely to be missed.

925. **Chatterji, Bhola**. A study of recent Nepalese politics. Calcutta : World Press, 1967. 190 p. map.

There is a dearth of authentic material describing the 1950-51 armed struggle for democracy in Nepal. The growth and development of this aspect of Nepalese history is quite fascinating as well as important. In this publication, an attempt has been made to delineate the complex patterns of contemporary Nepalese politics and to place them in proper perspective. The narrative rests on hitherto unused primary sources, particularly the experiences of the man who had been in the forefront of the struggle.

926. **Chauhan, R.S.** The political development in Nepal, 1950-70. New Delhi : Associated Publishing House, 1971. 336 p. bibliog.

A study of the revolution of 1950 and the subsequent political development up to 1970. The conflict between traditions & modernity is highlighted.

927. **Darshankar, Arjunrao Y.** Leadership in panchayati raj : a study of Beed District. Jaipur, India : Panchsheel Prakashan, 1979. 202 p. bibliog.

A study of the Bir District of Nepal. It is a revision of the author's thesis presented to Marathwada University in 1977.

928. **Goyal, Narendra.** Political history of Himalayan states : Tibet, Nepal, Bhutan, Sikkim, and Nagaland since 1947. 2nd ed. New Delhi : Cambridge Book and Stationery Stores, 1966. 179 p.

Chapters 3 to 7 deal with Nepal.

929. **Kaphley, Indra Prasad.** Fundamental bases of panchayat democratic system. Kathmandu: The Author, 1967. 242 p.

A description of the panchayat democratic system (local-government) in the light of western concepts.

930. **Karajnit, Surya Man.** Panchayat democracy. Kathmandu : Saraswati Lama [1973?]. 142 p. Available from Monal Stationery Mart, Kathmandu.

Discusses the panchayat political system in Nepal.

931. **Khanal, Yadu Nath.** Nepal in 1972 : a search for a new base camp? *Asian Survey*, vol. 13, no. 2 (Feb. 1973), pp. 211-216.

An analytical account of Nepal's domestic and foreign policy after the death of King Mahendra. The author expresses his confidence that King Birendra's genuine interest in the country's economic development is sure to bring changes in the economy.

932. **Khanal, Yadu Nath.** Nepal, transition from isolationism. Kathmandu : Sajha Prakashan, 1977. 298 p.

The reminiscences of an educationist and statesman on the recent political transformation of Nepal.

933. **Koirala, Bishweshwar Prasad.** Ājako rāshṭriya cintana : vaktavya, Sam. Su. Ā. lāī sujhāva, ra antaravārtaharūko saṅkalana. Place of publication? Madhav Mani Rajabhandari, 1980. 36 p.

A collection of statements, proposals and interviews given to Sam. Su. A., a political group, by Bishweshwar Prasad Koirala, former Prime Minister of Nepal, He discusses the controversial change in Nepal's form of government and other related issues.

934. **Kriesberg, Victor.** Rishikesh Shaha's dismal enterprise. Kathmandu : Publisher?, 1976. 22 leaves. bibliog.

A critique of '*Nepali politics, retrospect, and prospect*', a work by Rishikesh Shaha, b. 1925, a Nepalese statesman, These are originally serialized in an English language daily of Nepal.

935. **Kumar, D.P.** Nepal, year of decision. New Delhi : Vikas Publishing House, 1980. 222 p. bibliog.

This book reviews the political conditions in Nepal and the directions of policy-making. The author describes the ideology of the conservative factions and of the new political forces and their struggle, to which the author gives his intellectual and emotional support. Nepal's positive characteristics and special circumstances and the role of tradition are also stressed by the author in a plea for a balanced approach towards the future, in which he believes the basic human values and democratic principles must ultimately triumph. A chapter is devoted to Nepal's changing relations with India and China.

936. **Lohani, Prakash C.** Nepal in 1974. *Asian Survey*, vol. 15, no. 2 (Feb. 1975), pp. 96-101.

Describes Nepal's economic, political, and diplomatic performance during 1974.

937. **Mahendra Bir Bikram Shah Deva.** Proclamations, speeches and messages [of] H.M. King Mahendra Bir Bikram Shah Deva. Kathmandu : Department of Publicity, Ministry of Information and Broadcasting, His Majesty's Government of Nepal, 1967. vol. 2.

This book was first published in six volumes under the title *Pages of history*. This volume covers: Dec. 1960-1965.

938. **Malhotra, Ram C.** The system of panchayat democracy in Nepal. Kathmandu : Ministry of Information and Broadcasting, Department of Information, 1966. 11 p. (Nepal today series, no. 2).

A leaflet based on a talk delivered by the author; it first appeared in the magazine *Ramjham* and was serialized in the daily *Rising Nepal.*

939. **Malla, Kamal Prakash** and **Kanaskar, Tej R.**, ed. Occasional papers in the humanities and social sciences.

For full entry refer to Languages and Dialects—Linguistic studies section.

940. **Manandhar, Mangal Sidhi.** Geopolitical basis of Nepal's existence.

For full entry refer to Geography—General section.

941. **Mantri-patro.**

For full entry refer to Encyclopaedias, directories, and who is who section.

942. **Mohsin, M.** and **Pashupati Shumshere J.B.R.** Some aspects of panchayat system in Nepal. Kathmandu : Department of Publicity, Ministry of Information and Broadcasting, 1966. 43 p. (Nepal today series, no. 5)

A collection of articles previously published in the *Nepalese Perspective.*

943. **The Monarchy in Nepal.** 2nd rev. ed. Department of Information, Ministry of Communications, His Majesty's Government. Kathmandu : The Department, 1977. 11 p.

The roles of the monarchy, panchayat democracy and its facets are presented from the government point of view.

944. **Nepal Recorder.** Kathmandu : Nepal Press Digest (Private) Ltd., 1977- irregular.

This is translation of basic documents on the Government and economy of Nepal. This supersedes *Nepal Gazette.*

945. **Okada, Ferdinand E.** Nepalese society and the panchayat system. *Pañcāyata Darpaṇa* (*Panchayat Darpan*), no. 15, vol. 5 (1975), pp. 85-88.

Analyses the panchayat system in a socio-political context.

946. **Panta, Shamba Bhakta.** Political aspects of panchayat democracy. *Pañcāyata Darpaṇa* (*Panchayat Darpan*), no. 15, vol. 5 (1975), pp. 15-23.

Describes the panchayat system in its political context.

947. **Shaha, Rishikash.** Nepali politics : retrospect and prospect. Delhi : Oxford University Press, 1975. 208 p. bibliog.

The author's career straddles politics, administration, and academics. This book consists of three chapters which although written aud published at different time, have been carefully revised and updated for publication in this form. The first chapter is concerned with the problems of nation-building in Nepal and suggests lines along which the country should proceed in order to modernize. The second chapter deals with the organization and working of panchayat politics, and the third and final chapter focuses on Nepal's foreign policy, its international relations and internal developments in historical perspective.

948. **Singh, Khadga Man.** A retrospect on democracy : party and panchayat. Place and Publisher not known, 1980. 32 p.

The author is a political activist. In this booklet, he has analysed Nepal's experience regarding democracy.

949. **Sinha, U.N.** Panchayat democracy of Nepal : in theory and practice. Kathmandu : Department of Information, Ministry of Communications, 1972. 140 p.

An introduction to panchayat democracy and its functional units, constitution, and social aspects.

950. **Thakur, S.B.,** comp. Panchayat : an annotated bibliography.

For full entry refer to Bibliographies section.

951. **Topics on panchayat :** a collection of articles on different aspects of panchayat democracy. Kathmandu : College of Education, 1967. 36 p.

A collection of three articles: *Individual freedom and panchayat democracy* by Ganesh Raj Singh; *Economic policy of the panchayat system* by B.P. Shreshtha; and *Some problems of decentralization under panchayat democracy* by U.N. Sinha.

952. **Tuladhar, Sugat Das.** The relativity of Nepalese problems. Kathmandu : The Author, 1977. 148 p. bibliog.

Relates to internal and external problems of Nepal.

953. **Verma, Yugeshwar P.** Nepal : progress and problems, 1972-80. Kathmandu : Pratibha Verma, 1981. 198 p. bibliog.

This book has grown out of author's interest in contemporary Nepalese life. The author was a journalist and had ample opportunity to record and comment on the changes in the country from close quarters. This book is an analytical study of events in Nepal during the period 1972-80.

954. **Yatri, Purna Prakash Nepal.** Setiañcala digdarśana : vividha anusandhānātmaka vishayasamanvita.

For full entry refer to Geography—General section.

25

POPULATION

STUDIES AND HISTORY

955. **Bista, Dor Bahadur**. People of Nepal. 2nd ed. Kathmandu : Ratna Pustak Bhandar, 1972. 210 p. map. bibliog.

An ethnological study of the peoples of Nepal.

956. **Burghart, Richard**. The role of kinship in the formation of Janakpurdham pilgrim groups. *Contributions to Nepalese Studies*, vol. 2, no. 1 (Feb. 1975), pp. 71-90.

Pilgrims and devotees of the Vaisnavite cult celebrate several religious festivals throughout the year in Janakpurdham, Nepal. Pilgrims from Nepal and Bihar, India, converge on Janakpurdham to celebrate the dramatic re-enactment of the *Ram-Lila* on these occasions. Most of the pilgrims travel in groups, and the purpose of this paper is to describe the role of kinship in the formation of these groups of Maithili pilgrims.

957. **Caplan, Lionel**. Land and social change in East Nepal : a study of Hindu-tribal relations. London : Routledge and Kegan Paul, 1970. 224 p. 4 maps. illus.

This book is based on thirteen months of field-work, undertaken between 1964-65 by a professional anthropologist. This study depicts the relationship between Brahmins and Limbus, examining the deep divisions that have arisen from their historic confrontation over land and their interdependence in economic and political activities. This is the first book about the Nepalese land system and Kipat tenure written in a critical fashion by an anthropologist. The book is important and valuable not only to those engaged in professional academic studies, but also administrators, social workers, and planners.

958. **Doherty, Victor S.** The organizing principles of Brahmin-Chetri kinship. *Contributions to Nepalese Studies*, vol. 1, no. 2 (June 1974), pp. 25-41.

A brief analysis of Brahmin-Chhetri kinship and its main principles. The article is based on a field survey conducted in Pokhara and the surrounding area.

959. **Gaborieau, Marc.** Les Musulmans du Nepal. *Objects et Mondes*, vol. 6, no. 2 (1966), pp. 121-132. illus.

This article, in French, describes the status of Muslims in Nepal. Muslims are a minority in Nepal and little has been written about them.

960. **Gaborieau, Marc.** Minorités Musulmanes dans le Royaume Hindou du Népal. Nanterre : Laboratoire D' Ethnologie, 1977. 282 p. 4 maps. bibliog. illus.

Hindus and Buddhists comprise most of the population of Nepal, a small portion is Muslims. The author discusses the status of Muslims during the political changes that took place in the reign of Prithvi Narayan Shah, 1723-75. In addition, religious practice and its local variations and economic conditions are studied. The most important part of the work is part two, which reviews the social and administrative rights of Muslims. This part also discusses the laws and statutes which assigned all Muslims to one caste, and gives information on the various sub-castes within the Muslims group.

961. **Goldstein, Melvyn C.** Preliminary notes on marriage and kinship. *Contributions to Nepalese Studies*, vol. 1, no. 2 (Feb. 1975), pp. 57-69.

A brief comparison of the kinship and marriage patterns of the Helambu Sherpas with the Sherpas of Khumbu and the Tibetans of Lhasa.

962. **Gurung, Nareswor J.** An ethnographic note on Nar-Phu Valley. *Kailash : a Journal of Himalayan Studies*, vol. 5, no. 3 (1977), pp. 229-244. map. illus.

Nar-Phu Valley is the most remote part of the Manang District. There are two villages Nar and Phu, situated ten kilometres apart, with a total population in 1971 of 850. The people of Nar-Phu have their own dialect and belong to an ethnic group locally called Nar-Phuth. The data for this ethnographic study was collected during fieldwork in Manang, sponsored by the Institute for Nepal and Asian Studies, Tribhuvan University.

963. **Hall, Andrew R.** Preliminary report on the Langtang region. *Contributions to Nepalese Studies*, vol. 5, no. 2 (June 1978), pp. 51-68. bibliog.

The author provides some basic ethnographic information on the little-known Langtang region of north-central Nepal and compares and contrasts the different groups living there in terms of kinship and ritual behaviour. Includes a calender of festivals.

964. **Hofer, Andras.** A settlement and smithy of the blacksmiths (kāmī) in Nepal. *Kailash : a Journal of Himalayan Studies*, vol. 4, no. 4 (1976), pp. 349-396. bibliog. illus.

A slightly revised version of the German original, which appeared in *Archiv fur Volkerkunde*, vol. 26 (1972). The author's observations were made in 1972 during a research visit to a Tamang community. The study was sponsored by Deutsche Forschungsgemeinschaft. The blacksmiths (*kāmī*) belong to the untouchable caste. In this article the author has described the *kāmī* and their settlement, the smithy, and the technology: materials, tools, the manufacture of an axe, a hoe and a copper water jug and other products of the *kāmī*.

965. **Jest, Corneille.** The Kuswar of Chaithali (central Nepal). Translated from the French by Andrew E. Manzardo. *Contributions to Nepalese Studies*, vol. 4, no. 2 (June 1977), pp. 1-45. bibliog. illus.

The Kuswar are members of the caste of fishermen, and the Kuswar village of Chaitali consists of sixteen houses above the valley of the Sun Kosi. In this article the author examines : the origins of the Kuswar; their social organization; religious beliefs; Bote, the Kuswar divinity; the dance of Ram; Kuswar and Danuwar; and the Kuswar and development.

966. **Macdonald, Alexander W.** Essays on the ethnology of Nepal and South Asia. Kathmandu : Ratna Pustak Bhandar, 1975. 317 p. bibliog. (Bibliotheca Himalayica, Series III, vol. 3).

This is a collection of fourteen articles by the author previously published in different periodicals. Of these, only one was originally in English, the others were in French translated into

English for this publication. The articles relevant to Nepal are: The healer in the Nepalese world; The Tamang as seen by one of themselves; An aspect of the songs of the Gaine of Nepal; Remarks of Nepali sung verse; Notes on two festivals among the Tharu of Dāṅg; The heirarchy of the lower jāt in the Mukti Ain of 1955; Nepalese notes: the Jamaipurnimā and the Gosāīkuṇḍa.

967. **Manzardo, Andrew E.** [et al.]. The Byanshi : an ethnographic note on a trading group in far western Nepal. *Contributions to Nepalese Studies*, vol. 3, no. 2 (Sept. 1976), pp. 83-118. map. bibliog. illus.

The Byanshi are lesser-known trading group who live in the district of Darchula, close to the borders of Nepal, India, and Tibet. They make their living by trading wool, yak tails, salt, grain, and other commodities across the Himalayas and over the border. In the summer the Byanshi live in their traditional homeland in Byans Panchayat in the northern section of Darchula; in the winter they migrate down to Khalanga Panchayat, the district headquarters of Darchula District. In this article, the author describes the summer home; the winter home; social organization; religion and ceremonies; and continuity and change in the Byanshi. Includes a calendar of festivals.

968. **Northey, William Brook** and **Morris, C. J.** The Gurkhas : their manners, customs, and country. Reprint. Delhi : Cosmo, 1974. 282 p. map. bibliog. illus.

A reprint of a book published in 1928 by John Lane, London. It describes historical, sociological, and anthropological aspects of Nepal, and includes a chapter on the Magars and their neighbours, the Gurungs. In addition, chapter 4 by R. L. Turner, examines the languages.

969. **Schuler, Sidney.** Notes on marriage and the status of women in Baragaon. *Kailash : a Journal of Himalayan Studies*, vol. 6, no. 2 (1978), pp. 141-152. bibliog.

The data was collected from the area of Kagbeni and Muktinath panchayats in Baragaon, Mustang District, but it does not cover Cuksang Panchayat of Baragaon. The indigenous language is a dialect of Tibetan and the people in the area are Gurung and Thakuri. The culture of Baragaon is closely related to, but not identical with, that of traditional Mustang. This paper attempts to systematize some of the variables which characterize marriage relationships in Baragaon. Particular emphasis has been given to traditional legal aspects rather than to ritual details.

970. **Shrestha, D. B.** [et al,]. Ethnic groups of Nepal and their ways of living. Kathmandu : The Authors, 1975. 90 p. 2 maps. illus.

Nepal is inhabited by diverse ethnic groups, who speak different languages, hold different faiths, and have different cultures. These ethnic groups are again split into castes and sub-castes, resulting in minor variations in their ways of living, language, and culture. The study is a preliminary socio-economic history of Nepal. The first portion provides data on the following ethnic groups : Kirats, Limbu, Rais, Dhangars, Sherpas, Satars, Sunwars, Danuwars, Mooshars, Darais, Tharus, Newars, Brahmans, Thakuris, Kshatriyas, Tamangs, Chepangs, Gurungs, Magars, Thakalis, Muslims, and Matwali Chhetris. The second half of the publication covers the social conditions and customs of the population of several districts and is a geographical-cultural study.

971. **Toffin, Gerard.** The peoples of the upper Ankhu Khola Valley. *Contributions to Nepalese Studies*, vol. 3, no. 1 (Jan. 1976), pp. 34-46. map.

The Ankhu Khola Valley is located about forty-five kilometers west of Kathmandu. This article discusses settlement, population groups, hierarchy and castes of the people of the Ankhu-Khola Valley.

972. **Upreti, Bedh Prakash.** Limbuwan today : process and problems. *Contributions to Nepalese Studies*, vol. 3, no. 2 (Sept. 1976), pp. 47-70. bibliog.

The spread of education and new economic opportunities after 1950, had a tremendous impact on the traditional socio-cultural and political systems among the Brahmins and Limbu of Limbuwan, eastern Nepal. This paper throws light on socio-cultural change among these peoples after 1950, examining the background and the forces of change.

973. **Vannini, Fulgentius.** Christian settlements in Nepal during the eighteenth century. Agra, India : Distributors : Capuchin Ashram, 1977. 145 p. map. illus.

A creditable study of Christianity in Nepal. As an Italian Capuchin, the author worked for thirty-five years in the dioceses of Allahabad and Lucknow, and this book is the product of many years of study and research. Although he draws from many original documents to make this study 'scientific', it is nevertheless pleasant reading and at times even thrilling. The study also throws ample light on the history of the church in north India. Includes 7 plates of illustrations.

974. **Vansittart, E.** The tribes, clans, and castes of Nepal. *Journal of the Asiatic Society of Bengal*, vol. 63, p. 1, no. 4 (1894), pp. 213-249.

Gives information on various tribes, clans, and castes of Nepal.

975. **Von Furer-Haimendorf, Christoph**, ed. Asian highland societies in anthropological perspective. New Delhi : Sterling Publishers Pvt. Ltd., 1981. 265 p.

Expanded versions of papers present at a 1978 New Delhi seminar on the Himalayan region. There are thirteen chapters in all, of which five deal with Nepal. These cover anthropological perspectives of Thakalis, Kham Nagar, Gurangs, and Sherpas. The publication also covers The law of debt in Nepal.

976. **Von Furer-Haimendorf, Christoph,** ed. Caste and kin in Nepal, India, and Ceylon. New Delhi : Sterling Publishers, 1978. 364 p.

An anthropological study of Hindu-Buddhist contact zones.

977. **Von Furer-Haimendorf, Christoph**, ed. Contributions to the anthropology of Nepal. New Delhi : Vikas, 1977. 260 p. map. bibliog.

This monograph presents some of the proceedings of a symposium held at the School of Oriental and African Studies, University of London, June 28-July 3, 1973. There were five participants from Nepal, seven from the UK, six from the USA, four from France, six from Germany, and two from Sweden. All the participants had done anthropological research on some aspects of Nepal.

978. **Von Furer-Haimendorf, Christoph**. Status and interaction among the high Hindu castes in Nepal. *Eastern Anthropologist*, vol. 24, no. 1 (Jan.-Apr. 1971), pp. 7-24.

979. **Wake, C.H.** and **Kumar, Mainali**. A brief profile of the Chirimar people of Belaspur Village, Banke. *Contributions to Nepalese Studies*, vol. 5, no. 1 (Dec. 1977), pp. 41-44. illus.

This article deals with a group of untouchables, the Chirimar, who are peculiarly isolated from the mainstream of development in Nepal, despite living almost in Nepalganj. The author discusses their origins, migratory pattern, occupation, social organization, and their ceremonial traditions.

ETHNIC AND MINORITY GROUPS

CHEPANGS

980. **Hodgson, B. H.** On the Chepang and Kusanda tribes of Nepal. *Journal of Asiatic Society of Bengal*, vol. 17, no. 2 (1848), pp. 650-658.

The Chepang and the Kusanda are two small tribes that live to the west of the Kathmandu Valley in Central Nepal. This brief description of the two tribes compares them with the inhabitants of Bhutan.

981. **Jest, Corneille.** Les Chepang, ethnie népalaise de langue tibéto-birmane. *Objects de Mondes*, vol. 6, no. 2 (1966), pp 169-184. illus.

A short study in French of the Chepangs. It includes a short description of their language

DURAS

982. **Adhikari, Rishi Kant.** The Duras of West Nepal. *Nepal Digest*, vol. 2, no. 11-12 (Oct. 1973-Jan. 1974), pp. 59-65.

A socio-economic study of the Duras, a small tribe living in the Lamjung District.

GURKHAS

983. **Adshead, Robin.** Gurkha : the legendary soldier. Singapore : Asia Pacific Press, 1970. 189 p. illus.

Chiefly concerns those soldiers enlisted in the following Infantry Regiments who have stood the test of time and to whom the book is dedicated: 2nd King Edward VII's own Gurkha Rifles; 6th Queen Elizabeth's own Gurkha Rifles; 7th Duke of Edinburgh's own Gurkha Rifles; 10th Princess Mary's own Gurkha Rifles.

984. **Forbes, Duncan.** Johnny Gurkha. Reprint.London : Hale, 1965. 208 p. maps. illus.

The author served as an officer with Gurkhas and here he describes all aspects of their life.

985. **Nepal and the Gurkhas.** London : Her Majesty's Stationery Office, Ministry of Defence, 1965. 158 p. maps. bibliog. illus.

Contains information about Nepal and her military people, the Gurkhas.

986. **Tuker, Francis Ivan Simms.** Gorkha : the story of the Gurkhas of Nepal. London : Constable, 1957. 319 p. illus.

A history of Nepal, nostalgic about the period of the British Empire, but with emphasis on the mountain tribes and castes recruited for the Gurkha Brigade.

987. **Vansittart, Eden.** The Goorkhās. 2nd rev. ed. New Delhi : Ariana Publishing House, 1980. 100 p. bibliog.

The Gurkha dynasty was established in the 16th century in the principality of Goorkha, and it gradually spread its influence over its neighbours through a series of fierce wars. More recently, the Gurkha soldiers have become a famous and popular constiuent of His Majesty's forces in Nepal. Because of this interest, the author of this work, first published in 1890, gathered information from various sources in order to establish as accurately as possible the history of the races, tribes, and clans of the fighting classes of Nepal, together with their customs and characteristics.

GURUNGS

988. **Andors, Ellen.** The rodighar and its role in Gurung society. *Contributions to Nepalese Studies*, vol. 1, no. 2 (June 1974), pp. 10-24.

The *rodighar*, or *rodi* house, can be described as a nightly social club, a semi-permanent dormitory where young people from the village congregate to sing, talk and joke. This article describes the organization and activities of the *rodi* house, outlining the integral part it plays in the economic, social, and ritual structure of Gurung society.

989. **Doherty, Victor S.** The organizing principles of Gurung kinship. *Kailash : a Journal of Himalayan Studies*, vol. 2, no. 4 (1974), pp. 273-301.

The Gurungs are primarily hardworking farmers who live in villages on the hills around the Annapurna Himalaya range. They represent one of the main Nepalese traditional cultures. In this article, the author discusses the circumstances and patterns of Gurung adaptation to city life in the rapidly modernizing Pokhara area, marriage customs and their social consequences, and the terminology of Gurung kinship.

990. **MacFarlane, Alan.** Resources and population : a study of the Gurungs of Nepal. Cambridge, England : Cambridge Universiry Press, 1976. 364 p. bibliog. illus. (Cambridge Studies in Social Anthropology, 12)

A detailed study of resources and population in the Gurung community of Nepal. Particularly important are chapters 11 and 12 which deal with the social structure and fertility.

991. **McHugh, Ernestine.** The women of Tebas : feminine perspectives in Gurung culture. *Kailash : a Journal of Himalayan Studies*, vol. 8, no. 1-2 (1981), pp. 45-69.

This article discusses the status of women in the Gurung community, with special reference to feminine perspectives on community, religion, and the life-cycle.

992. **Pignede, Bernard.** Les Gurungs : une population himalayenne du Népal. Paris : Mouton, 1966. 414 p. 2 maps. bibliog. illus.

This book in French describes the life of the Gurungs, their society and religion.

KIRATS

993. **Chemjong, Iman Singh.** History and culture of the Kirat people. Phidim, Nepal : Tumeng Hang and Chandraw Hang, 1966-67. 2 vols. vol. 2 has imprint : Kathmandu : Pushpa Ratna Sagar, 1967.

Kirat is the name of an ancient tribe of Nepal, and the Limbus and Lepchas claim to be descendants of this tribe. They are settled in eastern Nepal and Sikkim, India. They have their own religion and well-developed philosophy, very similar to late Vedic monism, with simple rituals. This book examines the history and culture of the tribe, and is an enlarged edition of author's *Kirat itihas*, published in 1948 in Kalimpong, India.

994. **Tandukar, Gopal Man.** Kiratese at a glance. Kathmandu : International Standard Books and Periodicals Store, 1980. 55 p. bibliog.

Describes the Kirati people of Nepal and adjacent areas. Lepchas and Limbus are considered to belong to this tribe. This small book throws light on the origins, socio-economic conditions, marriage and funeral ceremonies, literature, etc. of the Kiratis, very little of which is familiar to the outside world.

995. **Uperti, P.R.** A review of the Kirat problem. *Nepalese Prespective*, vol. 9, no. 3 (Sept. 1973), pp. 3-8.

An essay on Kirati people and their origins.

KUSUNDAS

996. **Hodgson, B.H.** On the Chapang and Kusanda tribes of Nepal.

For full entry refer to Population—Ethnic and minority groups—Chepangs section.

997. **Reinhard, Johan.** Apercu sur les Kusuṇḍa, peuple chasseur du Nepal. *Objects et Mondes*, vol. 9, no. 1 (1969), pp. 89-106.

In a village near Gorkha in central Nepal, the author, in the spring of 1968, managed to make contact with a few Kusunda. Very little is known about this population, which has nearly disappeared. In the past, they were nomadic and lived mainly by hunting and gathering; today, for all practical purposes, they live a sedentary life. The author gives a brief summary of what remains of their culture.

998. **Reinhard, Johan.** The Ban Rajas—a vanishing Himalayan tribe. *Contributions to Nepalese Studies*, vol. 4, no. 1 (Dec. 1976), pp. 1-22. bibliog. illus.

Ban Rajas (forest kings), or Kusunda, is the grandiose name for what today amounts to a few widely scattered and economically impoverished families. It is ironic that this tribe is becoming known merely as a disappearing cultural group. In this article the author presents some information which he collected during his travels in Nepal, both older material and more recent findings. He discusses the origins of the Ban Rajas, their kinship terminology, life style, rituals, medicine, religion, and language.

LEPCHAS

999. **Gorer, Geoffrey.** Himalayan village : an account of the Lapchas of Sikkim. London : Michael Joseph, 1938. 510 p. illus.

Although the author based his account on field-work in Sikkim, what he says is applicable to the Lepchas across the border in Nepal. The illustrations, include portraits.

1000. **Takanilamu, Nima**. Lepchā jatiko utpati au sṛshtiko eka jhalko. Darjeeling, India : Shyam Brothers, 1968. 49 p.

This booklet is based on *Lepcha Namthar*, a traditional history of the Lepchas, which has never been published and is only available in manuscript form. The author of this work recounts the mythological creation and historical origins of the Lepcha tribe as part of the Kirat tribe of Sikkim, Ilam (Nepal), Bhutan and, Darjeeling.

LIMBUS

1001. **Jones, Rex L.** and **Jones, Shirley Kurz**. The Himalayan women : a study of Limbu women in marriage and divorce. Palo Alto, California : Mayfield, 1976. 155 p. bibliog. illus. (Explorations in world ethnology)

This book is based on twenty-four case-studies of marriage and divorce of women in Limbuan, a community in the far-eastern part of Nepal. The authors describe Limbu marriage as a process rather than an act, involving not only the motivations and goals of husband and wife but those of the ambient society as a whole. There is a high divorce rate and the death rate for males is much higher than for females: therefore, many women are widows and heads of households. Although the main emphasis is on women, the life-style of men and women in Limbu society is also discussed.

1002. **Jones, Shirley Kurz** and **Jones, Rex L**. Limbu women, divorce and the domestic cycle. *Kailash : a Journal of Himalayan Studies*, vol. 4, no. 2 (1976), pp. 169-184. bibliog.

The field research for this study was conducted by the authors in 1967-69 in the area of Tehrathum Bazar, eastern Nepal. The authors examine the problem of Limbu marital stability from a women's perspective. After a brief introduction, they describe the ethnographic setting, the Limbu women's role in production, divorce, and economic independence. In conclusion they support the theory that socio-cultural and not biological variables determine the position of women in society.

1003. **Sagant, Philippe.** Le paysan Limbu : sa maison et ses champs. Paris : Mouton, 1976. 404 p.

An extremely interesting and valuable study of the Limbus in French. Most of the work is an impressively detailed and painstaking account of Limbu agricultural practices, calendar customs, and habitat. But the material is organized around an over-all question: when, how, and why was Limbu ecology transformed so rapidly?

1004. **Sagant, Philippe.** Pretres Limbu et categories domestiques. *Kailash : a Journal of Himalayan Studies,* vol. 1, no. 1 (Mar. 1973), pp. 51-75. illus.

This article, in French with an English summary, examines the structure of Limbu households, with a view to formulating the differences between the *Phedangma* and the *Rijuwa*, the two main categories of Limbu priests in eastern Nepal.

MAGARS

1005. **Hitchcock, John T.** The Magars of Banyan Hill. New York : Holt, Rinehart & Winston, 1966. 115 p. map. bibliog. illus. (Case studies in cultural anthropology)

This series of case studies is designed for students in the social sciences. This work is an anthropological study of two Magar communities in Nepal. It includes a glossary and six illustrations of Pandera Thum (Banyan Hill) and the culture of the Magars living there.

1006. **Hitchcock, John T.** Sub tribes in the Magar community in Nepal. *Asian Survey,* vol. 5, no. 4 (1965), pp. 207-215.

Discusses problems of interpretation presented by the Magar sub-tribes.

1007. **Jiro, Kawakita.** The hill Magars and their neighbours : hill peoples surrounding the Ganges plain. Tokyo : Tokai University Press, 1974. 484 p. maps. illus.

An account of the people living in the Kali Gandaki region, which separates Dhaulagiri and Gandaki anchals in western Nepal, along the Jomoson trail. The field-work was done during 1963-64. This is mainly an account of the relationship between the peoples of the area and their environment, with only passing reference to the Magars.

1008. **Kihara, Hitoshi,** ed. Peoples of Nepal Himalaya. Kyoto: Fauna and Flora Research Society, Kyoto University,

1957. 425 p. map. illus. (Scientific Results of the Japanese Expedition to Nepal Himalaya, 1952-53, vol. 3)

Presents ethnographic notes of varying validity, by members of a Japanese scientific expedition that travelled through parts of Nepal inhabited by Magras. The comments on the relationship between culture and environmental features is useful and suggestive.

1009. **Molnar, Augusta.** Marital patterns and women's economic independence : a study of Kham Magar women. *Contributions to Nepalese Studies*, vol. 6, no. 1 (Dec. 1978), pp. 15-29.

A preliminary report on marriage among the Kham speaking Magars of western Nepal. The author describes their marital patterns and explores the interrelation between the patterns and women's economic independence. The data for this paper was collected in Thabang Panchayat as part of the author's research for a Ph. D. degree on the Kham Magar. Includes nine case histories.

NEWARS

1010. **Chattopadhyay, K.P.** An eassy on the history of Newar culture. Kathmandu : Educational Enterprise, 1980. 119 p.

The material for this book was originally published in the *Journal of the Asiatic Society of Bengal*, vol. 19 (17 Oct. 1924). The study is one of the basic documents for studying the history and culture of the Newars.

1011. **Nepali, Gopal Singh.** The Newars : an ethno-sociological study of a Himalayan community. Bombay : United Asia Publications, 1965. 476 p. map. bibliog. illus.

The Newars of Nepal have a high level of material culture and a distinctive social organization. Though stray references to them are available in the pioneering accounts of Levi, Hodgson, Oldfield, K.P. Chattopadhyaya, and others, there has been no systematic ethno-sociological study on the subject. This monograph, which earned the author a Ph.D at Bombay University, makes an attempt to fill in this gap. The author uses the functional approach and the descriptive method to advantage, and this is particularly evident in his treatment of caste, religion, and kinship. In addition, the author covers the Newars and their interaction with the various other ethnic groups of the politically significant cis-Himalayas region, and discusses the similarity of certain cultural traits between the Newars and the distantly placed Nayars of Malabar.

1012. **Regmi, Jagadish Chandra**, comp. and ed. The Newars.

For full entry refer to Bibliographies section.

1013. **Shakya, Hemraj**. Nepāla-saṃskṛtiyā mūlukhā. Lalitpur, Nepal : Chandra Laxmi Devi Shakya, 1969. 124 p. bibliog.

The Newars living in the Kathmandu Valley rightly claim to be the original inhabitants of a vast region surrounding Kathmandu. They have their own distinctive language, culture, and traditions, and the civilization of modern Nepal owes much to this community. The author investigates every aspect of Newar culture, and also describes how religious traditions, both Brahmanic and Buddhist, have been shaped in Nepal by Newar culture. He also traces the development of the Newari script.

1014. **Sresthacharya, Iswaranand**. Newar kinship terms in the light of kinship typology. *Contributions to Nepalese Studies*, vol. 4, no. 2 (June 1977), pp. 111-128.

According the Schusky, there are two major ways to classify kinship systems: one which classifies the systems according to the terms used for addressing one's cousins, and one which classifies the systems according to the terms which one uses for one's parents and their siblings. This study examines the Newar kinship system from these two points of view. It includes a glossary of Kirtipur-Nagāā-Pāngā Newari kinship terms.

1015. **Von Furer-Haimendorf, Christoph**. Elements of Newar social structure. *Journal of the Royal Anthropological Institute of Great Britain and Ireland*, vol. 86 (1956), pp. 15-38.

Contains much material on the society of the Newars, the Tibeto-Burman-speaking people who founded Nepalese civilization.

RAIS

1016. **Barnouw, Victor**. Eastern Nepalese marriage customs and kinship organization. *Southwestern Journal of Anthropology*, vol. 11 (1955), pp. 15-30.

A study of the marriage customs of the Rais, based on information obtained in Darjeeling, India. Together with Magars, Gurungs, and Limbus, Rais formed most of the Gurkha Brigade.

1017. **McDougal, Charles**. The Kulunge Rai : a study in kinship and marriage exchange. Kathmandu : Ratna Pustak Bhandar, 1979. 170 p. maps. bibliog. illus. (Bibliotheca Himalayica : series III, vol. 14)

This monograph is a socio-anthropological study of the Kulunge Rais, an ethnic group of eastern Nepal. The field research upon which it is based was made possible by a post-doctoral fellowship from the National Science Foundation, Washington, D C, and by a grant from the London Cornell Project for South and Southeast Asian Studies, financed jointly by the Carnegie Corporation of New York and by the Nuffield Foundation. The research was conducted between December 1964 and December 1965 in eastern Nepal.

1018. **McDougal, Charles.** Structure and division in Kulunge Rai society. *Kailash : a Journal of Himalayan Studies*, vol. 1, no. 3 (Sept. 1973), pp. 205-225.

An anthropological study of the Kulunge Rais of Solukhumbu District, Nepal. It describes their environment and settlement patterns, economic organization, marriage customs, etc.

RAUTES

1019. **Bista, Dor Bahadur.** Encounter with the Raute : the last hunting nomads of Nepal. *Kailash : a Journal of Himalayan Studies*, vol. 4, no. 4 (1976), pp. 317-327. illus.

The Raute are believed to be the last tribe of nomadic hunter-gatherer in Nepal. They travel as far as Deukhuri in the south, Pyuthan in the east, and Achham in the west, but they have never crossed the lower Himalayan range to the north. The author visited their winter camp in the lower hills of the Himalayan region during January-February 1972. In this article he recounts his experiences during his trek and describes the Raute way of life and social habits.

1020. **Reinhard, Johan.** The Raute : notes on a nomadic hunting and gathering tribe of Nepal. *Kailash : a Journal of Himalayan Studies*, vol. 2, no. 4 (1974), pp. 233-271.

The Raute are a hunter-gatherer group in western Nepal, the last hunting and gathering tribe in Asia. They will not allow contact with anyone outside the tribe because they believe that their hunting god will become angry and their hunting will be ruined. Somehow the author managed to become honourary brother of the leader, and spent two weeks with the tribe. Based on his observations, the author describes physical and cultural environment, history and language, economic and material culture, social structure, politics, life-cycle, religion, relations with villagers, and cultural change.

SHERPAS

1021. **Axelsen, Hans Guldberg.** The Sherpas of the Solu District : a preliminary report on ethnological field research in the Solu District of north-eastern Nepal. Copenhagen : The Author, 1977. 71 p.

Based on field research during 1972-73, the author attempts to give information on all aspects of Sherpa culture in Solukhumbu District: monastic life, religious festivals, archaeological remains, social structure, material culture, and economic development, etc.

1022. **Oppitz, Michael.** Myths and facts : reconsidering some data concerning the clan history of the Sherpas. *Kailash : a Journal of Himalayan Studies,* vol. 2, no. 1-2 (1974), pp. 121-131.

An attempt to explain the historical development of Sherpa society. The study was made in the Solukhumbu region of eastern Nepal.

1023. **Von Furer-Haimendorf, Christoph.** The Sherpas of Nepal : Buddhist highlanders. London : John Murrary; Berkeley, California : University of California, 1964. 298 p. map. bibliog. illus.

An excellent account of the hillmen who figure in mountaineering ventures, by the doyen of anthropologists who write on Nepal. The illustrations include portraits.

THAKALIS

1024. **Gauchan, Surendra and Vinding, Michael.** The history of the Thakaali according to the Thakaali tradition.

Kailash : a Journal of Himalayan Studies, vol. 5, no. 2 (1977), pp. 97-184. map. bibliog. illus.

The Thakali-speaking people live in the Mustang District, where the language is spoken in different dialects by three separate groups. Although the members of all three groups refer to themselves as Thakali when dealing with outsiders, they call themselves by the individual group names when conversing with other Thakali-speaking people. The best-known of the three groups refer to themselves as Tamhaang or Tapaang; the second group is known as Puntan: and third group is called Thin, Shyaangtan or Chimtan. In this article the authors describe the history of Thakalis.

1025. **Manzardo, Andrew E.** and **Sharma, Keshav Prasad.** Cost-cutting, caste and community : a look at Thakali social reform in Pokhara. *Contributions to Nepalese Studies*, vol. 2, no. 2 (June 1975), pp. 25-44. bibliog.

Historically, the Thakalis were a marginal people living just outside the ethnic and economic sphere of the Kingdom of Mustang, but some have now migrated to other parts of Nepal. Very little have been published about the Thakalis who migrated, and this article fills that gap. The author's emphasis is on one of the main institutions responsible for social reform: Thakali Samaj Sudhar Sangh (Thakali Social Reform Organization) of Pokhara. The article describes the structure and functions of Thakali Samaj Sudhar Sangh in some detail.

1026. **Vinding, Michael.** A preliminary report on kinship terminologies of the Bodish section of Sino-Tibetan speaking peoples. *Kailash : a Journal Himalayan Studies*, vol. 7, no. 3-4 (1979), pp. 191-225. bibliog.

The field-work for this article was undertaken in Nepal in 1972 and from 1975 to 1978: it was financed by Danish Research Council for the Humanities under the Danish government. The purpose of this report is to present ten types of kinship terminology of the Bodish section of Bodish division of Sino-Tibetan speaking peoples. These kinship terminologies are: the Tamang Thakali, the Mawatan Thakali, the Yhulkasummi Thakali, the Darjeeling Tamong, the Nyesyangba, the Nar-Phu, the Chusangtan, the Baragaun Tibetan, the Gyasumdo Tibetan, and the Helambu Sherpa.

1027. **Vinding, Michael.** The Thakali household and inheritance system. *Contributions to Nepalese Studies*, vol. 7. no. 1-2 (Dec. 1979- June 1980), pp. 21-45. bibliog.

This article describes and analyses the household system among the Thakalis. It first examines the economics of the household and the inheritance system. Next, the frequency of different household types is analysed in relation to residence pattern and the development cycle of the household.

THARUS

1028. **Bhatta, Dibya Deo.** The Tharus, an aboriginal tribe in Nepal. *Asian Student*, 12 May 1973.

Asian Student is an English-language weekly, published in San-Francisco, California. This article describes the Tharu people and discusses their culture, marriage customs, and economy.

1029. **Srivastava, S.K.** The Tharus, a study in culture dynamics. Agra : H.K. Kapur, 1958. 343 p. maps. illus. (Distributed by New Order Book Co.)

A study of the culture of the Tharus, a tribe in Nepal.

TIBETANS

1030. **Aris, Michael.** Report on the University of California Expedition to Kutang and Nubri in northern Nepal in autumn 1973. *Contributions to Nepalese Studies*, vol. 2, no. 2 (June 1975), pp. 45-87. illus.

The author, together with John Cepelok and Joe Clack, made an expedition to the Tibetan districts of Kutang and Nubri at the headwaters of the Buri Gandaki River in northern Nepal, during October and November 1973. Their work was sponsored by University of California at Berkeley and financed jointly by the National Geographical Society and University of California at Berkeley. The main aim of the project was to make a general survey of Tibetan Buddhist culture in the area. This is the report of their work, with details of their travelling.

1031. **Aziz, Barbara Nimri.** Tibetan frontier families : reflections of three generations from D'ing-ri. New Delhi : Vikas Publishing House, 1978. 292 p. illus.

An anthropological study of the inhabitants of D'ing-ri, a village on the Tibet-Nepal border. It includes a detailed description of descent and residence systems and of the variety of marriage practices. The book presents an example of one of the many population groups in Nepal involved in the ancient and on-going process of migration.

1032. **Goldstein, Melvyn C.** Population, social structure and strategic behaviour : an essay on polyandry, fertility, and change in Limi Panchayat. *Contributions to Nepalese Studies*, vol. 4, no. 2 (June 1977), pp. 47-62. bibliog.

This paper is firstly concerned with 'coping' behaviour, and focuses on how individuals attempt to gain their personal and social objectives through the use of social and material resources. Secondly, it examines the operation and components of ecosystems, with particular emphasis on the role of social and cultural factors in such systems. The data presented here was collected by the author in Limi Panchayat, Humla District, during field studies undertaken in 1974 and 1976. Though Limi Panchayat is a part of Nepal, the people of Limi are linguistically and culturally Tibetan.

1033. **Jest, Corneille.** Dolpo : communautés de langue Tibétaine du Népal. Paris : Centre National de la Recherche Scientifique (CNRS), 1975. 481 p. 8 maps. bibliog. illus. (Cahiers népalais)

The author visited Dolpa four times during 1960-67. He begins by discussing the physical setting and milieu of Dolpa, and then gives a detailed analysis of the means of production and economic life. Finally he examines the social life of the inhabitants, Tibetan speaking community of Dolpa, and their religious concepts, institutions, and practices.

1034. **Jest, Corneille.** Tarap, une vallée dans l'Himalaya.

For full entry refer to the Country and its people section.

GENERAL SOCIAL SURVEYS

1035. **The Analysis of the population statistics of Nepal.** Kathmandu : Government of Nepal, National Planning Commission Secretariat, Central Bureau of Statistics, 1977. 208 p. map.

A statistical analysis of the 1971 population census.

1036. **Bourini, A.K.** The demographic sample survey of Nepal, 1974-1975 : survey method and findings : report. Kathmandu : United Nations Office of Technical Co-operation and United Nations Fund for Population Activities, 1976. 77 p.

A survey estimating the population growth rate of Nepal and its components : fertility, mortality, and both domestic and international migration. Mimeographed.

1037. **Bourini, A.K.** The demographic sample survey of Nepal : second year survey, 1976 : report. Kathmandu : United Nations Office of Technical Co-operation and United Nations Fund for Population Activities, 1976. 34 p.

A report on the results of the second year of the demographic sample survey in Nepal. The first phase of this survey was intended to last for three years, 1974-77, in which six rounds of interviews were to be conducted. Afterwards, a new sample was selected and followed for three more years. Data collection for the second-year survey started in January 1976 and was completed in December 1976. Mimeographed.

1038. **The Demographic sample survey of Nepal** : third year survey, 1977-78. Population Division; Central Bureau of Statistics. Kathmandu : His Majesty's Government of Nepal, National Planning Commission Secretariat, Central Bureau of Statistics, 1978. 33 p.

This report presents the results of the third year of the Demographic Sample Survey of Nepal; the survey undertook two rounds of follow-ups on all the respondents throughout the period of the survey. Fifteen districts were selected: two from the mountains, nine from the hills, and four from the Terai. A complete enumeration of the households was carried out in the wards selected from certain panchayats representing the districts. Altogether a total of 191 wards were selected from the fifteen districts.

1039. **Kanaskar, Vidya Bir Singh.** Population projection for Nepal, 1970-2000. Kathmandu : Centre for Economic Development and Administration, Tribhuvan University, 1980. 61 p.

This study was funded by WHO and sponsored by the Steering Committee of the Health for All by the Year 2000/Basic Minimum Needs and the HMG/WHO Management Group. It is the outgrowth of a broader project, 'Health for all by the year 2000'. The study has overcome the inadequacies of existing population estimates for Nepal and attempted to project Nepal's population upto the year 2001. It also presents estimates of population by geographic regions: the mountains, the hills, and the Terai. Mimeographed.

1040. **Mid-term population sample survey, 1976** : National level result. Kathmandu : Central Bureau of Statistics, His Majesty's Government, National Planning Commission Secretariat, 1979. 45 p.

The mid-term population sample survey of 1976, an inter-census survey, was first of its kind. The primary objective was to provide up-to-date estimates of: the population by age and sex, the economically active population by profession, the literacy rate, migration, and other miscellaneous statistics. A secondary objective was to establish some guidelines for future estimates of population, by drawing on representative samples to get reliable national estimates.

1041. **National In-service Training Workshop on Population Education for Panchayat Trainers, 29 January to 8 February 1980** : report and training manual. Lalitpur, Nepal : Central Panchayat Training Institute, Population Education Project, Ministry of Home and Panchayat, His Majesty's Government, Nepal, 1980. 1 v.

The proceedings, recommendations, and summary reports of the workshop on population education for panchayat trainers. In all, forty-four participants attended the workshop, which emphasized the need for accelerating development by effectively checking population growth. The main purpose of the workshop was to encourage the spread of population, education and family planning into rural areas.

1042. **Population and development** : proceedings of the Seminar on 'Population and Development' organized by Centre for Economic Development and Administration, Kathmandu, July 28-30, 1971. Kathmandu : Centre for Economic Development and Administration, 1971. 201 p. (CEDA study series. Seminar paper, no. 2)

1043. **Population census, 1971**. Kathmandu : His Majesty's Government, National Planning Commission Secretariat, Central Bureau of Statistics, 1975. 5 vols.

Vol. 1: *General characteristic tables*; vol. 2: *Social characteristic tables in 2 parts*; vol. 3: *Economic characteristic tables in 2 parts*; vol. 4: *Female fertility characteristic tables*; vol. 5: *Selected locality tables, major urban.*

1044. **Population of Lumbini Zone by districts and panchayats.** Compiled by Central Bureau of Statistics. *Statistical Bulletin : Nepal*, vol. 9 (1974), pp. 5-31.

A statistical account of the population of the Lumbini Zone.

1045. **Population projections for Nepal, 1971-1986.** Kathmandu: His Majesty's Government, National Planning Commission Secretariat, Central Bureau of Statistics, 1974. 13 leaves.

This projection is in continuation to *Population projection for Nepal, 1961-1981.* In this report, the whole country is divided into twelve physical divisions, whereas in earlier one, there were only eight divisions. This useful projection will provides population estimates required by planners, administrators, scholars, and others.

1046. **Reports [1] National Level Orientation** Seminar on Population Education for Senior HMG Officers, 2-6 July 1979. [2] National Level Orientation Seminar on Population Education for Heads of Departments, Other Public Officials, and Community Leaders, 15-21 August 1979. Lalitpur, Nepal : Central Panchayat Training Institute, Population Education Project, Home and Panchayat Ministry, HMG, Nepal, 1979. 216 p.

A joint report on two national-level seminars on population education through panchayats, co-operatives, and other training institutions. The project was sponsored by His Majesty's Government of Nepal, ILO, and UNFPA. These reports are of national importance and will be very useful for socio-economic development planning.

1047. **Thapa, Yadab S.** Effects of population growth on government expenditure. Kirtipur, Nepal : Centre for Economic Development and Administration, 1978. 118 p. bibliog.

Population growth is one of the main factors affecting the impact of government expenditure on economic development. This study attempts the difficult task of assessing the relationship between government spending and demographic change. It examines the impact of population growth on the government's expenditure and on its attempts to estimate what proportion of its investment will be absorbed in maintaining existing per capita levels of income. Mimeographed.

26

PROFESSIONAL PERIODICALS

1048. **Bulletin (Nepal Bank Limited).**

For full entry refer to Finance & Banking section.

1049. **The Economic Journal of Nepal.**

For full entry refer to Economy—General Studies section.

1050. **The Economic Monthly.**

For full entry refer to Economy—General Studies section.

1051. **Education and Development.**

For full entry refer to Education section.

1052. **Education Quarterly.**

For full entry refer to Education section.

1053. **Geographical Journal of Nepal.** Kirtipur, Nepal : Geography Instruction Committee, Institute of Humanities and Social Sciences, Tribhuvan University, 1978- annual.

An academic journal containing articles on all aspects of geography of Nepal. Very useful for teachers and students of geography.

1054. **The Himalayan review.** Kirtipur, Nepal : Nepal Geographical Society, 1968- annual.

Includes scholarly articles on the geography of Himalaya. Some volumes are issued in combined form.

1055. **Isdoc Bulletin.**

For full entry refer to Industry section.

1056. **The Journal of Development and Administrative Studies.**

For full entry refer to Administration and local government section.

1057. **Journal of Humanities and Social Sciences**. Pokhara, Nepal : Institute of Humanities and Social Sciences, Tribhuvan University, 1978- quarterly.

An academic journal, publishes articles in English and Nepali.

1058. **Journal of Natural History Museum.**

For full entry refer to Libraries and museums section.

1059. **Journal of Nepal Engineers' Association.** Kathmandu : Nepal Engineers' Association, 1969- semiannual.

Includes articles in English. The publication was suspended for some time.

1060. **Journal of the Institute of Medicine.** Kathmandu : Institute of Medicine, 1979- semiannual.

Includes articles in English and Nepali.

1061. **Journal of the Nepal Medical Association.** Kathmandu : Nepal Medical Association, 1962- bimonthly.

From 1962-72, this was a quarterly publication. Includes articles in English and Nepali. Some numbers are issued in combined form and some numbers are accompanied by supplements.

1062. **Journal of the Nepal Research Centre.**

For full entry refer to Literature—History and criticism Section.

1063. **Kailash : a Journal of Himalayan Studies.**

For full entry refer to Country and its people section.

1064. **NAFA Art Magazine.**

For full entry refer to Arts section.

1065. **The Nepal Journal of Forestry.**

For full entry refer to Flora & Fauna section.

1066. **Nepal Journal of Management.**

For full entry refer to Industry section.

1067. **Nepala Kanuna Paricarca=Nepal Law Review.** Kathmandu : Tribhuvan University, Institute of Law, 1977- quarterly.

A useful academic periodical for teachers and student of law. Includes articles in English and Nepali.

1068. **Nepalese Economic Journal.** Kathmandu : Nepal Rastra Bank, Bankers Club, 1979- three number a year.

Nepal Rastra Bank is a government owned bank. The banks in Nepal have an association known as Bankers Club which is a part of Nepal Rastra Bank. This periodical gives information regarding economic conditions of Nepal which are very useful for the bankers as well as for general public.

1069. **Nepalese Journal of Agriculture.** Lalitpur, Nepal : Nepal Agricultural Association, 1966- annual.

A scholarly journal that publishes articles on agriculture in Nepal.

1070. **Newsletter (Nepal Nature Conservation Society).** Kathmandu : Nepal Nature Conservation Society.

Gives information concerning Nepal Conservation Society and includes intellectual articles on nature conservation in Nepal.

1071. **Prasasana : the Nepalese Journal of Public Administration.** Lalitpur, Nepal : His Majesty's Government of Nepal, Public Administration Department, 1968- three number a year.

From December 1968 till June 1974 (vol. 1, no. 1—vol. 5, no. 2), this was a semiannual publication. Publishes scholarly articles in English and Nepali on public administration of Nepal.

1072. **Research bulletin (Tribhuvan University).** Kirtipur, Nepal : Tribhuvan University, Research Division, 1975- semiannual.

Publishes academic articles on all aspects of research.

1073. **Tribhuvan University Newsletter.** Kirtipur, Nepal : Research Division, Rector's Office, Tribhuvan University, 1976- semiannual.

This publication was started on December 14, 1966 and gives news of Tribhuvan University.

1074. **Vanijya samsara.** Kirtipur, Nepal : Tribhuvan University Commerce Association. annual.

A scholarly journal publishes articles on commerce and industry of Nepal.

1075. **Voice of History.** Kirtipur, Nepal : Tribhuvan University History Association, 1975- annual.

Publishes scholarly articles in English and Nepali.

27

RELIGION

CEREMONIES & RITUALS

1076. **Bennett, Lynn.** Sitting in a cave : an analysis of ritual seclusion at menarche among Brahmans and Chhetris in Nepal. *Contributions to Nepalese Studies*, vol. 6, no. 1 (Dec. 1978), pp. 31-45. illus.

Sitting in a cave (*Guphā basne*) is a rite of passage among Brahmans and Chhetris of Nepal that marks the transition of a girl at menarche from a pre-sexual to a sexual being. The author describes and analyses the rituals, and includes a case study.

1077. **Bouillier, Veronique.** Funeral observances of a group of non-ascetic sunyasi in central Nepal. *Contributions to Nepalese Studies*, vol. 3. no. 2 (Sept. 1976), pp. 35-45. illus.

The author examined the life-cycle rituals of *Giris*, a sub-group of Sannyasis including their funeral rites, which are most important. The *Giris* do not cremate their dead, as Hindu tradition dictates, but rather, they bury them, as is the rule among ascetics. But the *Giri's* funeral rites are completely opposed to the ascetic tradition, and this article describes these rites among *Giris*.

1078. **Jest, Corneille.** Chez les Thakali, ceremonie consacree aux ancetres du clan. *Objects et Mondes*, tome 9, fasc. 1 (1969), pp. 59-68. illus.

The author describes the two-days ceremony in honour of the ancestors which takes place among the Thakali, tribal people, in their home at the beginning of the seventh month. The first day is devoted to a ritual for good luck; on the second day, the Thakali medium interferes. After driving evil influence from the house, a cock is sacrificed in the ground floor, and a ram on the roof-top terrace. The ritual ends with a procession.

1079. **Locke, John K.** Newar Buddhist initiation rites. *Contributions to Nepalese Studies*, vol. 2, no. 2 (June 1975), pp. 1-23. illus.

The author witnessed the *bare chuyegu* initiation ritual at the Machindra Baha in Kathmandu. In this article, he presents a description of the rites as he saw them performed, in the belief that any understanding of the sociological and religious phenomena of Newar Buddhism must begin with a factual account of the religion as it is practised today. Initiation rites at Machindra Baha are held at irregular intervals, and the ceremonies take place on five different days spread over an eight-day period.

1080. **Ortner, Sherry B.** Sherpas through their rituals. Cambridge, England : Cambridge University Press, 1978. 195 p. bibliog. illus. (Cambridge studies in cultural systems, 2; Anthropological studies of systems of meaning, 2)

A study of Sherpas and their religion.

1081. **Pant, Mahes Raj.** Puṣyābhiṣeka. *Journal of the Nepal Research Centre*, vol. 1 (Humanities) (1977), pp. 93-116

It is known from the *Gopālarāja Vaṃśāvalī* (the *Bendall Vaṃśāvalī*) and other historical documents that some of the Nepalese kings who reigned in the period between 1167-1381 underwent a consecration known as *Puṣyābhiṣeka*. But the term *Puṣyābhiṣeka* has been difficult to define authentically in the context of Nepalese history. For this reason, this paper was prepared to define the term *Puṣyābhiṣeka* on the basis of the *Śāstras*, a rite prescribed in *Atharvaveda*.

1082. **Toffin, Gerard.** Jako : a Newar family ceremony. *Contributions to Nepalese Studies*, vol. 2, no. 1 (Feb. 1975), pp. 47-56. bibliog.

At Pyangaon, a Newar village to the south of Kathmandu, the two *saṃskāra* (nāmakarṇa and annaprāsanna) are celebrated in one ceremony which is called *Jako* in Newari and which takes place six month after the birth of a girl and seven months after the birth of a boy. In December 1971, the author observed this *Jako* ceremony for a girl, which lasted for two days. He describes the performance of this ceremony in detail.

1083. **Tuladhar, Sumon Kamal.** Gwaye da tayegu : an initial ritual of the Samyaka Guthi. *Contributions to Nepalese Studies*, vol. 7, no. 1-2 (Dec. 1979- June 1980), pp. 47-70. bibliog. illus.

The *gwaye da tayegu* ritual is just one part of the *Samyaka* ritual, but it gives a panoramic view of *Vajrayāṅa* Buddhism and the social organization of the Buddhist Newars. This article discusses the rituals carried out in the *gwaye da tayegu* ceremony on 15 January 1979. This ritual announced the *Sāmyaka* ceremony which was observed on 15 January 1980. This article is based on author's field observations of *gwaye da tayegu* and on consultation with key informants who were in charge of the *Samyaka* ceremony. The author also discusses some of the key elements of the ritual in relation to other features of the religious and social life of Newar Buddhists.

DEITIES

1084. **Allen, Michael.** The cult of Kumari; virgin worship in Nepal. Kathmandu : Institute of Nepal and Asian Studies, Tribhuvan University, 1975. 67 p. bibliog. illus.

This monograph is the outcome of author's research on 'Society and religion amongst the Newars of Nepal'. This is the most comprehensive study of the cult of the Kumari, the 'virgin goddess'. He has tried to show the deep significance of the cult in the socio-religious life of the people of the Kathmandu Valley. This is a very useful monograph for those interested in Nepalese cultural history. It includes 27 plates and 2 diagrams.

1085. **Bista, Khem Bahadur.** Le culte du Kuldevata au Nepal en particulier chez certains Ksatri de la vallée de Kathmandu. Paris : Centre National de la Recherche Scientifique, 1972. 169 p. map. bibliog. illus.

A study of the practices and purposes of the worship of Kuldevata (the divinity worshipped by those of Chhetri lineage) in Nepal. The Chhetris are one of the highest castes in Nepal. This work is in two parts: a general descriptions of the Chhetries, and a description of the worship of Kuldevata in Nepal. This work also provides an analytical study of the different sub-castes of the Chhetris. The text in French, with a preface in English. Includes 18 illustrations, 4 tables.

1086. **Detmold, Geoffrey** and **Rubel, Mary.** The gods and goddesses in Nepal : a traveller's guide to the Hindu and Buddhist deities in the Kathmandu Valley of Nepal, with a comprehensive glossary to aid in their identification. Illustrated by Brenda H.T. Ching. Kathmandu : Ratna Pustak Bhandar, 1979. 120 p. bibliog.

An introduction to Hindu and Buddhist deities of Nepal, which also gives information on the general principles of Hinduism and Buddhism and on the place of the various gods. Includes a glossary; details on the symbols, handposes, and position of the deities for identification; and line drawings.

1087. **Gaborieau, Marc.** Note préliminaire sur le dieu Maṣṭā. *Objects de Mondes*, vol. 9, no. 1 (1969), pp. 19-50. illus.

Maṣṭā is a god worshipped in western Nepal in the Karnali Zone. This article summarizes the main legends about Maṣṭā and studies the organization of the principal shrines dedicated to the god. This article furnishes insight into the popular religion of western Nepal, a subject which to date has not been studied by anthropologists.

1088. **Locke, John K.** Karunamaya : the cult of Avalokitesvara-Matsyendranath in the valley of Nepal. Kathmandu : Sahayogi Prakashan for Research Centre for Nepal and Asian Studies, Tribhuvan University, 1980. 524 p. bibliog. illus.

Matsyendranath, a deified personality, was a yogi of the Natha sect. He is worshipped both in India and Nepal by Buddhists and Brahmins alike—the Buddhists accept him as an incarnation of Bodhisattva Avalokitesvara This is the first extensive study, on the cult of Matsyendranath and it throws much light on the history, rituals, and festivals of the cult, as well as on its socio-cultural setting. The book includes 74 illustrations, some in colour, of the rituals, temples, and festivals associated with the cult and also a glossary and an appendix containing hymns in Sanskrit.

1089. **Rubel, Mary.** The gods of Nepal : an introduction to the deities of Hinduism and Buddhism with a glossary to aid their identification. Kathmandu : Bhim Ratna Harsha Ratna, 1968? 52 p bibliog.

This is an introduction to Hindu and Buddhist deities of Nepal. Gives information regarding the general principles of Hinduism and Buddhism and the place of their various gods. Includes glossary, details about the symbols, handposes, and position of the deities for identification.

1090. **Sagant, Philippe.** Tâmpunmâ, divinité limbu de la forêt. *Objects et Mondes*, vol. 9, fasc. 1 (1969), pp. 107-124. map. illus.

The author briefly describes the main aspects of Tampunma, a Limbu forest divinity. He sketches out the forest divinity position in the pantheon and the manner in which the Limbu of the Mewa Khola imagine the divinity. He notes the times at which the deity is invoked and describes the ceremonies of worship.

1091. **Sharma, Buddhi Sagar.** Devatā citrasaṅgrahātmaka. Edited by Babu Krishna. Kathmandu : Bir Pustakalaya, 1962. 165 p. illus. (Purātatva prakāśana mālā, 10)

This volume is part one of a larger work which deals with temples and images in Nepal according to tantric traditions, chiefly Brahmanic. It presents line drawings illustrating all the deities worshipped in Nepal and northern India. Names of the deities are also given, with illustrations.

GENERAL STUDIES

1092. **Aris, Michael.** Autobiographies of three spiritual masters of Kutang. Thimphu : Kunsang Topgay, 1979. 789 p.

In 1973, the author headed an expedition to the areas of Kutang and Nubri in northern Nepal, situated along the upper reaches of the Buri Gandaki River. One of the objects of this expedition was to photocopy manuscripts and block prints in Tibetan relating to the local history of the area, and this work presents five fascimile texts from among the findings. The texts are autobiographies of three Nying-mapa lamas of Kutang and date from 1668 to 1767. The texts illustrate the expansion of Tibetan Buddhism in the Himalayan areas and provide information on the local life of Kutung and its neighbouring districts.

1093. **Aryal, Mukunda Raj**. The development of Solarcult and Shivabhaskara in Nepal. *Nepalese Culture*, vol. 1 (1979), pp. 29-34. bibliog.

Śiva is one of the Hindu trinity and Bhaskara is a name for Surya (sun). This article for general reader explains why Bhaskara, the Surya, is addressed as Śhivabhaskara.

1094. **Berglie, Per-Arne**. Preliminary remarks on some Tibetan "spirit mediums" in Nepal. *Kailash : a Journal of Himalayan Studies*, vol. 4, no. 1 (1976), pp. 85-108. bibliog. illus.

Describes the curing of the sick and the counteracting of harmful forces by *dpa' bo*, Tibetan spirit medium. The study was undertaken during 1970/71 and concerns four *dpa' bo* living in a settlement for Tibetan refugees.

1095. **Buddha dharma va Bauddha tirtha.** Kathmandu : Yurimaya, Suvarna Kesari, 1976. 63 p.

Nepalese Buddhists, a sizeable proportion of the population, cherish great respect for the holy places associated with Gautama Buddha, both in Nepal and India, and they undertake pilgrimages to such places at the first available opportunity. This Newari work describes such holy places and gives accounts of travel to them. The author's name is not given in the work. It is particularly interesting because it unfolds some traditional beliefs and rituals related to pilgrimage which are typically Nepalese.

1096. **Burghart, Richard**. Bairagi mandals. *Contributions to Nepalese Studies*, vol. 3, no. 1 (Jan. 1976), pp. 63-104. bibliog.

The word *mandal* here means a formally constituted organization. The followers of Hindu saint, Swami Ramanand of the 14th century, are known as Ramanandi or *bairagi* (the desireless) started a *mandal* and also organised regional based *mandals*. In this article, the author describes: the officers of mandal (Sri Mahant); the election of *Sri Mahant*; the *bhandara* (feast); the privileges of *Sri Mahant* and the function of the *mandal*. He then examines three *mandals*: the Nilpur *mandal*, the Suja *mandal*, and the Janakpur Bhavan Kuti mandal. Of these, the first is the type commonly found and the second and third are somewhat unique variations of the common type. Includes a glossary.

1097. **Chemjong, Iman Singh.** Yākathuṅa cukamuka sāmajika Mundhum ; Kirāta darśanako sārāṃsa = Summary of Kirat philosophy. Atharia Chugva, Nepal : Khagendra Singh Limbu, 1969. 38 p.

The Limbus of Sikkim and eastern Nepal are deemed to be the main branch of the ancient Kirat community and they have retained the religion and philosophy of that great tribe. The religious philosophy of the Limbus is well developed and unique in many respects. Their basic religious work, *Mandhum* (knowledge), is still not translated into any other language. This book in Nepali, summarizing the philosophy of the Limbus, is of great importance.

1098. **Corneille, Jest.** Traditions et croyances religieuses des habitants de la vallee de Tichrong (nord-ouest du Nepal). *Ethnographie*, no. 65 (1971), pp. 66-86. illus.

Tichurong, the area around the Bheri River located between 2,000 and 3,500 metres north of the Dhaulagiri Range, constitutes an ethnical unit. The legends, myths, local religious traditions and economy of the inhabitants of Tichurong are presented, with illustrations. The text is in French.

1099. **Dharmacharyya, Dharma Aditya.** Buddhism in Nepal. *Buddhist India*, vol. 2, no. 4 (Dec. 1928), pp. 251-258.

A papar read at the 17th congress of International Orientalists held at Oxford on Aug. 27, 1928.

1100. **Dietz, Siglinde.** The fifth chapter of Nāgārjuna's Ratnāvalī. *Journal of the Nepal Research Centre*, vol. 4 (Humanities) (1980), pp. 189-220. bibliog.

Among the manuscripts which were microfilmed by the Nepal German Manuscript Preservation Project, there was a copy of the *Ratnāvalī* written by the Madhyamaka philosopher Nāgārjuna. *Ratnāvalī* is a very popular didactic text. This presentation of the fifth chapter of Nāgārjuna's *Ratnāvalī* contains transliterated Sanskrit text, followed by a Tibetan translation. At the end, philological commentary is also given.

1101. **Eliade, M.** Shamanism : archaic techniques of ecstasy. Translated from French by Willard R. Trask. Rev. ed. New York : Bollingen Foundation, 1964. 610 p. (Bollingen series, 76) (Distributed by : Pantheon Books, New York)

A translation of *Le chamanisme et les techniques archaiques de l'extase*. Shaminism, as described by most scholars, is pre-eminately a magico-religious phenomenon of Siberia and central Asia, and the word 'shaman' comes originally from the Tungusic word *saman*, meaning 'one who is excited, moved, raised' and was borrowed into English from the Russian. The term is descriptive of the shaman's most basic attribute shaking, or an 'ecstatic trance'.

1102. **Fournies, A.** The role of the priest in Sunuwar society. *Kailash : a Journal of Himalayan Studies*, vol. 2, no. 3 (1974), pp. 153-166.

The Sunuwars are a Sino-Tibetan tribe, belonging to the Bodic group. In Sunuwar society, the priest is known as *Naso*. This article describes the position of *Naso*, how his successor is chosen, the paraphernalia of the *Naso*, and the conducting of rituals. It also highlights the significant changes taking place in the religious practices of Sunuwars.

1103. **Gutschow, Niels** and **Shrestha, Krishna Prasad.** The svamgu loham in Bhaktapur — a contribution to the study of the Newar concept of space. *Kailash : a Journal of Himalayan Studies*, vol. 3, no. 1 (1975), pp. 61-65. illus.

This *svamgu lohām* legend connected with the installation of three Bhairava stones mentions the Bhimsen temple Tacapāl, the Chupin Ghāt, and Mangal Ghāt. The stones at these three sites are meant as a device to unify the town. To worship these stones, or even to walk through the town, is understood as over-coming history and realizing integration. To worship is to perform integration in time and space. These stones, which are placed in line, realize a concept of space which serves to characterize Bhaktapur as a habitat, not around a core, but along a line.

1104. **Hitchcock, John T.** and **Jones, Rex L.** Spirit possession in the Nepal Himalayas. Translations of French articles by Harriet Leva Beegun. New Delhi : Vikas Publishing House, 1976. 401 p. map. illus. bibliog.

This anthology, the result of recent field-work by sixteen anthro-pologists, contains accounts of all forms of spirit possession and shamanism found among the peoples of Nepal. In the last few years this relatively new field has drawn an ever-increasing international body of anthropologists attracted by the complexity and variety of the phenomenon. The social, religious, psychic, and therapeutic aspects of spirit possession are dealt with on a broadly regional and ethnic basis, and the collection is completed by contributions on Lamaist spirit possession and historical observations. There are ninteen essays in all.

1105. **Journal of Nepal Research Centre.**

For full entry refer to Literature—History and criticism section.

1106. **Kloppenborg, Ria.** Theravāda Buddhism in Nepal. *Kailash : a Journal of Himalayan Studies*, vol. 5, no. 4 (1977), pp. 301-321.

The modern Theravāda movement in Nepal has been given little attention by students of Buddhism. This study is based partly on written sources but mainly on observation and interviews carried out during several visits by the author to Nepal. During these visits the author has collected information from many Theravādin monks, nuns, and laymen. This study is limited to the description of the history and the present status of Nepalese Theravāda.

1107. **Levi, Sylvain.** Le Nepal : étude historique d'un Royaume Hindou. Paris : E. Leroux, 1905. 395 p. illus.

Describes Nepal and gives information on political, judicial, economic organization, and Hindu and Buddhist religious practices of the people of Nepal.

1108. **Nepalarajakiya-Virapustakalayasthahastalikhita-pustakanam brhatsucipatram.**

For full entry refer to Libraries & Museums section.

1109. **Okada, Ferdinand E.** Ritual brotherhood : a cohesive factor in Nepalese society. *Southwestern Journal of Anthropology*, vol. 13 (1957), pp. 212-222.

An account of ritual brotherhood among various groups in Nepal and suggestions about its function.

1110. **Oldfield, H. Ambrose.** Sketches from Nepal, historical and descriptive, with an essay on Nepalese Buddhism and illustrations of religious monuments and architecture.

For full entry refer to History—General section.

1111. **Schuler, Sidney.** Yaks, cows, and status in the Himalayas. *Contributions to Nepalese Studies*, vol. 6, no. 9 (June 1979), pp. 65-72. bibliog.

The cow has a special position in Hindu society. The purpose of this paper is to examine the status of yaks and cows among non-Hindus living within the boundaries and along the peripheries of Hindu societies in Nepal.

1112. **Smith, Warren W.**, ed. Mythological history of the Nepal Valley from Svayambhu Purana. Translated from the Sanskrit by Mana Bajra Bajracharya. Kathmandu : Avalok Publishers, 1978. 78 p. map. bibliog. illus.

Describes the mythological history of Nepal. Includes *Naga and serpent symbolism* by the editor.

1113. **Snellgrove, David L.** Buddhist Himalaya : travels and studies in quest of the origins and nature of Tibetan religion. Oxford : Bruno Cassirer ; New York : Philosophical Library, 1957. 324 p. maps. illus.

This book contains an excellent chapter on Buddhism in Nepal.

1114. **Snellgrove, David L.** Himalayan pilgrimage : a study of Tibetan region by a traveller through western Nepal.

For full entry refer to Tourism & travellers' accounts—Travellers' accounts.

1115. **Sudarshan, Bhikshu.** Caitya-pūjā. Kathmandu : Heramaya Shakya, 1980. 28 p.

It is a religious duty of all Buddhists to worship sacred monuments built on relics of the Buddha. This Newari work fully describes such worship, its purpose, its rituals, and its variations.

1116. **Sumangala, Bhikkhu.** Buddha-dharma=Buddhist meditation. Lalitpur, Nepal : Mo. Shilpakar, 1974. 80 p.

A sizeable proportion of the population in Nepal professes Buddhism in some form or other. This book presents articles by the author on Buddhism in English, Nepali, and Newari.

1117. **Von Furer-Haimendorf, Christoph.** A nunnery in Nepal. *Kailash : a Journal of Himalayan Studies*, vol. 4, no. 2 (1976), pp. 121-154. illus.

Bigu gompa (a nunnery) is in Bigu village. *Bigu gompa*, locally known as *Tashi gompa* (its full name is *Tashi-Chime-ga-tsel bikung*—Pleasure garden of deathless good fortune). *Tashi gompa*, like many monastic institutions in Nepal, is a relatively recent foundation and in it Sherpa and Tamang nuns live together. The author visited the nunnery in 1974, and in this article, he describes the history of *Tashi gompa*, its economic base, the structure of the *gompā*-community with its twenty-seven nuns, and the relations between the *gompa* and the village community.

1118. **Watanbe, K.** The Nepalese nava dharms and their Chinese translations. *Journal of the Royal Asiatic Society*, (1970), pp. 663-664.

Miscellaneous information regarding the philosophy and practices of Mahayana Buddhism in Nepal.

1119. **Watters, David E.** Siberian shamanistic traditions among the Kham-Magars of Nepal. *Contributions to Nepalese Studies*, vol. 2, no. 1 (Feb. 1975), pp. 123-168. bibliog. illus.

The Kham-Magars are people of ancient Mongolian descent who inhabit the upper tributaries of the Sāni Bheri, Bari Gād, and Mari Khola on the southwestern flank of the Dhaulagiri massif. Shamanism, as described by most scholars is a magico-religious phenomenon of Siberia and central Asia. In this article, the author has described shamanistic traditions among the Kham-Magars.

1120. **Yatri, Purna Prakash Nepal.** Setīañcala digdarśana : vividha anusandhānātmaka vishayasamanvita.

For full entry refer to Geography—General section.

RELIGIOUS SITES

1121. **Bajracharya, Badree Ratna.** Śrī Lum Madhi Ajimāyā vaṃśāvali = The short history of Bhadrakalika. Kathmandu : Vajracharya Adhyaya Mandal, 1981. 12 p.

Bhadrakali is a deity worshipped by both Hindus and Buddhists in Nepal. This Newari publication presents the traditional history of the Bhadrakali temple at Kathmandu.

1122. **Bajracharya, Purna Harsha.** Swayambhu : the light of Nepal. 2nd ed. Kathmandu : Swayambhu Improvement Society, 1973. 7 p.

This leaflet presents a brief history and description of Swayambhunath, the Buddhist pilgrimage centre located on a hillock near Kathmandu.

1123. **Macdonald, Alexander W.** A little-road guide to the holy places of Nepal. Part 1. *Kailash : a Journal of Himalayan Studies*, vol. 3, no. 2 (1975), pp. 89-144.

A Tibetan-language work, presented here in both transliterated and original forms. The original text was loaned to the author in September 1969 by 'Khrulzig rin-po-che. The author plans to issue a second part of this study, which will contain an annotated translation. This article will be very useful to Tibetologists interested in Nepal.

1124. **Majupuria, Trilok Chandra** and **Majupuria, Indra.** Pashupatinath, the divine glory of the guardian deity of Nepal. Gwalior, India : M. Devi, 1981-82. 272 p. bibliog. illus.

Lord Pashupatinath is the guardian deity of Nepal, which is predominantly a Hindu country, and the King of Nepal prays to Lord Pashupatinath for the welfare of his people and country. The temple of Pashupatinath is believed to have been established in the 1st century, if not earlier. In this work the authors throw light on the legends, history, sculpture, and many other facts and myths about the temple, that have remained unknown or unexplored for many years.

1125. **Regmi, Jagadish Chandra**, ed. Temples of Kathmandu. Kathmandu : Culture Centre,1972. 40 p.

Besides presenting a cursory survey of the existing temples of the Kathmandu Valley, this booklet also presents, in bibliographical form, a history of religions and religious sects during the ancient and mediaeval (c. 464-1475) periods. The classified list of the important existing temples also serves the same purpose.

1126. **Reinhard, Johan.** Khembalung : the hidden valley. *Kailash : a Journal of Himalayan Studies*, vol. 6, no. 1 (1978), pp. 5-35. map.

Guru Rinpoche, the Indian Buddhist yogi is believed to have established several 'hidden valleys', known as *beyul* in Tibetan, while he travelled through the Himalayas. The exact number of *beyul* is not known. Of those *beyul* thought to exist in Nepal, Khembalung must be one of the best known among Buddhists. During October and November 1977 the author, along with eleven companions, decided to gather information concerning this hidden valley and to locate it if at all possible. In this article the author describes the legend and his journey, and gives a translation of the Tibetan text concerning Khembalung. The final section of the article presents the original Tibetan text.

1127. **Roy Chaudhury, Pranab Chandra**. Temples and legends of Nepal. Bombay : Bharatiya Vidya Bhavan, 1972. 93 p. illus. (Bhavan's Book University, 176)

Describes both Hindu and Buddhist temples and legends of Nepal.

1128. **Shakya, Ratna Jyoti**, tr. and comp. A brief introduction to Shiva Deva sanskarita Om Kuli Shri Rudra Varna Mahavihar. Lalitpur, Nepal : Sangha Ratna Shakya, Hira Kaji Shakya, Bhim Ratna Shakya, 1980. 25 p. illus.

A history of the Rudra Varna Mahavihar (Okubahal), a Buddhist monastery in Patan, founded by Shiva Deva in the 6th century. The book has been reconstructed from old Newari manuscripts.

1129. **Slusser, Mary**. Kathmandu : a collection of articles. Kathmandu : American Women of Nepal [1972?]. 46 p. maps.

Collection of articles, previously published in the bulletin of the American Women of Nepal, are concerned with religious sites and monuments in Kathmandu Valley.

1130. **Stoddard, Robert H**. Perceptions about the geography of religious sites in the Kathmandu Valley. *Contributions to Nepalese Studies*, vol. 7, no. 1-2 (Dec. 1978-June 1980), pp. 97-118. map.

The author discusses the topic under the following headings: Nature of geography, Perceptions of sacred space, Geographic characteristics of some cosmologies, The spatial arrangement of selected sacred sites in the Kathmandu Valley, Perceptions of sacred sites, and Conclusions.

1131. **Sudarshan, Bhikshu.** Mahābuddha : chagū adhyayana. 2nd rev. ed. Kathmandu : Bahadur Shakya, 1980. 31 p.

Discusses the religious and historical importance of Mahābuddha, a Buddhist shrine in Kathmandu.

1132. **Tshampa Ngawang of Drumpa**. Places of pilgrimage in Thag (Thakkhola). Edited and translated with an introduction by David Snellgrove. *Kailash : a Journal of Himalayan Studies*, vol. 7, no. 2 (1979), pp. 75-170. maps. illus.

This Tibetan text, presented here with an English translation, relates to various religious sites in the land of Thag, now in the Mustang District. Being close to Tibet, Thag was influenced by Tibetan language and culture.

1133. **Wylie, Turrell.** A Tibetan religious geography of Nepal. Rome : Instituto Italiano per il Medio ed Estremo Oriente, 1970. 66 p. map. bibliög. (Serie Orientale Roma, 42)

This study is based on the Nepali section of *Dzam-gling-rgyas-bshad* by Bla-ma Btsan-po. The term geography, as used here, means little more than a guide book for pilgrims. The book gives succint directions to sacred locations, describes the holy objects found in each, and refers to important ecclesiastic associations.

TEXTS

1134. **Abhidhanottara tantra** : a Sanskrit manuscript from Nepal. Reproduced by Lokesh Chandra. New Delhi : Sharada Rani, 1981. 160 p. (Śata-piṭaka series : Indo-Asian literature, v. 263)

An early mediaeval text of the Vajrayana school of tantric Buddhism, chiefly devoted to the worship of Yoginī (the mother goddess). This text is in all probability a continuation of the tradition of Cakrasaṃvara-tantra. This is reproduced from a manuscript preserved by Professor Raghuvira.

1135. **Asta-sahasrika prajnaparamita** : a Sanskrit manuscript from Nepal. Reproduced by Lokesh Chandra. New Delhi : Sharada Rani, 1981. 177 p. (Śata-piṭaka series : Indo-Asian literature, v. 265)

A canonical text of Mahayana Buddhism as practised in Nepal, it is regarded as one of the nine dharmas. This Sanskrit work is reproduced from the collection of Professor Raghuvira.

1136. **Bajracharya, Devanand**. Svayambhū darśana : Nevā bhāshā śloka, Mālinī chanda. Maru Pigannani, Nepal: Shubharatna Tamrakar [1963?]. 14 p.

A poem describing the religious importance of (Śrīsvayambhū Mahācaitya) Swayambhu, a Buddhist shrine in Kathmandu. It is devotional literature and useful for research purposes.

1137. **Bajracharya, Mohanraj**. Gokarṇeśvara Vītarāga kathā. Lalitpur, Nepal : Sanukaji Vajracharya, 1980. 21 p.

The legend of Gokarneshvar Prince, a mythical character, retold in Newari. It glorifies the importance of rites for the dead (*śraddha*) according to the religious practices of the Buddhist Newars and is an interesting work for the cultural anthropological studies of the community.

1138. **Bhattarai, Muralidhar,** comp. Manushya aura usakā dhyeya = Man and his goal. Kathmandu : Shri Annapurna Press [1961?]. 64 p.

Describes the goal of life according to the Hindu religion. It comprises select Sanskrit and Hindi poetical passages, with English translations and notes in Hindi and English.

1139. **Chemjong, Iman Singh**. Kirāta-mandhuma. Kirāta ko Veda. Palnavam, India : Rajendra Ram [n.d.]. 108 p.

The Limbu community settled in eastern Nepal and Sikkim are known as Kirats. Unlike other tribal peoples, Kirats have a written sacred book, believed to be revelation, which is called *Mundhum* (knowledge). The author, a famous linguistic and historian of the Kirati civilization, has issued this first printed edition of this sacred book in the Kirata language (Devanagari script), along with a Nepali translation. This publication provides sufficient material for the study of Limbu religion.

1140. **Dharmacharya, Dharma Aditya.** Discovery of Dharma Samuccaya in Nepal. *Buddhist India,* vol. 2, no. 1 (Mar. 1928), pp. 34-42.

The Dharma Samuccaya is the greatest work of its kind in Buddhist literature. In this article, the author has described its discovery and this manuscript belongs to 1193 A.D. The original manuscript has title: Dharma Samuccaya nāma dharmaparyāya meaning the exposition of the law known as the Dharma Samuccaya *or* the compendium of the law.

1141. **Gorakhabodha**, tathā 84 siddhamadhye carpatanātha-viracitam : Carpataśatakam. Edited and translated by Nara Hari Nath ; assistant editor : Chandra Nath Yogi. 2nd ed. Kashi, India : Sri Gorakhanatha Pustakalaya, 1964, 48 p. (Gorakshagranthamālāyāḥ saptāśititamam; pushpam 87)

The Gorakhanathies form an important religious sect in India and Nepal. It has two branches: one followed by orthodox Hindus, and one by tantric Buddhists of Nepal. In both, eighty-four *śiddhas*, i.e. realized souls, are accepted as authorities of the traditions. The present work comprises two Sanskrit treatises. First outlines the philosophy and practice of Gorakhanath sect according to the orthodox school and the second is attributed to Charpatinatha, who is not known to other traditions of the sect.

1142. **Karandavyuha and other texts** : Sanskrit manuscripts from Nepal. Reproduced by Lokesh Chandra. New Delhi : Sharada Rani, 1981. 170 p. (Śata-piṭaka series : Indo-Asian literature, v. 268)

This work comprises *Kāraṇḍavyūha*, a Mahayana canon, some protective spells efficacious for magical achievements (*dhāraṇīs*), canonical legends of Buddha (*avadānas*). and prayer-books of the Vajrayana sect of Mahayana Buddhism in Nepal. The *avadānas* are ascribed to the celebrated Kashmiri Buddhist scholar Sarvajñamitra. *Kāraṇḍavyūha* has been published earlier but the other texts are hitherto unpublished, and the *avadānas* are particularly important. The work is reproduced from the collection of Professor Raghuvira.

1143. **Panca-raksa** : two Sanskrit manuscripts from Nepal. Reproduced by Lokesh Chandra. New Delhi : Sharada Rani, 1981, 260 p. illus. (Śita-piṭaka series : Indo-Asian literature, v. 267)

A collection of five classical protective spells (*dhāriṇīs* or *rakṣās*) efficacious for magical achievements; their use is prevalent in the Vajrayana sect of Mahayana Buddhism in Nepal. The work is reproduced from the collection of Professor Raghuvira.

1144. **Satkarmaratnavali.** Girvan Juddha Bikram Saha Deva; Ram Nath Acharya; Damodar Koirala. Kathmandu : The Compilers [1969?]. 4 vols. Available from Valmiki Sanskrit College, Kathmandu.

King Girvan Juddha Vikram Shah Deva, a great scholar of religion, thought it necessary to give a difinitive form of the rituals to the people, and the present work is the outcome of his attempt. This work includes the necessary rituals, domestic rites of the four castes, tantric rituals, spiritual practices, and occasional and ceremonial worship of various deities — Saivites and Shaktas in particular. The mantras to be applied, the liturgical procedures, and objects are all described in the traditional way. This manual is still followed in the orthodox circle, and it is very useful for the study of the Brahmanic religious practices in Nepal.

1145. **Shakya, Hem Raj.** Śrī Hiraṇyavarṇa Mahāvihārasthita piṇḍipātra-abhilekha.

For full entry refers to History—Archives, sources, and inscriptions section.

1146. **Singh, Renu Lal.** Fundamental values. Kathmandu : Ratna Pustak Bhandar, 1964. 57 p.

A presentation of moral, intellectual, and spiritual values and their relevance in today's world situation.

1147. **Singh, Renu Lal.** The right life, or, Swadharma, as taught by Shree Shivapuri Baba, a fully enlightened soul. Kathmandu : Govinda Prasad Pradhan, 1975. 60 p.

Presents the teachings of Shivapuri Baba (Govindananda Bharati), 1826-1963, a Hindu religious leader.

1148. **Stuti-bhajana grantha.** Translator H.B. Chhetri, P.B. Gurung, F.J. Phyarala. Darjeeling, India : Eric Benjamin, 1977. 252 p.

A Nepali version of the Psalms of the Old Testament.

28

SOCIAL SERVICES, HEALTH, AND WELFARE

1149. **Baral**, M.R. ed. The child in Nepal. Kathmandu: Nepal Medical Association, 1979. 204 p.

Contains papers presented at a seminar organized by the Nepal Medical Association on the occasion of the International Year of the Child. These concern with the health facilities and the health conditions of children in Nepal.

1150. **Bennett, Lynn.** Sex and motherhood among the Brahmins and Chhetris of east-central Nepal. *Contributions to Nepalese Studies*, vol. 3, special issue, pp. 1-52. illus.

A revised version of an earlier paper entitled *Pregnancy, birth, and early child rearing: health and family planning attitudes and practices in a Brahman-Chetri community*, which the author wrote under the direction of Dr. Ferdinand E. Okada and which was published as paper no. 9 in the Remote Areas and Local Development Department/UNICEF Research-cum-Action Project series in October 1974. The author collected data from July 1972 to September 1974 as part of the field research for her doctoral dissertation at Columbia University.

1151. **Blustain, Harvey S.** Levels of medicine in a central Nepali village. *Contributions to Nepalese Studies*, vol. 3, special issue, pp. 83-105.

This study was undertaken in Lig Lig Dumre village, western Gorkha District, a community made up of Muslims and Chhetris. The article is concerned with local concepts of illness and its causes and analyses the complex interaction between these traditional concepts and the new techniques of medical practice brought about by the development of the health-delivery systems in Nepal.

1152. **Dixit, Hemang**, comp. and ed. Medical bibliography of Nepal.

For full entry refer to Bibliographies section.

1153. **Gautam, Prasanna Chandra**. Health problems in Karnali Zone : a hospital-based comprehensive study. Kathmandu : Remote Areas and Local Development Department, Government of Nepal/UNICEF, 1974. 53 leaves. (Research-cum-Action Project paper—Remote Areas and Local Development Department, His Majesty's Government of Nepal/UNICEF; no. 6)

Karnali is a hilly area not much known about the natural resources as well as the people living there to the other part of the world. This is a study investigating health conditions in the Karnali region.

1154. **Health service long term plan and the various roles of medical graduates**. Kathmandu : Centre for Educational Research, Innovation, and Development, National Education Committee, Nepal [1979?]. 14 leaves.

These are proposals, short notes, and occasional papers on health service groups, a long-term health service plan, hospitals in the plan, and house offership. This plan was approved by the government, although it elaborated on the concept of health service groups and in certain ways modified it.

1155. **JNMA souvenir** : ninth All Nepal Medical Conference of the Nepal Medical Association, Janakpurdham, 1-4 March 1979. chairman : B.N. Jha; editor : Sanjib Dhungel. Kathmandu : Nepal Medical Association, 1979. 134 p. map.

This is a special issue of *Journal of the Nepal Medical Association*, vol. 17, no. 1. It contains articles on medicine with special reference to Nepal.

1156. **Joshi, Durga D.** Veterinary public health hazards in Nepal. Kathmandu : Chandra Kumar Bhattarai, 1973. 87 p. illus.

An investigation into public health hazards in Kathmandu caused by unhygenic methods of meat and milk distribution. Information is provided about animal diseases that may be transmissible in humans. The author presents suggestions for improving the present conditions.

1157. **Journal of the Institute of Medicine.**

For full entry refer to Professional periodicals section.

1158. **Journal of the Nepal Medical Association.**

For full entry refer to Professional periodicals section.

1159. **Miller, Casper J.** Faith-healers in the Himalayas : an investigation of traditional healers and their festivals in Dolakha District of Nepal. Kathmandu : Centre for Nepal and Asian Studies, Tribhuvan University, 1979. 201 p. 2 maps. bibliog. illus.

This book deals with traditional faith-healers, called *jhānkrīs*, and their clients in the district of Dolkha, Janakpur Zone in north eastern Nepal. The author carried the out field-work from October 1974 to August 1978. During this time, he interviewed traditional healers of various ethnic groups (Tamang, Sherpa, Thami, Jirel, Chetri, and Kami). The author's main purpose was to investigate the functions of *jhānkrīs* that distinguish them from other specialists like priests and doctors, and to discover what kind of organization they have among themselves.

1160. **National Seminar on Women's Decade, 27-30 May 1979 : proceedings.**

For full entry refer to Employment and Manpower section.

1161. **Nepalarajakiya Virapustakalayasthahastalikhitapustakanam brhatsucipatram.**

For full entry refer to Libraries and Museums section.

1162. **Okada, Ferdinand E.** Notes on two Shaman-curers in Kathmandu. *Contributions to Nepalese Studies*, vol. 3, special issue, pp. 107-112.

'Case-books' of two Tamang shamans, who practise among different ethnic groups in the Kathmandu Valley. The author records which illnesses were treated by these urban healers and points out that in Kathmandu, at least, curing is not a primary occupation. The shamans work at their practices only part-time, spending most of their time in other economic pursuits.

1163. **Peters, Larry G.** Shamanism and medicine in developing Nepal. *Contributions to Nepalese Studies*, vol. 6, no. 2 (June 1979), pp. 27-43. bibliog.

The major social function of the shaman in Tamang society is the diagnosis and treatment of illness. This paper first describes indigenous categories of illness and examines the unique relationship that exists between modern medicine and shamanism in the Kathmandu Valley. Secondly, it examines the curing practices of Tamang shamans.

1164. **Pradhan, Bina** [et al.]. Child development study in Nepal : implications for policy and training. Kathmandu : Centre for Economic Development and Administration, Tribhuvan University, 1980. 141 p. bibliog.

The International Year of the Child provided the impetus for this project, entitled Child Development Study in Nepal, Implications for Policy and Training. Two case studies on Nepalese children are presented in this report and these are based on the data collected in the Status of Women in Nepal Project, undertaken by the Centre for Economic Development and Administration. This study was sponsored by the Social Welfare Development Centre for Asia and the Pacific (SWDCAP).

1165. **Proceedings of the Seminar on Traditional Medicines and Role of Medicinal Plants, Kathmandu, August 2-3, 1979.** Editorial board: S.R. Adhikary, chief editor, and others, Kathmandu : Nepal Pharmaceutical Association, 1979. 124 p.

This English and Nepali publication is a special issue of the *Journal of the Nepal Pharmaceutical Association*, 1979. The individual papers are: 'Concept and present status', 'Prospects in the national health case plan', 'Role of medicinal plants', 'Problems of evaluation of safety and efficacy', 'Problems in quality control and standardisation', 'Action programme and international cooperation for development.

1166. **Report of Phase I of the SWDCAP/CPTI Workshop on the Development of Materials for the Training of Paraprofessionals, Panchayat Development Training Institute, Kalbalguri, Jhapa, Nepal, 4 Dec.-12 Dec. 1978.** Lalitpur, Nepal : Central Panchayat Training Institute, 1978. 14 leaves.

The general objective of the workshop was to 'Train the social work educators, community development and rural development trainers in the preparation of indigenous training materials for a more effective role in identifying, analyzing, and combating the problem of poverty'.

1167. **Report of the Seminar on Nutrition Programme, April 4-6, 1977**. Edited by : Padma Shrestha. Lalitpur, Nepal : Central Panchayat Training Institute [1977]. 71 p. illus.

This was the first Seminar on Nutrition Programme in Nepal. The main objectives of the seminar was to co-ordinate the nutrition programmes of different governmental and non-governmental agencies and implement them in an integrated manner at the local level.

1168. **Shrestha, Ramesh** and **Shrestha, Mathura**. Report of a study in the primary health care unit (district) of Nuwakot, Nepal. Kathmandu : Health, Manpower Development Research Project, 1979. 101 p. (Rural Health Needs, study no. 3)

This report is the third publication of the Institute of Medicine, Health, Manpower Development Research Project. It identifies the health needs and health situation in the Nuwakot District. The findings in this district survey further emphasize the need for expansion of government health services.

1169. **Skjerven, Ove**. A demographic and nutritional survey of two villages in the upper Rolwaling Valley. *Kailash : a Journal of Himalayan Studies*, vol. 3, no. 3 (1975), pp. 295-301.

As part of a broad scientific study of the upper Rolwaling Valley, undertaken during October-November 1973 by a Scandinavian expedition, two villages, Beding and Simigon, were examined in terms of demographic and nutritional characteristics. Beding is a purely Sherpa village and Simigaon is about half Sherpa and half other ethnic groups, mostly Tamangs. The results of the survey are presented, together with a discussion and summary.

1170. **Stablein, William**. A medical-cultural system among the Tibetan and Newar Buddhists : ceremonial medicine. *Kailash : a Journal of Himalayan Studies*, vol. 1, no. 3 (1973), pp. 193-203.

In this article, the author briefly delineates the basic units which make up a medical-cultural-system, as symbolized by language and myth in ritual. He suggests that these units are fundamental to the *Vajrayāna* ritual complex, which is used for curing more than for any other reason. The article is partially the result of the author's field-work in Kathmandu, carried between 1968-71.

1171. **Stone, Linda.** Concepts of illness and curing in a central Nepal village. *Contributions to Nepalese Studies*, vol. 3, special issue, pp. 55-80. bibliog.

This description of illness and its treatment is based on research carried out in the village of Dhungagaun, located fifty miles north-west of Kathmandu, in Nuwakot District, Bagmati Zone. The author discusses local beliefs about the causes of illness, concentrating on the cultural and psychological aspects of illness.

1172. **Stone, Linda.** Cultural repercussions of childlessness and low fertility in Nepal. *Contributions to Nepalese Studies*, vol. 5, no. 2 (June 1978), pp. 7-36. bibliog.

The field-work was carried out in Nepal during 1973-75, under a fellowship granted by the Foreign Area Fellowship Program of the Social Sciences Research Council. Kingsley Davis was the principal investigator. The paper is divided into the following sections: Women and children : gradations in the stigma of childlessness; Parents and sons; Alternatives and options; 'Secondary wives by orthodox marriage; Secondary wives by elopement; Brothers and sons : the root of the problem; Adoption; The 'house-son-in-law'; Childlessness and social options: some comparisons with sub-Saharan Africa; and Childlessness and social change in Nepal.

1173. **Susta manasthitibata pidita = The retarded.** Kathmandu: Human and National Development Service, 1980. 80 p.

Presents case studies of mentally retarded children in Nepal.

1174. **Traditional and prevailing child-rearing practices among different communities in Nepal.** Contributors : Sudha Paneru, Basundhara Dhungel, Jitpal Kirat, Deon Prasad Rajaure, edited by Sudha Paneru. Kirtipur, Nepal : Centre for Nepal and Asian Studies, Tribhuvan University, 1980. 117 p. bibliog.

This work is part of a larger study, *Status of Children in Nepal* sponsored jointly by the Child Welfare Co-ordinating Committee/

Nepal and UNICEF/Nepal as a part of the International Year of the Child, 1979. The contents are : Introduction and methodology, The Thakuris, The Newars, The Sherpas, The Tharus, Conclusion and recommendation.

1175. **Wake, C.J.** Health services and some cultural factors in eastern Nepal. *Contributions to Nepalese Studies,* vol. 3, special issue, pp. 113-126.

A large-scale study of health conditions as perceived by health workers and villagers in four districts in eastern Nepal — Solukhumbu, Dhankuta, Jhapa, and Dhanusa. Some of the cultural implications of the Fifth Five Year Plan as applied to health services in the four districts are also reviewed.

29

SOCIETY AND SOCIAL STRUCTURE

1176. **Acharya, Meena.** Statistical profile of Nepalese women : a critical review. Kathmandu : Centre for Economic Development and Administration, Tribhuvan University, 1979. 101 p. bibliog. (Status of women in Nepal : vol. 1 : Background report, pt. 1)

This background report, part one in a series of monographs, presents a national statistical profile of Nepalese women. Specifically, it draws upon the available statistical data on women's economic, educational, and health status and on their childbearing and childrearing roles, and then translates the data into a unified portrait of Nepalese women today.

1177. **Bhattarai, Tara Deva.** A review of the community development programme in Nepal. Jawalakhel, Nepal : Central Panchayat Training Institute, Research Division, [1976?]. 51 leaves. bibliog.

This book was originally a M.Sc. thesis presented to the Department of Sociology and Anthropology, Michigan State University, in 1960. The contents are: Rural social structure of Nepal; Administrative structure of Community Development Department; Nature and function of development organization; The conspicuous position of village development worker; and Contribution of social science in community development.

1178. **Bista, Dor Bahadur.** Padipur : a central Terai village. *Contributions to Nepalese Studies*, vol. 3, no. 1 (Jan. 1976), pp. 1-32.

The village of Padipur lies on one side of a road running between two district headquarters in the central Terai. There are 155 households in the village. The article describes the village and covers: location, origins and history, the population, social structure, the dacoity, elections, agriculture, land tenancy, crops and livestock, the agricultural calendar, religious beliefs, economic development, education, government, the panchayats, etc.

1179. **Borgstrom, Bengt-Erik.** Kitini Gaon Panchayat : a presentation. *Contributions to Nepalese Studies*, vol. 1, no. 2 (June 1974), pp. 1-9.

Kitini Gaon Panchayat is located on the south eastern fringe of the Kathmandu Valley, about eighty miles from the headquarters of Lalitpur District Panchayat in Patan. This article is a socio-economic study of the Kitini Gaon Panchayat.

1180. **Bouillier, Veronique.** Economic relationships between occupational castes and high castes in central Nepal. Translated from the French by Sarah Duke. *Contributions to Nepalese Studies*, vol. 4, no. 2 (June 1977), pp. 99-110. bibliog. illus.

The facts presented here were gathered in Kattike Deurali Village Panchayat, Kabhre Palanchok District. This village, with the exception of two Newari families, is populated only by the following Nepalese castes: Jaisi Bahun, Chetri, Giri, Kami, Sarki, and Damai. Kami, Sarki, and Damai are occupational castes and the others are treated as high castes. This is the study of economic relationships between the three occupational castes and the other castes.

1181. **Campbell, J. Gabriel** [et al.]. The use and misuse of social science research in Nepal. Kirtipur, Nepal : Research Centre for Nepal and Asian Studies, Tribhuvan University, 1979. 153 p. bibliog.

A survey of the rapidly growing field of social science research in Nepal. The authors argue that research methods used in the West need to be adapted to suit Nepal's culture and the conditions prevailing in the country. In particular, believe that some of the social science data that is generated for development planning runs the risk of being both superficial and inaccurate. After scrutinizing current research methods used in Nepal and evaluating the validity of the data obtained, the authors suggest ways in which the quality and usefulness of social science research can be improved.

1182. **Caplan, A. Patricia.** Priests and cobblers : a study of a social change in a Hindu village in western Nepal. San Francisco : Chandler, 1972. 103 p. 2 maps. bibliog. illus. (Studies in soci al and economic change)

The author examines some of the economic and political changes which have taken place in Duari village, Belaspur District, western Nepal. The field work was conducted from January to December 1969. In presenting some general conclusions, the author makes some comparisons with other studies of social change in villages of India and Nepal.

1183. **Contributions to Nepalese studies.** Kirtipur, Nepal : Research Centre for Nepal and Asian Studies, 1973- semiannual.

This is journal of the Research Centre for Nepal and Asian Studies, Tribhuvan University. Includes scholarly articles in English and Nepali on Social Sciences and humanities in Nepal. Also includes papers, review articles, and short reviews of new books on Nepal.

1184. **Das, Shanta.** Basibiyāmlo : nibandha-saṅgālo. Kathmandu : Nav-Aloka Prakashan, 1980. 43 p.

A collection of controversial essays on various social and other contemporary problems of Nepal by a very talented writer.

1185. **Fisher, James F.**, ed. Himalayan anthropology: the Indo-Tibetan interface. The Hague : Mouton Publishers, 1978. 567 p. illus. (World anthropology)

This publication is divided into four parts: part one contains articles discussing general issues that affect the whole area; part two deals with groups or topics which are part of the South Asian tradition ; the third part is devoted largely to Central Asia, and the fourth part focuses on the Newars of Nepal, who in many ways exemplify the syncretistic nature of Himalayan society. The contributors are anthropologists, political scientists, linguists, sociologists, and students of comparative religion, from both Western and Eastern countries.

1186. **Gaborieau, Marc.** Le Nepal et ses populations. Brussels : Editions Complexe, PUF, 1978. 312 p. maps. bibliog.

A comprehensive look at Nepal in historical, anthropological and sociological terms. Part one deals with the geographical setting and historical development; part two examines the diversity of the population; and part three tackles the problems faced by a country of such diversity when confronted with the political aims of national unification.

1187. **Ghimire, Durga**, ed. Women and development. Kathmandu : Centre for Economic Development and Administration, Tribhuvan University, 1977. 77 p.

The proceedings of the seminar on women and development organized by Centre for Economic Development and Administration under the auspices of International Women's Year. The articles and comments contain a great deal of detailed information on traditional values and social norms, prevailing discriminatory laws, absence of equal opportunities for women.

1188. **Gutschow, Niels** and **Kolver, Bernhard.** Ordered space concepts and functions in a town of Nepal. Wiesbaden, GFR : Kommissionsverlag Franz Steiner GmbH, 1975. 59 p. 3 maps. bibliog. illus. (Nepal Research Centre. Publications, 1)

An attempt to outline the relations between tangible functions and abstract concepts in a Hindu city. The object of this study is the town of Bhaktapur (formerly known as Bhatgaon), a place which has not yet been greatly affected by Westernization. Includes a list of Bhaktapur castes.

1189. **Hitchcock, John T**. Some effects of recent change in rural Nepal. *Human Organization*, vol. 22, no. 1 (1963), pp. 75-82.

Discusses the socio-economic problems in Pandera Thum zone.

1190. **Household baseline study resource conservation and utilization project**. Prepared for His Majesty's Government of Nepal, Department of Soil and Water Conservation and the United States Agency for International Development by the Agricultural Projects Services Centre. Kathmandu : The Centre, 1980. 182 leaves.

Summarizes the findings of the baseline survey conducted in the three catchment areas of Kulekhani, Daraundi, and Upper Kaligandaki. The report covers demographic, economic, social, and environmental concerns. An attempt is made to present information on existing conditions among rural households in terms of these four categories.

1191. **Jha, Makhan**. Civilization & complex societies in South Asia. Varanasi, India : Kishor Vidya Niketan, 1981. 92 p. bibliog.

An anthropological study of South Asia, with special reference to the pilgrimage centres in India and Nepal, industrial society, the urbanization of the traditional city, the Vedic ashrams of ancient Rishis and their cultural contributions, etc.

1192. **Majupuria, Indra**. Nepalese women. Kathmandu : M. Devi, 1982. 304 p. bibliog. illus.

An account of the status and role of Nepalese women in all aspects of society: religious, social, economic, political, and legal.

1193. **Malla, Kamal Prakash**. The road to nowhere : a selection of writings, 1966-1977.

For full entry refer to Literature—Texts section.

1194. **Malla, Kamal Prakash** and **Kanaskar, Tej R.**, ed. Occasional papers in the humanities and social sciences.

For full entry refer to Languages and Dialects—Linguistic studies section.

1195. **Nepalese Society** : an introductory account of the main specialities of different ethnic and occupational groups of Nepalese society. Kathmandu : National Museum of Nepal, 1975. 51 p. bibliog. illus.

An introduction to the various ethnic and occupational groups in Nepal, examining their customs, environment, languages, and cultures.

1196. **Nepali samaja** : Nēpalī samajakā tehra jāti tathā peśāgata jātaharūko saṅkshipta paricaya. Kathmandu : National Archives, 1975. 57 p. illus.

A study, in Nepali, of the various ethnic groups and professional classes in Nepal.

1197. **Okada, Ferdinand E.** The kinship basis of a Nepalese rural ward. *Contributions to Nepalese Studies*, vol. 4, no. 1 (Dec. 1976), pp. 23-38. map. bibliog. illus.

Discusses function and processes of the social structure of rural Nepal. The author selected Ward 7 of Makaibari in the Kathmandu Valley and studied the structural patterns of kinship there. He suggests that the situation found in this ward is essentially the same as found in most of the rural wards in the midland hill zone of Nepal and that, whether or not the localities are physically separated, distinct kin groups can, in the main, be identified in association with distinct localities.

1198. **Parmar, Y.S.** Polyandry in the Himalayas. Delhi : Vikas, 1975. 191 p.

Describes polyandry as practised in the Himalayas and analyses its psychological, biological, and economic causes.

1199. **Poffenberger, Mark.** Patterns of change in the Nepal Himalaya. Delhi : Macmillan Company of India, 1980. 117 p. bibliog.

This work first explores how social and demographic conditions have interacted to cause increasing population growth over the past 200 years; secondly, it analyses the impact of population growth on hill ecosystems. Finally, the author attempts to establish how localized hill communities are responding, both in terms of their economic behaviour and fertility rates, to pressures resulting from the interaction of demographic, ecological, and socio-economic forces. The study found that a number of widely held theories of demographic change do not effectively explain the forces behind the demographic change in Nepal. The author suggests alternative approaches to the analysis of population patterns.

1200. **Pradhan, Bina.** Institutions concerning women in Nepal. Kathmandu : Centre for Economic Development and Administration, Tribhuvan University, 1979, 140 p. bibliog. (Status of women in Nepal. Vol. 1 : Background report, pt. 4)

This background report describes the current programmes set up by the government and private organizations to benefit women in Nepal. These organizations are: the Nepal Women's Organization; the Women's Services Co-ordination Committee; the Women's Affairs Training and Extension Centre of the Ministry of Home and Panchayat; the Social and Cultural Centre for Women: the Mother's Club, and the Business and Professional Women's Club. Also included is the Equal Access of Women to Education project of the Ministry of Education. Each institution's history, goals, leadership, membership patterns, organizational structure, programmes, forms of environmental linkages, and extent of resource mobilizati on are described and analysed.

1201. **Putnam, April M.** The tea shop as an arena of ethnic interaction in Nepal. *Contributions to Nepalese Studies*, vol. 2, no. 1 (Feb. 1975), pp. 11-17.

The author in her field-work observed that the tea shops lining the feeder roads to Narayangad, Chitwan District's main bazar town, provide an excellent arena for studying interaction between the different caste/ethnic groups of the Rapti Valley resettlement area. The tea shop is not only a place for relaxation and refreshment, but also a forum for discussions ranging from local gossip to world affairs, and a place to conduct business. Low castes are permitted at these tea stalls, but are treated differently. The author describes a particular tea shop in this article, analysing the behaviour patterns and conversations.

1202. **Raj, Prakash A.** A Nepalese discovers his country. Kathmandu : Sajha Prakashan, 1979. 112 p.

Discusses the social, economic, political, and cultural transformation of Nepal since 1951.

1203. **Rana, Kamal.** Status and role of women in the organised sector on the situation in Nepal. Kathmandu : Social Services National Coordinating Council, Nepal, [1977]. 38 p.

In Nepal women are often discriminated against, and men have more prestige, power, and privilege. But the direct measurement of status is a difficult and complex problem. This study was undertaken to highlight certain problems of women in Nepal.

1204. **Regmi, Jagadish Chandra.** People of Nepal. Series no. 2. Assisted by Sheshraj Shiwakoti. Kathmandu: Office of the Nepal-Antiquary, 1981. 193 leaves.

This mimeographed publication is a special issue of *Nepal-Antiquary: Journal of Socio-historical Research and Digest* (April 1981) and replaces no. 31-35. Rather misleadingly titled, this collection includes not only ethnological studies of some of the peoples of Nepal—Lepchas, Kirats, Gurungs, Sunuwars, Rajabamshis, and Muslims but also articles on history, current affairs, law, foreign affairs, Himalayan archives, Oriental women, and US, contributions to Nepal.

1205. **Report on Repati Baseline Survey.** Prepared for His Majesty's Government of Nepal and the United States

Agency for International Development by the Agricultural Projects Services Centre. Kathmandu : Agricultural Projects Services Centre, 1980. 2 vols. map.

This mimeographed report summarizes the findings of the Rapati Baseline Survey in its four main areas: demographic, economic, social, and environmental. The survey was intended to get information on existing conditions among rural households, in each of the four categories. It was conducted in the five administrative districts of the Rapti Zone. Household types were classified according to the total cultivated land owned by the households, but in a few places, the reporting was based on ethnic groups.

1206. **Rural women in today's horizon** : a report on the National Workshop for the Promotion and Training of Rural Women in Income-Raising Group Activities, 5-7 February 1979, Mujelia, Janakpur, Nepal. Chandni Joshi, assisted by Ganesh Chandra Adhikari; Raman Raj Mishra. Kathmandu : Social Services National Co-ordination Council, Women's Services Co-ordination Committee, Nepal, [1979?]. 68 p.

The women involved in the income-raising project, representatives of the Women's Services Co-ordination Committee and the U.N. Agencies, and the four case-study writers constituted the participants in the workshop seminar. During the first two days of the seminar, four case-studies 'Agro-based cottage industry', 'Vegetable farming', 'Ginger production', and 'Handicraft', were presented to show how women were successfully able to raise their income. The women in the workshop were then divided into four discussion groups in order to consider the case-studies and to prepare plans for future programmes on the income raising activities of rural women.

1207. **Sharma, Prayag Raj**. Caste, social mobility, and Sanskritization : a study of Nepal's old legal code. *Kailash : a Journal of Himalayan Studies*, vol. 5, no. 4 (1977), pp. 277-299. bibliog.

This article examines the broad features of the process in Nepal. The analysis is based on the old legal code, called the *Ain* or *Mulki Ain*. A description of the Sanskritization process is also presented, based on general observations of this phenomenon around present-day Nepal or in the recent past.

1208. **Sharma, Prayag Raj.** Nepal : Hindu-tribal interface. *Contributions to Nepalese Studies,* vol. 6, no. 1 (Dec. 1978), pp. 1-14. bibliog.

Attempts to critically review and clarify the problem of Nepal's Hindu-tribal relationships. The author suggests the usual approch; emphasizing a sharp Hindu-tribal dichotomy, suffers from a lack of historical perspective. By combining historical and anthropological approaches, the author tries to demonstrate that the ethnic groups in Nepal are more interrelated than divided and that the notions of 'Hinduand 'tribal' are perhaps better understood as a continuum than as a dichotomy.

1209. **Sharma, Prayag Raj,** ed. Social science in Nepal : a report on the Seminar on Social Science held in the Institute of Nepal and Asian Studies, T.U., in October 1973. Kathmandu : Institute of Nepal and Asian Studies, Tribhuvan University, 1974. 215 p.

The contents are: 'Geography in Nepal' by Soorya Lal Amatya; 'Sociology and anthropology in Nepal' by A. W. Macdonald; 'The state of anthropology in Nepal' by Khem Bahadur Bista; 'The development of sociology in Nepal' by T. S. Thapa; 'History in Nepal : reflections of a working historian' by Dr. Ludwig F. Stiller; 'Development of the study of political science in Nepal', by B.C. Malla; 'Public Administration in Nepal' by Dr. Prachanda Pradhan; and 'Economics in Nepal' by Dr. P.P. Timilsina.

1210. **Shrestha, Indira.** Annotated bibliography on women in Nepal.

For full entry refer to Bibliographies section.

1211. **Shrestha, Vihari Krishan.** Karṇālī loka saṃskṛti. vol. 3: jana jīvana. Kathmandu : Royal Nepal Academy, 1971. 114 p. 2 maps.

The volumes in this series attempt to bring to light the civilization, economic and social conditions, history and geography of the Karnali Zone. This volume deals with the people of Karnali with particular reference to Diyar Village. It gives information about the life of the people in general, folk culture, the culture of the higher strata of the society and the aristocracy. In addition, the origins of the ancient races, tribes, and families are traced. Various systems of marriage, Hindu rites and ceremonies with local variations, popular religion, etc., are also discussed.

1212. **Stone, Linda.** Food symbolism in Hindu Nepal. *Contributions to Nepalese Studies*, vol. 6, no. 1 (Dec. 1978), pp. 47-65. bibliog. illus.

This study is based on fieldwork in the rural community of Dhaungagaun, located in the hills of central Nepal. Brahmans and Chhetris predominate in Dhungagaun. They all practise farming and follow Hindu religious practices. The author offers here an interpretation of food symbolism among Brahmans and Chhetris, based on comparisons. He attempts to show that there is a consistency in the use of food symbols throughout these different cultural realms. These patterns then suggest a broader interpretation of how food symbols become a medium through which certain basic ideological principles of Brahman-Chhetri society are expressed.

1213. **Von Furer-Haimendorf, Christoph.** Caste in the multi-ethnic society of Nepal. *Contributions to Indian Sociology*, vol. 4 (1960), pp. 12-32.

Discusses the variations of the caste system peculiar to Nepal.

1214. **Wake, C.J.** Bikas : evolution in Nepal. Kathmandu : Research Centre for Nepal and Asian Studies, Tribhuvan University, 1980. 186 p. bibliog. illus.

Bikas mean evolution. The author looks with an anthropologist's eye at the changes that modernization has brought to the people of Nepal, their hopes and frustrations, and their achievements. The changes in political development, political and administrative processes, land use and agricultural development, economic development, education, health services, and culture and development are discussed in this book.

1215. **Women in Nepal.** Kathmandu : International Women's Year Committee, Nepal, 1976. 115 p.

A collection of articles by various people. It includes the speeches of government officials.

1216. **Women of Nepal** : approaches to change : a seminar sponsored by U.S. International Communication Agency and Centre for Economic Development and Administration, May 17-18, 1978, Kathmandu. Kathmandu : Tribhuvan University, Centre for

Economic Development and Administration, 1978. 95 p. bibliog.

A collection of background papers, plenary papers, and workshop recommendations from the seminar. The papers include descriptions of the various women's organizations in Nepal, a comparison with the women's movement in America, and observations on the women's movement in Nepal.

30

SPORTS AND RECREATION

1217. **Rana, Ina Shumshere** and **Dixit, Mani.** Those were the days. Kathmandu : Sharda Prakashan Griha, 1977. 168 p. 1 map.

Experiences of hunting by the authors in India and Nepal Includes illustration.

1218. **Shyam Bahadur K.C.** and **Kumar, Uttam.** Sports in Nepal. Kathmandu : National Sports Council, 1975. 106 p.

This is the translation of Nepali work 'Nepālamā khelakūda'. Gives details about the sport activities in Nepal. Includes illustrations.

31

TOURISM AND TRAVELLERS' ACCOUNTS

GUIDEBOOKS

1219. **Amatya, Jagadish Man Singh.** Picturesque Nepal. 3rd rev. ed. Kathmandu : Ratna Pustak Bhandar, 1970. 128 p. illus.

A fully illustrated handbook for tourists.

1220. **Amatya, Jagadish Man Singh.** Pokhara Valley : trekking and Annapurna : Dhaulagiri area. Kathmandu : Man Kumari Amatya, 1970. 174 p. illus.

Pokhara Valley is in central Nepal, ninety miles north-northwest of Kathmandu. This book is useful guide to the Dhaulagiri area of Pokhara Valley.

1221. **Bajracharya, Manik Lal.** A catalogue on Nepal. Kathmandu : Eastern Trading and Investment Company, 1973. 281 p. illus.

A guidebook for tourists.

1222. **Bezruchka, Stephen.** Guide to trekking in Nepal. Foreword by Edmund Hillary. 4th ed. Seattle, Washington : The Mountaineers ; Kathmandu : Sahayogi Press, 1981. 256 p. maps. bibliog. illus.

A comprehensive, authoritative guide for the trekkers. Also provides information on planning treks and on the individual trails. The author includes details on Nepali language, culture, customs, and natural history.

1223. **Bista, Soma Dhoj** and **Satyal, Yajna Raj.** Nepal travel companion. Kathmandu, 1967. 153 p. illus.

A useful travel guide issued during International Tourist Year.

1224. **Elliott, J.H.** Guide to Nepal. 2nd ed. Calcutta : W. Newman, 1963. 122 p. maps. bibliog. illus.

A useful guidebook for tourists.

1225. **Iozawa, Tomoya.** Trekking in the Himalayas. Translated by Michiko U. Kornhauser and David H. Kornhauser. Tokyo : Yama-Kei, 1980. 208 p. maps. illus.

This book was originally published in Japanese in 1976 under the title: *Himaraya torekkingu.* The author trekked throughout the Himalayas and made a full study of the area before writing this book. Most other books deal wtth portions of the Himalayas, but this book discusses the whole range of 3,500 kilometers. The information was collected during the author's four visits to the Himalayas between 1970-75, and all the descriptions are supported by excellent maps, sketches, and illustrations.

1226. **Malla, Kamal P.** Kathmandu, your Kathmandu. Kathmandu : Nepal Press, 1967. 15 p.

Information on Kathmandu for tourists. The essay describes the history, religion, culture, and political conditions of Kathmandu, and the natural resources around Kathmandu are examined in detail.

1227. **Maskay, Pushkar Lal.** Guide to Bhaktapur : the town of devotees. Kathmandu : The Author, 1962. 59 p. map. illus.

Bhaktapur (formerly known as Bhadgaon) is a place of historical importance and is famous for its abundance of mediaeval art and architecture. It is one of the three most important towns of Nepal and was established in about 889 AD during the time of Raja Anand Dev. In the past the town was inhabited by *Bhaktas* which mean devotees, and hence Bhaktapur is called 'The town of Devotees'. This guidebook describes Bhaktapur's people, cottage industries, temples, gods and goddesses, local dances and festivals, etc.

1228. **Nepal, an interesting account to foreigners.** Kathmandu : Department of Publicity, Ministry of Information & Broadcasting, 1966. 61 p. illus.

A useful travel guide.

1229. **Nepal in pictures.** Kathmandu : His Majesty's Government of Nepal, Department of Publicity and Broadcasting [1963?]. illus.

A useful guidebook.

1230. **Raj, Prakash A.** Kathmandu and the Kingdom of Nepal. Victoria, Australia : Lonely Planet, 1980. 160 p. maps. illus.

Widely available, this informal guide is intended primarily for budget travellers. It contains useful and practical advice on locating accommodation and restaurants, travelling by public transport, and shopping, along with information on tourist sites, trekking, local customs, etc. Includes a glossary of Nepali terms and a list of local festivals.

1231. **Raj, Prakash A.** Nepal on two dollars a day : a guide for the tourist. Kathmandu : The Author, 1973. 143 p. maps. illus.

A guide for the tourists.

1232. **Raj, Prakash A.** Nepal on $ 4 a day. 2nd ed. Kathmandu : R.C. Joshi, 1975. 153 p. maps.

A guidebook for travellers. This is a revised and updated edition of *Nepal on two dollars a day* by the same author.

1233. **Rana, Pramode S.J.B.** Your guided companion = Votre renseignement guide = Auskunfte fur touristen. Kathmandu : Jore Ganesh Press, 1971. 54 p. 4 maps.

A guide to the Kathmandu Valley in English, French, and German.

1234. **Rieffel, Robert.** Nepal, namaste. 2nd rev. ed. Kathmandu : Sahayogi Prakashan, 1975. 225 p. illus.

A guidebook containing general information.

1235. **Rouvre, Evrard de.** Guide touristique et artistique. Paris : Éditions Robur, 1975. 255 p. map. bibliog. illus. (Le Monde en Poche)

A very useful handbook on Nepal for French speaking tourists.

1236. **Shrestha, A.P.** Colourful Palpa : its potential for tourism. Tansen, Nepal : Palpa Research Centre, [1974?]. 23 p. map. illus.

Palpa District is situated in Lumbini Zone of Nepal. This book describes its tourist sites.

1237. **Shrestha, D.B.** and **Singh, C.B.** Picturesque Kathmandu : some places of interest in the Kathmandu Valley ; some illuminating facts. 2nd rev. and enl. ed. Kathmandu : The Authors, 1971. 123 p. map. illus.

A tourist guide which describes Kathmandu Valley in pictures, with particular reference to temples and tourist sites.

1238. **Thapa, Udhir Samsher.** Know Nepal and Nepali. Kathmandu : Shail Thapa, 1971. 120 p. maps. illus.

A guide to Nepal and the Nepali language.

1239. **Williams, L. F. Rushbrook,** ed. A handbook for travellers in India, Pakistan, Nepal, Bangladesh and Sri Lanka (Ceylon). 22nd rev. ed. London: John Murray; New York : Barnes & Noble, 1975. 762 p. illus.

Among the many new features in this edition is a long section on Nepal. The author provides expert coverage of many special subjects.

TRAVELLERS' ACCOUNTS

1240. **Baker, Michael H. C.** Journey to Kathmandu. London : David & Charles, 1974. 167 p. illus.

Describes a journey from England to Kathmandu.

1241. **Bernstein, Jeremy.** The wildest dreams of Kew : a profile of Nepal. Photographs by Claude Jaecoux. London : Allen & Unwin, 1970. 186 p. bibliog. illus.

This traveller's account describes the history, land, and people of Nepal.

1242. **Eskelund, Karl.** The forgotten valley : a journey into Nepal. London : Redman, 1959. 187 p. map. illus.

An account of the author's travels.

1243. **Freshfield, Douglas W.** Round Kanchenjunga : a narrative of mountain travel and exploration.

For full entry refer to Geography—General section.

1244. **Hillary, Louise.** High time. London : Hodder and Stoughton, 1973. 192 p. map. illus.

A Descriptive account of travel in the Everest region of the Himalayas.

1245. **Marnham, Patrick.** Road to Kathmandu. London : MacMillan, 1971. 160 p. map.

An account of the author's journey from Istanbul to Kathmandu by road.

1246. **Mineau, Wayne.** The fever peaks. London : Davies, 1962. 217 p. maps. illus.

The author's experiences in Nepal, together with a brief history of Nepal after the Gurkha conquest.

1247. **Morris, John.** A winter in Nepal. London : R. Hart-Davis, 1963. 232 p. illus.

An account of the authors travels in Nepal which includes detailed descriptions of Kathmandu, Patan, and Bhadgaon (Bhaktapur). The author was an army officer who served with Gurkhas, and this enabled him to thoroughly study the Gurkhas and their life and customs. This makes the travels account more interesting.

1248. **Oldfield, Henry Ambrose** and **Oldfield, Margaret Alicia.** Views of Nepal, 1851-1864. Kathmandu : Ratna Pustak Bhandar, 1975. 53 p. illus. (Bibliotheca Himalayica; Series III, vol. 5)

Selected sketches and paintings by a British Resident surgeon and his wife. These are presently in the collection of the India Office Library, London.

1249. **Sakya, Karna.** Dolpo : the world behind the Himalayas. Kathmandu : Sharda Prakashan Griha, 1978. 198 p. maps. bibliog. illus.

Dolpo is situated in Dhaulagiri Zone of Nepal. This is a narrative of the author's expedition to Dolpo.

1250. **Snellgrove, David L.** Expériences népalaises. *Objects et Mondes*, vol. 6, no. 2 (1966), pp. 91-120. illus.

An article in French recounting the author's travels. He describes Nepal with special reference to shrines and architecture.

1251. **Snellgrove, David L.** Himalayan pilgrimage : a study of Tibetan region by a traveller through western Nepal. Oxford : Cassirer, 1961. 304 p. maps. bibliog. illus.

A study of the history and development of Buddhism which includes the author's account of his travels through the remote regions of west Nepal.

1252. **Temple, Richard.** Travels in Nepal and Sikkim. With a new introduction by J. Gordon Temple. Reprint. Kathmandu : Ratna Pustak Bhandar, 1977. 131 p. 3 maps. illus. (Bibliotheca Himalayica; series I, vol. 20)

A reprint of the chapters dealing with Nepal and Sikkim in *Journals kept in Hyderabad, Kashmir, Sikkim and Nepal*, vol. 2 (1887), p. 151-262, published in London, and an article on the Lake Region of Sikkim published in the *Proceedings of the Royal Geographical Society*, no. 4 (June 1881), pp. 326-40. It first appeared in book form in 1887. In 1874-77, Sir Richard Temple was Lieutenant Governor of Bengal, and in May 1876 he toured Nepal. This book contains the author's remarks on the tour.

1253. **Tucci, Giuseppe.** Journey to Mustang, 1952. Translated from the Italian by Diana Fussell. 1st English ed. Kathmandu : Ratna Pustak Bhandar, 1977. 85 p. map. illus.

The first English translation of *Tra giugle a Pagode*, first published in Rome in 1953. This is an account of the Tucci Nepal Expedition from Kathmandu to Pokhara and back again via Tatopani, Mustang, Baglung and Rumminidei.

1254. **The Visit of Prince Waldemar of Prussia to Nepal in February and March 1845.** Translated by Per Kvaerne. *Kailash : a Journal of Himalayan Studies*, vol. 7, no.2 (1979), pp. 35-50.

Prince Waldemar visited Ceylon, India, and Nepal in 1844-46, and his diary of this journey, edited by Alexander von Humboldt and published posthumously in Berlin in 1853, contains a chapter on Nepal. This is the first English translation of the prince's account of his visit to Nepal, which took place between 5 February and mid March 1845.

TOURISM

1255. **Khumbu region tourism study**. Kathmandu : Industrial Services Centre, 1979. 124 p. illus.

Khumbu region is in the Sagarmatha Zone. This report is a condensed version of a four-volume study; it gives the summaries and conclusions of the tourist development plan, examines the engineering and investment proposals, discusses the economic and financial implications, and finally looks at organization and management. The report covers the design of the project, land-use planning, the projected demand, policy and implementation, and also includes a list of consultants and six statistical appendixes.

1256. **Uprety, Dilli Raj** and **Uprety, Bhagwati**. Le royaume du Népal = Nepāla. Kathmandu : B. Uprety. 1974. 160 p. map.

This French publication describes the history of Nepal with particular reference to tourist sites. The publication was issued on the coronation occasion of Birendra Bir Bikram Shaha Deva, b. 1945.

32

TRADE

1257. **Adhikari, Krishna Kant.** A brief survey of Nepal's trade with British India during the latter half of the nineteenth century. *Contributions to Nepalese Studies*, vol. 2, no. 1 (Feb. 1975), pp. 187-196.

Nepal's trade at this time was limited to India and Tibet, and through Tibet, there was some trade with China. However, there was no registered trade between India and Nepal until 1875. This article discusses the trade between Nepal and India which was confined mainly to export and import goods, the duties levied on such goods, and other matters relating to trade.

1258. **Aziz, Barbara N.** Preliminary research report on anthropological explorations of the eastern Himalayas. *Contributions to Nepalese Studies*, vol. 5, no. 1 (Dec. 1977), pp. 45-53. map.

This report is presented as an introduction to the trade economy of the Arun Valley, eastern Nepal. In compiling this material, the author has tried to provide quantification of the processes described and also attempted to draw attention to this powerful and telling transport economy, suggesting that further attention in this area will yield a deeper understanding of the hill economy as well as some direction for later economic developments.

1259. **Bajracharya, Manik Lal.** Nepal, 1972-73 : trade and information directory. Kathmandu : Eastern Trading and Investment Co., 1973. 591 p.

A comprehensive directory, which provides general information on various aspects of Nepal with an emphasis on development trends, trade, and treaties. The trade directory section contains a detailed list of trade professionals, industries and manufacturers and exporters.

1260. **Banskota, Narrottam Prasad.** Indo-Nepal trade and economic relations.

For full entry refer to Foreign Relations section.

1261. **Export promotion directory of Nepal.**

For full entry refer to Encyclopaedias, directories, and who's who section.

1262. **Kiriella, T.B.A.** Selected markets for medicinal herbs from Nepal : report on mission. Kathmandu : Trade Promotion Centre, 1981. 17 p.

This report is the outcome of a market study tour undertaken under the auspices of the International Trade Centre ITC—UNCTAD/GATT, Geneva, The mission was undertaken at the request of the Trade Promotion Centre by the ITC Market Development Adviser, Mr. T.B.A. Kiriella during March and April 1980. The report contains the prospects for marketing major Nepalese medicinal herbs in the Federal Republic of Germany, Switzerland, and Great Britain.

1263. **Manzardo, Andrew E.** Ecological constraints on trans-Himalayan trade in Nepal. *Contributions to Nepalese Studies*, vol. 4, no. 2 (June 1977), pp. 63-81. map. bibliog.

Discusses the trade between Nepal and trans-Himalayan areas by the different communities of Nepal. The article mentions the restrictions on trade across the northern border of Nepal since the early 1960 and their effect. The author agrees with the views of Dr. Haimendorf on certain points, and differs with him on others. Haimendorf's views are also discussed here.

1264. **Nepal Journal of Management.**

For full entry refer to Professional periodicals section.

1265. **Nepal Trade Directory.**

For full entry refer to Encyclopaedies, directories, and who's who section.

1266. **Nepal's trade agreements** : as of force in July 4, 1980. Trade Promotion Centre, Nepal. 3rd ed. Kathmandu : The Centre, 1980. 122 p.

This publication includes documents and other relevant information on Nepal's trade agreements with Bangladesh, Bulgaria, China, Egypt, Korea, Pakistan, Poland, Sri Lanka, Great Britain, the U.S.A., the U.S.S.R., and Yugoslavia.

1267. **Operations manual for Nepalese economic affairs officers stationed abroad.** Trade Promotion Centre, Nepal. Kathmandu : The Centre, 1981. 42 p.

This manual was prepared by Nepalese diplomats with commercial responsibilities and stationed abroad, by senior officials of the Ministries of Foreign Affairs and Finance, and by officials of the Trade Promotion Centre during a workshop held in Kathmandu from 2 to 11 May 1979; consultations on trade representation service held in Kathmandu from 29 August to 15 September 1979; and a workshop in Geneva from 20 to 30 November 1979. These events were conducted by the International Trade Centre, UNCTAD/GATT for trade promotion of Nepal.

1268. **A Profile on Australian tariff preferences.** Compiled by the Trade Promotion Centre. Kathmandu : The Centre, 1974. 33 p.

In 1974, the government of Australia introduced a generalized system of tariff preferences which made eligible for beneficiary status, 138 developing countries, including Nepal. The system covers dutiable semi-manufactures, manufactured goods and handicrafts. This publication introduced the above scheme to those in Nepal who were engaged in exporting handicrafts to Australia. Also includes a list of duty free arrangements made by the government of Australia. Mimeographed.

1269. **Report on trade flow survey of agricultural commodities, particularly cereal grains in Nepal, 1971/72.** Sponsored by His Majesty's Government of Nepal, National Planning Commission, Kathmandu. Kathmandu : His Majesty's Government of Nepal, Ministry of Food, Agriculture, and Irrigation, Department of Food and Agricultural Marketing Services, 1970 42 p.

This study was undertaken in seventy-five district of Nepal in order to identify the origin, destination, and volume of trade of major agricultural commodities, particularly cereal grains and potatoes. The report reveals that there was a significant flow of grains from the Tarai to the Hills, and the volume of interdistrict movement was equally significant in equalizing supply and prices.

1270. **Report on Workshop in Trade Information for Business, Biratnagar, 11-12 November 1980**. Kathmandu : Trade Promotion Centre, 1980. 6, 6 p.

The workshop was organized under the auspices of the Trade Promotion Centre in collaboration with the International Trade Centre, UNCTAD/GATT, Geneva, the Industrial Services Centre, Kathmandu, and the United Nations Industrial Development Organization, Vienna. The main aim of this workshop was to introduce businessmen to various types and services of trade information available on exportable products and on trading countries of interest. Mimeographed.

1271. **Schuler, Sidney**. Migratory traders of Baragaon. *Contributions to Nepalese Studies*, vol. 5, no. 1 (Dec. 1977), pp. 71-84.

This is a preliminary report, discussing seasonal migratory trading patterns of the population of Baragaon. Baragaon is an area located along a traditional trade-route between Tibet, the middle hills of Nepal, and the plains region of the Nepalese Terai and northern India. The villages concerned are located in the Kagbeni and Muktinath Panchayats in the central part of Mustang District, Nepal.

1272. **Selected documents on land-locked developing countries**. Trade Promotion Centre. Kathmandu : The Centre, 1976. 88, 30 p.

The Trade Promotion Centre of Nepal has endeavoured to compile the principal documents and international resolutions and recommendations relating to land-locked developing countries as of August 1972. This publication would be useful to provide an insight and impetus, in particular, to ameliorate the conditions affecting the export growth of a land-locked country such as Nepal. Mimeographed.

1273. **Singh, Ramesh** and **Bista, Nirmal K.** Ad hoc conference report on implications of the new foreign trade policy measures on Nepalese economy. Kirtipur, Nepal :

Centre for Economic Development and Administration, Tribhuvan University, 1978. 71 leaves. (CEDA occasional paper) (International relations series, no. 1).

This mimeograph publication is the outcome of the proceedings of a conference on the 'Implications of the new foreign trade policy measures on Nepalese economy' organized by the International Relations Group of the Centre for Economic Development and Administration during April 1978. In addition to the conference proceedings, a few other relevant articles are included in this publication to make it more useful.

1274. **Srivastava, S.B.** An appraisal of foreign trade statistics, 1962-1963. Kathmandu : Central Bureau of Statistics, Ministry of Economic Planning, His Majesty's Government, 1964? 10 leaves.

This mimeographed leaflet discusses problems regarding imports and exports, export trade to overseas countries, the balance of trade, and invisible trade.

1275. **Stiller, Ludwig F.** A note on Himalayan trade. *Journal of the Tribhuvan University*, vol. 7, no. 1 (Nov. 1972), pp. 1-34.

A historical review of Nepal's trade with Tibet and China.

1276. **Trade and industrial directory of Nepal.** Compiled and edited by Adri Trade Link. Kathmandu : Adri Trade Link, 1973. 485 p.

Provides useful information on various aspects of trade, industry, and commerce and includes a detailed list of industrial firms, exporters and importers, and similar trading concerns.

1277. **Von Furer-Haimendorf, Christoph.** Himalayan traders : life in highland Nepal. London : John Murray, 1975. 316 p. 7 maps. bibliog. illus.

In this book, the author shows in striking detail how trading patterns operated over a very wide range of communities. The first four chapters of the book are in some respects a sequel to the author's *The Sherpas of Nepal* (London : John Murray, 1964); while they cover subjects additional to those already dealt in there, they also describe modifications of social arrangements brought about by recent years. Chapters 5-8 deal with: the Bhotias of the Arun and Tamur regions; highlanders of the

Dhaulagiri Zone; traders of Karnali Zone; and trade and social relations. The chapters provide an overall view of the socio-economic conditions among a sample of Tibetan-speaking high-altitude dwellers and amplify the very meagre ethnographic information on the Buddhist border tribes.

1278. **What Nepal offers**. Trade Promotion Centre, Nepal. 2nd ed. Kathmandu : The Centre, 1978, 67 p.

The basic objective of this book is to pr.sent a glimpse of Nepal's leading exportable commodities, which, over the past few years have successfully entered the overseas markets. These include jute and jute goods, medicinal herbs and spices, hides and skins, and handicrafts.

33

TRADITIONAL CUSTOMS, FESTIVALS AND COOKERY

1279. **Anderson, Mary M.** The festivals of Nepal. London : George Allen & Unwin, 1971. 288 p. bibliog. illus.

Feasts and festivals truly constitute a way of life for the people of the valley of Nepal. The book is the result of author's five years stay in Nepal and studing the meaning of the ancient processions and rituals, the mythological, religious, and historical backgrounds of the ceremonies, and the wealth of delightful legends and folk-tales surrounding them. The author aimed to have a survey of the living tradition and the legends surrounding them which are current among the people and not to go in their historical backgrouud. The author has described only *36* festivals where as several are celebrated in Nepal. The book presents a delightful account of the folk religion of the people of Nepal as embodied in their festivals.

1280. **Bennett, Lynn.** The wives of the Rishis : an analysis of the Tij-Rishi Panchami women's festival. *Kailash : a Journal of Himalayan Studies*, vol. 4, no. 2 (1976), pp. 185-207. illus.

Tij-Rishi Panchami is actually comprised of two separate festivals on the 3rd and 5th day of the bright half of Bhadau (August-September). In this article, the author has described about the origin of this festival, what is the importance, and how it is celebrated.

1281. **Bista, Kham Bahadur.** Tîj ou la fête des femmes. *Objects et Mondcs*, tome 9, fasc. 1 (1969), pp. 7-18. illus.

Tij is a festival of women which falls in the month of August. The author shows how Nepalese women are attached to an old custom, which is believed to ensure long life and prosperity for their husbands. He stresses the three phases in the celebration of Tij : a copious evening meal; a day of strict fasting with a pilgrimage to a temple dedicated to Śiva; the observance of Pañcami for purification.

1282. **Ghimire, Premalata.** A note on the Nepalese Satar festivals of Soharai and Patamela. *Contributions to Nepalese Studies*, vol. 7, no. 1/2 (Dec. 1979/June 1980), pp. 9-19. bibliog. illus.

The Satars live in Morang and Jhapa districts in the eastern-most part of Nepal's Terai. Satars and Santals of Bihar are of the same origin. *Soharai* and *Patamela* are Satars' main festivals. *Soharai* is a festival of cattle and is observed for six days in the month of Magh (January/February). *Patamela* is celebrated in honour of Lord Mahadeva during the last week of Chaitra (March/April) or the first week of Baisakh (April/May) and continues for three days. This article explains the origin of these festivals and how these are celebrated.

1283. **Goodman, Jim.** Guide to enjoying Nepalese festivals. Kathmandu : Kali Press, 1981. 118 p. bibliog.

This is an introductory survey of religious celebration in Kathmandu Valley. This guide introduces the curious to some of the many aspects of the Nepalese festival. This contains all the information one needs to both follow events and understand them, as well as the background essential to make further inquiries on one's own. The basic research on most of the festivals listed here was originally done by Mary Anderson.

1284. **Jest, Corneille.** Le fête du Janaipurnimâ à Pâtan. *Objects et Mondes*, tome VI, fasc. 2 (1966), pp. 143-152.

Janaipurnima is a well known local Śaivite festival of Patan, Lalitpur. The festival is observed by all the castes and Buddhist Newars in the months July/August on full moon night. In this article which is in French languagc, the author has described the importance of this festival and how this festival is celebrated by the people.

1285. **Kirpatrick, William.** An account of the Kingdom of Nepaul, the substance of observations made during a mission to that country in the year 1793.

For full entry refer to History—General section.

1286. **Lall, Kesar.** Nepalese customs and manners. Kathmandu : Ratna Pustak Bhandar, 1976. 59 p.

In Nepal, several tribes and clans stay together. Apart from those, who have their origin in Nepal, some are migrated from India, some are from Tibet, and some are from China. They have their own social life and customs and speak different languages and dialects. This publication is the study of customs and manners of all the tribes and clans of Nepal.

1287. **Locke, John K., S.J.** Rato Matsyendranath of Patan and Bungamati. Kathmandu : Institute of Nepal and Asian Studies, Tribhuvan University, 1973. 118 p. bibliog. illus. (Historical series ; no. 5)

This is a very comprehensive study on the chariot festival—*Ratha Jatra* or *Rato Matsyendranath* in Patan. It is a colourful and fascinating festival usually beginning some time in April and lasting until the first week of June. For the people of Patan and the surrounding farming communities this is one of the most important social and religious events of the year. It marks the beginning of the rainy season and Matsyendranath is looked upon as the dispenser of the annual rain. Along with the historical and religious description of the festival, the author has analysed the festival with cultural and anthropological stand-point. This study has revealed the details of the cult of Matsyendranath and the sources for the study .

1288. **Macdonald, Alexander William.** Notes sur deux fêtes chez les Thâru de Dâṅg. *Objects et Mondes,* tome 9, fasc. 1 (1969), pp. 69-88. illus.

The author describes briefly two well-known festivals (i) Holi; (ii) Magh Sankranti; as he saw these among the Tharus of Dang, inner Terai, western Nepal in 1967. The celebrations of Tharus of Dang differ from other communities of the same area.

1289. **Majupuria, Indra.** Joys of Nepalese cooking : a most comprehensive and practical book on Nepalese cookery : 344 easy-to-make, kitchen tested recipes. Gwalior, India : S. Devi, 1980-81. 328 p. illus.

The Nepalese food is essentially traditional in type and has grown in the form of an art inherited from mother to daughter. House-wives take pride in their skill to cook the traditional dishes. The purpose of this book is to make Nepalese cuisine known to the outside world. Title on spine : Nepalese cooking.

1290. **Majupuria, Indra** and **Majupuria Trilok Chandra.** Marriage customs in Nepal : ethnic groups, their marriage custom and traditions. Kathmandu : Indra Majupuria, 1978. 206 p. bibliog. illus.

In this book the authors have discussed the marriage customs in different ethnic groups of Nepal. They have noted differences and variations, nay the sharper ones, in the marriage customs not only of races, castes, or subcastes but even in different families also. These differences are due to migration, education, and other influences. During the course of this study, they have not considered the money given in the dowry, compensation, fine for adultery, etc., as these vary from place to place and involve the financial status of the persons.

1291. **Majupuria, Trilok Chandra** and **Gupta, S.P.** Nepal : the land of festivals : religious, cultural, social, and historical festivals. New Delhi : S. Chand & Company Ltd., 1981. 152 p. bibliog. illus.

The main purpose of this book is to present the different festivals observed in Nepal. The festivals of Nepal are not only very colourful and mysterious but also involve long preparations. These festivals are religious, historical and based on various folk-lores and interesting legends. Nepal observes quite a number of festivals and one can always witness either festival or jatra (procession) throughout the year.

1292. **Mikame, Kiyotomo.** A note on the Phaguwaa Festival of Chitwan Tharu. *Kailash : a Journal of Himalayan Studies*, vol. 7, no. 3-4 (1979), pp. 227-246. bibliog.

This research was conducted on a ten-day field trip in March 1979 in Surtaanaa Village, Khairahani Gaun Panchayat, Chitwan District of Southern Nepal. The people of the area are called Tharu and their language is Tharu of Indo-Aryan group. The main aim of this study is to give a preliminary indications of the *Phaguwaa Festival* of the Chitwan Tharu as celebrated in March 1979. This festival is also known as *Hori* or *Holi* and relates to a new year of the Tharus.

1293. **Millot, Jacques.** Le bétel au Népal. *Objects et Mondes*, tome VI, fasc. 2 (1966), pp. 153-168.

This article is in French language and gives details about the traditional practice of chewing of betel leaf, its use and preparation in Nepal. Includes illustrations.

1294. **Nepali-khana = Nepālī-khānā.** Kathmandu : Field Training Course, Summer Institute of Linguistics, Tribhuvan University, 1970 or 71. 26, 15 p.

A guidebook for Nepalese cooking. This is issued as an appendix to the Jungle camp cookbook of Summer Institute of Linguistics.

1295. **Sheffield, Meg** and **Shaha, Siddhanta.** Nepali cooking : a short essay including recipes. *Kailash : a Journal of Himalayan Studies*, vol. 6, no. 2 (1978), pp. 127-139.

The authors discuss in this article the type of food generally liked in Nepal and also describe how to prepare boiled rice, lentil sauce, mixed vegetables, potato chutney or pickle, cooked tomatto chutney, potato and cauliflower pickle, pickled tomato and peas, lamb and mutton curry, mutton curry, cabbage and potatoes, green leafy vegetable, yoghurt pudding, and rice beer. Nepali food is well balanced in its components and distinctively flavoured. It is not hot.

1296. **Shrestha, D.B.** and **Singh, C.B.** Some prominent festivals in Nepal. Kathmandu : The Authors, 1972. 54 p. illus.

Discusses in brief the prominent festivals in Nepal.

1297. **Tailhet, Jehanne H.** The tradition of the Nava Durga in Bhakatpur, Nepal. *Kailash : a Journal of Himalayan Studies*, vol. 6, no. 2 (1978), pp. 81-98. illus.

Literary translation of Nava Durga is nine Durgas. Durgas are the various demonic representations or manifestations of Pārvati, the sakti of Śiva in the tantric tradition. Nava Durga is a ceremony that is ritually marked by a set of masks, which, on public occasions, are worn and danced with. These masks are unique to Bhaktapur (Bhadgaon) and they have special properties that distinguish them from most mask traditions. The author has discussed in this paper, the process of making these masks and their contextual levels of folk meaning. These ceremonies and rituals integrate many ideologies and beliefs, a number of which concern the agricultural cycle. This 200 years old tradition of Nava Durga in Bhaktapur is loosing its importance due to the changes in beliefs of the persons and also gathas (who have been given the honour of dancing) want more offerings now.

34

TRANSPORT

1298. **Kathmandu traffic-transport** : analysis and recommendations. Department of Housing & Physical Planning. Kathmandu : The Department, 1973. 59 leaves. 16 maps.

This study is conducted by the Transportation Planning Unit of the Department from October 1972 to July 1973. Vehicular registration and accident data were obtained from the Traffic Police, whereas Department of Roads provided traffic flow data. Further assistance was provided by the Statistical Unit. This report analysis the information about Kathmandu traffic and transport, and makes necessary recommendations how the results of surveys and data available can be used for the formulation of proposals. Mimeographed.

1299. **A Pre-feasibility study on trolley transport as an alternative to oil based land transport**. Project-in-charge : Tika P. Pokharel; members: Abullaish, Binod K. Karmacharya. Kirtipur, Nepal : Tribhuvan University, Centre for Economic Development and Administration, 1976. 125 p.

This study is related to Kathmandu-Birgunj, Biratnagar-Dharan, and Butaul-Bhairahawa roads. Mimeographed.

1300. **Ropeway feasibility study** (Chatra-Bhojpur and Pokhara-Baglong). Centre for Economic Development and Administration. Kathmandu : The Centre, 1972. 31, 11, 11 p.

This is a feasibility study of wire-rope transportation between Chatra-Bhojpur and Pokhara-Baglong, with reference to cost effectiveness and freights, etc.

1301. **Seminar-cum-Workshop on Transport Project Analysis, May 3-July 3, 1971.** Kathmandu : Centre for Economic Development & Administration, 1971. 1 vol.

These papers which are in English and Nepali relate to the transportation problems in Nepal. Has spine title: Transport project analysis.

INDEX

The index includes all the possible access points : authors, joint authors, editors, compilers, titles, parallel titles, alternate titles, and important series. All the index entries are referred to the entry number in the text of the Bibliography. Initial articles are ignored in filing.

णाणं

पयासयं

2470

भारतीय ज्ञानपीठ

1944